I Want to Live in
SPAIN

Mark Harrison

UKA PRESS, LONDON

Most UKA Press Books are available at special quantity discounts for bulk purchase for sales promotions, premiums, fund-raising, or educational use. Special books, or book excerpts, can also be created to fit specific needs.

For details, write: Special Markets, UKA Press, 55 Elmsdale Road, London, E17 6PN, or email: andrealowne@ukauthors.com

Published by the UKA Press
55 Elmsdale Road, Walthamstow, London, E17 6PN, England
Olympiaweg 102-hs, 1076 XG, Amsterdam, Holland
St. A,108, 2-5-22 Shida, Fujieda, Shizuoka, 426-0071, Japan

First published in Great Britain by the imprint UKA Press: 2004
Second, Revised Edition: 2005
This Edition published by the independent UKA Press: 2007

The UKA Press World Wide Web site is
www.UKAPress.com

A CIP catalogue record for this book is available from the British Library
ISBN   978-1-905796-07-6   (1-905796-07-2)

Edited by Don Masters, A.St, UKA Press,
Book Design by Don Masters
Cover Design by Peter J. Merrigan
Cover Photograph © Mark Harrison
Printed in the United Kingdom of Great Britain
2 4 6 8 10 9 7 5 3 1

For Vivien ~
and Mike and Joy, who proved that lasting
friendship can emerge from unlikely beginnings
and survive an author's temerity,
and Don Masters, Editor of the UKA Press ~
for
Making Many Things Possible

Foreword

For a brief period in my life I trained as a chef in a small provincial hotel in Cheshire. I loved it.

My mentor was a rather unadventurous chef, more adept at preparing two hundred portions of chicken in white wine for a wedding than creating anything original. Then one Sunday the owner of the hotel was entertaining a few friends at a private dinner and the chef was given carte blanche to prepare what he liked.

This was real cooking and I volunteered to help in the kitchen and wait on the tables. The next thing I knew, I was walking into the dining room with a dozen fillet steaks impaled on a ceremonial sword and flaming in burning brandy that trickled down and singed the sleeve of my waiter's jacket.

Mum's cooking (brilliant though it was) would never seem the same again. Sadly perhaps, I chose the route of steady work and job security instead of pursuing my love of food. Who knows whether I would have reached the heights of the culinary arts, or whether I would still be churning out prawn cocktails and black forest gateaux to compliant wedding guests.

Luckily my impromptu move to Spain has given me the time to re-kindle my love affair with food and to share some of my favourite recipes in this book.

*In my first ten months in Spain I trimmed down from just over 15 stones to 12½. But, more importantly, I've maintained my weight for more than two years. Viv has lost weight too (not that she really wanted to, but then I'm in charge of cooking). Now, I don't even think about what I eat, but I stick to a few simple rules and enjoy the best food I've ever had in my life. At the end of this book, if you're still with me, I'll tell you how it works.

Chapter One

I Want to Live in Spain

'I want to live in Spain,' said Viv, one Saturday night as the wind howled and the rain lashed against the windows.

'Me, too.' I replied, stabbing a wing of guinea fowl. 'I was right about the cream,' I added. Cream, herbs, tomatoes, bacon, wild mushrooms – the recipe was turning out a treat. 'Here, have some more.' I ladled another scoop onto her plate.

'*I want to live in Spain.*'

I laughed, and reached for the wine.

I didn't imagine for a single second that Viv had just set in motion an unstoppable roller coaster, or that the endless wind and rain were nothing compared to what Spain had in store.

We had no reason to go and live in Spain, for a start.

In fact, we had no great ambition to leave Britain, and had never seriously thought of living abroad, other than an occasional dalliance with the idea of buying a holiday home somewhere.

Our house, Heath Lodge, in Lingfield, Surrey was a modest Victorian cottage with a half-acre garden surrounded by mature trees – limes, horse chestnuts and sycamores. Our neighbours were a comfortable distance away and the trees gave us a degree of privacy we cherished.

Opposite the house was the site of the Edenbridge and Oxted Agricultural Show; over a hundred acres of flat farmland that hosted around 30,000 visitors every August Bank Holiday. Despite the noise, and the dust, and the mud on the road, and the traffic congestion, and the animal rights protesters outnumbered by the police, we had learned to live with the Show; after all, it was just two days a year. We always went along, to spend part of each day in the Vice-Presidents' hospitality pavilion, flashing our paid-for badges and feeling uncomfortable as we mingled with the jodhpurs and riding boots who mingled with the floral print frocks, tweed jackets and Panama hats.

For the rest of the year, the Show Ground was empty and we were free to roam with Jessie, our six year-old German Shepherd, so long as we didn't upset the sheep or Paddy the Oxted Shepherd.

By most standards, we lived a privileged life. Ever since we had bought Heath Lodge ten years earlier, I would, from time to time, stand at the gate looking up the shingle drive at the black-and-white gables and rosemary-tiled roof, finding it hard to believe that this was really ours. But it was, and we assumed that this was where we would spend the rest of our days.

Then came that winter.

It seemed to rain and blow non-stop for six months – and that wind and rain, although I was no more than fuzzily aware of it when Viv tossed her comment about living in Spain across the table, had already set the roller coaster spinning down the tracks.

The first problem was Viv's fear of the roof. We pruned back the trees at Heath Lodge every five years or so, but they always recovered to engulf the house and block out much of the daylight, especially in summer when in full leaf – and in winter, when there was not so much daylight to block out.

Listening to the wind blow, as it did on many days and nights that winter, Viv became increasingly convinced that one of the trees would crash through the roof. It had reached the stage where she often couldn't sleep, listening to the wind howling through the branches as they scraped against the picturesque and expensive lichen-covered tiles.

One branch in particular hit more savagely every night.

I would say things to reassure, such as, 'Don't worry, we can claim from the insurance. If it smashes in, we can get a new roof.' This kind of remark seemed to have an effect, since Viv regularly reported that she'd been haunted by my suggestions; once claiming she'd spent the entire night pinned to the bed by a bulky sycamore branch, gazing up at the sky where the roof had once been, *waving an insurance claim form*, while 'You just lay there like a log.' (Then she got annoyed, when I laughed.)

Probably, though, it was not just this ever more-threatening racket on the roof.

There was also our spongy, moss-choked lawn; underwater for most of that winter, we looked as if we were floating on a lake. And our dog, Jessie, was constantly wet and muddy from her walks, so we had to listen to the washing machine and the drier as they competed around-the-clock to see which could cope the more noisily with the old towels we used to dry her off.

Everything was unrelentingly wet, dark and cold that winter.

Then I became ill. Nothing serious, just a bout of flu, but it forced me to take two days off, my first in more than sixteen years working for one of the London Boroughs. I couldn't seem to shake it, even after visiting the doctor for the first time in a decade. Antibiotics, prescribed after my third visit, failed to improve my fuzzy head and catarrh-choked chest.

The office was in chaos, as usual.

For ten years I'd expanded my empire, taking on disjointed responsibilities; usually willingly, and in return for more pay.

I was constantly juggling to keep the projects afloat, cutting corners and taking risks (never a good idea in the structured, over-regulated world of local government). I compensated for my inadequacies by working longer and longer hours.

Despite this, I'd have been happy to see out my career in local government. I still had ambitions to go further (though this depended on my boss retiring in the next few years), but I was approaching fifty and I had a very good salary with all the fringe benefits, and thirty-one years in the local government superannuation fund. I was very satisfied. Viv had a part-time job in the civil service, with a similar pension to look forward to.

Well, no one in their right mind would think of giving all that up, and we didn't.

But the flu lingered for more than five weeks. I dragged myself from bed each morning to be on the M25 by seven o'clock, and arrived home between seven and eleven. Apart from a few words in the morning, Viv and I hardly spoke during the week. Weekday evenings usually consisted of a snatched meal before I fell asleep in front of the television, sometimes after stopping off for a couple of beers and some male bonding on my way home.

Weekends were not much better. I never seemed to have the time or the inclination to get things done. I had long since lost interest in the usual weekend tasks of mowing, maintenance, bits of DIY. I still did them, but at top speed so I could justify a round of golf on Sunday mornings.

On Saturday nights, though, if we were not seeing friends, Viv and I always took time to have a meal together. This was something we'd done throughout our 29 years of marriage.

I always prepared the meal, because cooking was the one activity that utterly absorbed me and never became a chore. As a teenager I'd worked in a small provincial hotel near home under a competent but unadventurous chef, and over the next twenty-five years, I occasionally dreamed of leaving the cosseted world of local government to become a restaurateur. But the comfort and safety of a regular salary and the promise of an index-linked pension had me shackled. So I settled for exercising my culinary ambitions by preparing elaborate meals most Saturdays.

We never seemed to tire of these evenings. Over the food, we'd linger over a decent bottle of wine and, into the early hours, not that I could always keep track of the topic, we talked.

It was during one such Saturday evening in January, towards the end of my bout of flu, when Viv raised the topic of Spain with her remark, 'I want to live in Spain.'

At first, I joked, as usual. Yes, we often lightly fantasised about the idea of chucking our jobs and heading overseas, but it was just that – a pipe dream.

She repeated it, this time. '*I want to live in Spain.*'

Nodding toward the windows where the rain lashed, she pulled her collar up, shivering. After a short laugh, I wondered if we were in for one of those long conversations we'd had before, about the rain and wind, and the damned roof.

I'd worked hard enough I thought, to be soundly irritated…but I'd downed enough wine to say, 'I've got enough on my plate without the weather,' and think I was funny. I drank more wine, plunged my fork into what was left of the guinea fowl I'd spent so much time cooking *to perfection*, and went on eating.

I thought that would be the end of it.

After all, the idea of the dinner was to relax over conversation, not to mull anything challenging. But Viv stared at me as if shooting darts across a channel of miscommunication, as if the 'live in Spain' thing was…well, certainly not serious, but…

As I glanced across at her, ready to bring the mood back to normal by asking, 'Want some more of my fowl sauce?' – a wild, but to my mind, completely practical idea hit me. *What if we were to sell Heath Lodge, pay off the mortgage and live off the balance until our pensions came through?*

I said, 'All right. Let's think about the Spanish thing tomorrow,' and got up to go and make coffee. I was sure I'd forget Viv's suggestion and my notion of how it could be done. But I'd set myself up for a sleepless night, weighing the pros and cons. (I'd not been sleeping well, in any case, what with the last of the flu, our thundering trees, and Viv's dreams haunting mine.)

There's a time in everyone's life when they need to take stock, it struck me…it was just that most people never got round to it.

Viv and I were a strong couple, but like many, we'd drifted into a routine dictated by habit rather than choice. It was not what either of us really wanted. Sure, we were comfortably off and had all the toys, lots of good friends and a busy social life. But our lives were dominated by the ten or twelve hours a day I spent at work and the other hours I spent thinking about it.

Toward morning, I thought, 'Hell, let's go for it,' and fell soundly asleep.

Several hours later I woke feeling strangely refreshed. After a second I remembered I'd worked it all out – exactly, down to the last – what was it? – lira or centivo.

I jumped out of bed humming: 'Oh, yes, we're off to sunny Spain, y Viva España.'

Viv looked at my excited face and joined in. Laughing, we danced around the bedroom; Jessie, too. Neither Viv nor I had any idea where all this would end, and didn't care. We were inspired.

I had a reputation at work for being what psychologists call a 'completer finisher.' I always saw things through to the end. A bit like Magnus Magnusson, what I started, I was going to finish.

So it was that after a quick breakfast, I went out to buy the Sunday Times, after which I phoned every advertisement in the paper for homes in Spain.

Why Spain? We were not sure, at first. Viv didn't really care. Spain had a carefree ring to it, she thought, but we would have liked Portugal or Majorca, too. However, these were both too expensive for the budget we were likely to have available to us, we quickly realised. France was a possibility, but the weather was not as good and the cost of living was significantly higher.

So we settled for Spain, though we didn't have any idea of where in Spain we wanted to live.

But gradually our reading and research on the internet led us to look seriously at the northern Costa Blanca.

Two things influenced our choice. The World Health Organisation recommended the climate as one of the healthiest in the world. Another big factor was the cost of property.

We refined our choice further by agreeing we didn't want to live on the coast (too busy, too many tourists), but liked the idea of going inland towards the mountains – up into the 'real Spain.'

Over the next few weeks I was plagued with phone calls from the advertisers I'd contacted.

'When are you coming to Spain?'...'Would you like to take advantage of a free inspection flight?'...'We've just released the next phase on a new urbanisation, you must come and see it.'

Property was selling fast, or so they said, and I needed to get out to Spain as soon as possible.

I was typically impatient to move forward and would have jumped on the first plane.

As ever, Viv was the calming influence, saying we needed to do more research, not least about getting a pet passport for Jessie and checking the status of our pensions.

In a casual aside, I mentioned to a golfing neighbour, Dave Saunders, that we were thinking of selling the house and he said he knew someone who might be interested.

'Send them round,' I said, not expecting anything to come of it.

A week or so later Brian and Linda Parkes came to see Heath Lodge. I'd met them before a couple of times, as they were friends of the Saunders and one of our other neighbours.

We left them to wander round the house and make up their minds, but in my heart I sensed they were going to buy it. When they'd finished looking, we talked about a price, and I put a value on the house which was fair, but not over-optimistic. More importantly, it would give us sufficient funds, by my calculations, to live fairly comfortably in Spain with no other income.

Linda was a tiny woman, but dynamic, and Brian was retiring and reticent, so I quickly discerned that Linda was the driving force of the partnership. I waited for her to begin negotiations.

Suddenly, Brian spoke up. He simply said they wanted to buy the place. I then began to feel that the contradiction of what I'd sensed about the couple indicated that this was meant to be. Fated. Then Brian said that they had a house to sell, though they didn't need a mortgage – and this was all just too neat. Almost as if something had happened to make it fall into place.

'I have dead relatives,' Brian explained.

'Oh,' I began, struggling to find the right response, 'then you won't have much use for the guest bedroom – '

Viv interrupted, 'I'll put the kettle on,' and the deal was done.

Now all I had to do was jump on the first plane.

We were due to take a weekend break in Milan in three weeks, and Viv, steadfast as ever, was not going to leave Jessie in kennels twice in one month. Jessie was not just a pet. To Viv, at least, she represented family, in the sense of being the one who came before everyone else, including me. For the last 20 years we'd never taken a holiday lasting more than four days – the longest Viv could bear to be parted from Jessie, or any of the three German Shepherds we'd previously owned and pampered.

Holidays consisted of weekend breaks, usually to European cities. Though we enjoyed them, Viv was always relieved to recover the dog from the kennels. In the circumstances, I booked a flight for myself to Valencia, using Airmiles we'd accumulated over the years.

I called an English agent to ask if he could book me a hotel, and arrange for me to meet his man in the Costa Blanca.

A few days later, I arrived at the Hotel Ramis in Ondara. I did wonder by then if I wasn't rushing a bit, but still, I thought, not really. I was only there to look, after all; not to buy anything.

'Typically Spanish,' Hotel Ramis was described. Basic, but with good service and excellent food. Above all, it was cheap and comfortable. But I spent a largely sleepless Friday night – listening to people come and go at all hours along the echoing, uncarpeted corridors. I was full of trepidation at the prospect of meeting my 'agent's man, name of Barry Small' on Saturday morning.

It struck me that though I'd visited Spain a few times, sampling wines and taking photographs, and I'd started brushing up my school-cum-wine-holiday Spanish a few days ago, I knew next to nothing about the place; still less about living in a foreign country. Hearing voices outside my door, not understanding a word they said, worked on my mind. I was a foreigner. I didn't belong. I'd make all sorts of mistakes. However, I knew I had to see it through and gradually, during the night, I convinced myself once more that living in Spain would be just like home, on a day-to-day basis, at least: after all, how different could it be?

I got up early, and my third cup of coffee had come and gone when the hotel doors flew open and to my great relief in walked a very English-looking type, whom I recognised at once. I held out my hand and introduced myself. A dapper gent with an RAF moustache, Barry wore a dazzling white polo shirt and a blazer, and looked very active and knowledgeable. Just the type I needed.

With a mobile phone clasped to his ear he chatted away in English, gesturing to me to wait. As soon as the conversation ended I introduced myself again, to have it confirmed that he was indeed a very active real estate agent. He planned, today, to show houses in and around Gandia and Oliva – just to the north of the Costa Blanca, on the Costa del Azahar.

As he quickly and clearly explained, that part of Spain was now becoming hugely popular, and it was much cheaper than the Costa Blanca. Just as he was giving me his card and explaining he was not Barry Small, the real Barry Small walked in. I tucked the card away and said I'd be in touch.

I have only a few prejudices, I always maintain, that give me negative first impressions.

Tattoos, body piercing and baseball caps back-to-front, fall into that category. So too, do people who succumb to that peculiarly British form of naffness – suede shoes, and spectacles on a string round the neck. Barry met both the last two criteria, complemented by the kind of cardigan my grandfather used to wear to catch the ash from his Woodbines as he dozed in front of television. Because of these long-established standards I found it difficult to warm to Barry at first, but oddly enough (Viv often likes to observe, in retrospect and completely wrongly, that I am first-impression challenged), over the next two days it dawned on me that the real Barry Small and I were going to be good friends.

Basically, Barry did not want to be, nor was he cut out to be, a property agent. He'd done the sort of interesting and exciting things in his life that, as he spoke, I knew at once I should have done myself – including, amongst other things, running a zoo and organising wild life safaris in Zimbabwe.

He loved living in the mountains of the Costa Blanca, he said, and was part of the community in the village of Castell de Castells, where he taught English to the local children. But his first love was photographing wild flowers, animals, and insects in different parts of the world. He had a collection of many thousands of slides and planned, one day, to do this for a living; organising visits for fellow enthusiasts and giving slide shows.

As well as having a thorough understanding of the property market, Barry was a mine of information about local history and the flora and fauna in the area. He waxed lyrical about the history of some of the local villages and the long-running conflict between the Moors and the Christians. He talked about life in those parts under Franco as if he had lived through the Civil War.

Once, in the mountains above the Jalon Valley, we screeched to a halt and Barry insisted I get out of the car so he could show me the world's smallest wild daffodil, growing at the side of the road. This tiny plant stood just ten centimetres tall, its flower the size of the nail on my little finger and a pungent scent. Barry rattled off the Latin name, 'narcissus requienii', and other names I couldn't understand, without hesitation (he gave them to me later, written down, for my collection of items to impress friends).

Our first day's inspection started along the coast, from Calpe in the south to Denia in the north.

My first viewing was of a stylish villa in a densely-built urbanisation overlooking Moraira. In the garden, by the pool, I noticed a separate structure, secured by an electronic roller shutter. An outdoor kitchen, I surmised. But the shutter rose to reveal a comprehensively-equipped bar with a full range of optics, a lever for pulling up the lager, and a professional-looking sound system.

'Pity the poor neighbours,' I said, fiddling with the controls, knowing Viv would have nothing to do with it. 'How does it work, Barry?' I'd never seen anything like it.

After Barry had guided me ('It is NOT STOCKED') away from the mechanical bar, he took me on to see many 'more pleasant properties' and a number of plots, without once giving me any kind of hard sell. It seemed, I thought, that he was almost as anxious as I was, to find out just what I was really looking for.

We had dinner that first Saturday night in one of the open-air fish restaurants by the harbour in Calpe. If this was a marketing ploy of Barry's, it was a very clever one, I thought, planning to bring all our friends here as soon as they arrived in Spain. There's nothing more likely to sell anyone the idea of the good life in this part of Spain, I realised, than eating outdoors and choosing from a huge selection of cheap, fresh fish.

But back to Barry. As we talked, I felt as if we'd known each other for years. I used all my descriptive powers to explain exactly what I was looking for in Spain; not just the kind of property I wanted, but exactly the kind of lifestyle we envisaged.

'We want to go up toward the mountains and see a bit of real Spain,' I said. 'None of this tourist stuff.'

At the end of dinner Barry remarked that there were 'coast people' and there were 'mountain people.'

'All the best people are mountain people,' he said, 'and I think you are one of them.'

I merely nodded, but at heart I agreed enthusiastically. This was irresistible.

Sunday morning was glorious: a cloudless sky, clear air and warm spring sunshine, as we headed off through the Jalon Valley and up into the hills. I began to feel a sense of belonging – or was it just that I so desperately wanted to change my life? Whatever it was, I felt envious of everyone I saw, enjoying what seemed to be the good life, and I couldn't wait to join in. I'd already made up my mind that I wanted to live in this part of Spain.

We viewed a couple of properties that were 'pleasant' enough, and a few that were way outside our price range, despite Brain assuring me that I had significantly over-estimated the cost of living in Spain. There was one splendid villa we saw, high up on the north side of the valley with spectacular panoramic views, but with a sheer drop of around 20 metres below the balcony and terrace. I tottered backward from the view, steadied myself on a chair, and explained to Barry that Viv suffered from paranoid vertigo, and could not even have climbed out of the car to view a place like this.

An hour later I first set eyes on the tiny village of Parcent, perched – reasonably solidly, I noted with relief – on a small hill, and surrounded by very beautiful mountains.

The fretwork Church spire reminded me of Thunderbird Five. It rose high above the irregular tiled roofs and was visible for miles around.

The higgledy-piggledy collection of pastel-painted houses was interspersed with pines and a few tall cypress trees, more reminiscent of Tuscany than Spain.

Approaching from Jalon and Alcalalí, the view of Parcent was seriously marred, however, by a derelict, two-storey, grey concrete structure punctuated by rows of uniform window openings, stretching for about seventy-five metres and topped with what looked like a corrugated asbestos roof. Two rusting metal silos towered by its side. This was (and still is) an eyesore.

Barry explained that it was a battery chicken house of the kind that Franco had built in many of the villages in the area.

In the 1930s, people in that area lived close to the poverty line and survived by eating wild plants and animals found in the hills. The chicken house was a means of providing much needed protein to an otherwise malnourished population. Equally important, it was a source of tax revenue to Franco.

This 'Chicken Shack' was an ugly pockmark in terms of size, scale and design. (I often wondered, later, why the authorities hadn't taken a bulldozer to it long ago. Then again, there were often rumours it was to be converted to town houses – but since this would only have perpetuated its incongruity and further spoiled the beauty of the road into Parcent, we eventually accepted it, particularly when we found it was 'a slice of history', 'unique and bizarre', to our 'Must photograph this!' friends).

Just beyond the Chicken Shack, Barry turned off, and drove for about 500 metres or so along a bumpy track that appeared to lead to into olive and orange groves.

At the end of this rough road, we came out to a small cluster of detached houses set in substantial plots. Most had mature gardens, and were separated by well-established hedges and walls.

Then I saw Casa Emelia for the first time.

Though from the road the house looked rather nondescript, something told me this was the one. By the time I'd wandered round to see the blue of the pool, the lush green of the blossom-sprinkled garden, and the backdrop of rolling, misty mountains, I'd made up my mind. The scent of jasmine and honeysuckle, a warm breeze, and a look inside only reinforced my first impression. It was a little old-fashioned, but it had character. A bit of DIY, and it would be perfect.

Barry showed me round a few more properties, but I wasn't really looking. That house was ours. I knew it.

The journey back to England was a chore. The only available flight was from Valencia to Palma, Majorca, then to Gatwick. I boarded the plane and took my seat, hoping the flight might not be full, but I spotted a young couple coming down the aisle, babe in arms, and sensed my luck was out. I'd hoped to recover some of the sleep I'd lost over the last two nights when I had tossed and turned with anxiety and excitement. It wasn't to be.

By the time I arrived home in the early hours of Monday morning I was exhausted, but excited enough to keep Viv from her sleep as I enthused about our life-to-be in Spain. I described Casa Emelia down to every last detail, even drawing out a floor plan from memory to show how precisely it fitted our needs.

Viv was hesitant, as I had expected.

'You said you were only going to look,' she said.

Obviously, I'd have to use all my powers of persuasion to overcome Viv's caution, although I didn't have quite the energy at two in the morning. But no matter. I'd easily manage that later.

Back at work on Monday, I had to tell a few white lies about my eventful weekend, though inside I was bursting to say something. I dashed out to Boots the Chemist at lunchtime to have the photographs developed within an hour, and rushed home early to renew the dialogue with Viv.

In 1991 I'd made my mind up that we were going to buy Heath Lodge the moment we pulled up outside the house. Even the ancient fittings, peeling paint and musty smell failed to diminish my enthusiasm, and despite Viv's initial reluctance, we eventually went ahead. So this was not unfamiliar territory for me.

I arranged the photographs across the table and pointed out all of Casa Emelia's most endearing features. I reported much of what I had discussed with Barry Small during my trip. 'Barry said this,' or 'Barry said that,' I repeated over and over; so much so that Viv renamed him 'Barry Said.'

We stayed up late that night discussing whether to buy the house, or be more cautious and wait.

I don't know whether it was my powers of persuasion, or that for the first time she trusted my judgement implicitly, or if I eventually wore Viv out, but on Tuesday morning I was on the phone to the agent to make an offer for the place.

This was 14th March, and Viv's only condition was that we would not move before October, mainly because she did not want to take Jessie to Spain in the heat of the summer. I would have gone the next day.

I did little work that Tuesday as I waited for a response. Eventually it came. Our offer was accepted. The problem was that the current owners didn't want to complete until September.

'That's most inconvenient,' I said, holding back the delight from my voice. I thought of trying to shave a bit more off the price in the circumstances, but decided not to over-egg the deal. Getting our preferred time of settlement offered to us was another step on the path, and it still seemed that all this was meant to be.

Soon, Casa Emelia was as good as ours.

The deposit was wired to Spain, and two weeks later we signed the contract with a completion date of 5th September. I should have been overjoyed, and in almost every way I was. A part of me occasionally wondered, 'What if Viv hates the place?' but it was too late to back out, and I dismissed the question every time I thought of it.

There was no need for me to give notice at work for some months, but I soon found it terribly difficult to keep the secret. The biggest problem was my involvement in a number of long-term projects.

I found myself at meetings with people saying: 'We need to do this by Christmas,' or 'Can you finish this for January?'

At first, I said to myself: 'Well, that won't be my problem, will it?' But I felt increasingly dishonest agreeing to do work that I wouldn't see through, so I decided to spill the beans after a couple of weeks, and did so after five days, unable to stop myself confiding in my close friend, Alan Bowness. From the way his eyes lit up, I was sure he was genuinely pleased and excited.

Spurred on, I tapped on the door of the Chief Executive.

After making sure he was seated comfortably with his tie loosened, which meant he'd finished his meetings for the day and would look at me and listen, I blurted it all out.

After a pause, during which, I suspected, he was trying to work out whether I was serious (I had a reputation for an unusual sense of humour), he stood up and gripped my hand.

'Congratulations. Good for you,' he said, his face a mixture of disbelief and relief.

I then spoke to each of my senior staff personally, and another mixture of disbelief and relief greeted the news.

I left the rest to the office grapevine and it didn't take long. Local government is packed with careful, cautious people, many of them more interested in their future pension than their current salary. So my decision was unusual, to say the least.

The reactions were interesting.

I was puzzled by the many people who congratulated me as if I'd won a promotion. I was irritated by those who said, 'You lucky bugger,' as if I'd won the lottery. I was unnerved by people who asked if I knew what I was doing, and wondered how I could throw away a successful career within sight of my pension. 'Very brave or very foolish,' was their reaction. I was not the least bit surprised by those people who said nothing, but just stared at me. They'd been doing that for years.

The next seven months were the most difficult of my working life. There were a million and one things to sort before the sale of Heath Lodge was completed and we could move to Spain, but I still had a job to do. I tried to maintain enthusiasm, and succeeded for the most part. In fact, I was still dictating memos to my secretary during the last hour of my last day at the office, only partly because I'd left everything important until the last minute.

The most irritating thing as my departure approached was the comment from a few people: 'What do you care; you won't be here after October.' I did care, very much, I thought; and I was determined not to leave having lowered my standards in the final few months. All the same, I found myself in a few situations thinking: 'Thank Christ I won't have to put up with this for much longer' – mainly, it must be said, in relation to my dealings with some of the local politicians.

The sale of Heath Lodge went as smoothly as we could expect, given England's antiquated conveyancing laws. Brian and Linda managed to find a buyer for their house and we exchanged contracts in June with a long completion date timed to coincide with our planned departure for Spain in October. Viv set about the task of obtaining Jessie's pet passport, arranging for the anti-rabies jabs and sorting out the paperwork with the Ministry of Agriculture, Fisheries and Food.

I took charge of everything else.

A Spanish bank account was opened; we obtained our Numeros de Identificacion de Extranjeros; the conveyancing moved forward; and direct debits were set up to pay all the bills for the house in Spain. (Fortunately, I pre-booked the pesetas at a fixed rate; an option that later saved us a considerable sum when exchange rates shifted unfavourably over the next few months.)

Jon, the owner of Casa Emelia could, Barry had explained, be a bit difficult. He hadn't exaggerated. Jon first sent a message that he wanted us to pay for every small fixture and fitting, and set ridiculous prices. I became annoyed. He then offered me his beat-up old Renault estate car, and his rubber driver's cushion. I became more annoyed. Next, I was offered a 'stainless steel soap dish with sink rack.' This made me furious. I e-mailed his agent asking for confirmation that 'the items mentioned in the sale particulars would be left in the house' and that I would *not* be expected to purchase extraneous items. The Spanish contract of sale was not specific on this point; or several others, as it turned out.

'How much are you willing to pay?' was the owner's response.

'*No*,' I announced to the agent. 'I do not want these things. I want only what is listed.' Finally, Jon agreed that, although this was business, legally at least, he supposed, the listed items were included in the sale price, and it was not necessary for me to purchase the extraneous items he called 'goods' (and for this sacrifice on his part, he was later to extract revenge…).

By May it was time for Viv to see Casa Emelia. We were well and truly committed by this time, and the visit had been delayed long enough. We flew to Alicante and made the trip north.

In contrast to the journey south from Valencia, which passes through lush green orange groves, the drive from Alicante is almost depressing. The scenery is arid, barren and dusty.

After the urban sprawl of the City, the A7 is flanked by quarries and cement works; needed, no doubt, to supply the booming market for holiday homes which were burgeoning atop every hillside with a view of the Mediterranean. Then there's the distant view of Benidorm which seems to be emulating Manhattan.

We stayed at the Parador in Javea. Up to this point, apart from the few occasional doubts which I'd dismissed, I had absolutely convinced myself that Viv would fall in love with Casa Emelia, just as I had. Suddenly, the night before we were due to visit the house, my confidence slipped. I allowed the thought to re-enter my head: 'Suppose she doesn't like it?'

Next morning, I drove the hired car along one of the narrowest and most twisty routes towards Parcent. Viv seemed to turn ashen as she peered over the precipices on both sides of the road.

'Oh, my God,' I thought. 'She *does* suffer from vertigo –'

I pretended not to notice, and kept driving. We approached the village. The Chicken Shack looked more hideous than ever. A towering stack of uncollected rubbish marked the turning to the development, and builders' rubble had appeared along the road to the house since my visit in March. The road, which I'd described as 'a little bumpy,' had been pot-holed into a cart track. To make matters worse, the sky was an evil grey. The whole scene was overcast, dull, filled with gloom. Even I was having second thoughts.

Viv's first glimpse of the house would not be inspiring, I knew, since its best features were hidden from the road.

'Just *wait until you see the garden*,' I said – to myself, as much as to her.

In that dreary light, even the garden, which I had described as 'cheery and colourful,' lay lifeless and despondent. Jon and his wife gave us coffee and left us to wander round unattended. I looked for any sign of enthusiasm on Viv's face, but found it hard to detect anything more than mild interest. She was still noncommittal as we left, after again declining any interest in buying the faded curtains and out-dated light fittings.

'Right. Let's just nip up the mountain and see the countryside where Jessie can be taken for walks,' I suggested, thrusting an arm upward in the manner of a confident guide.

Clambering up the rough track through the pine trees, though, I realised I should have told Viv to pack some sturdy shoes. Hiking boots would have been best. But at least the views were spectacular, and I chatted to Viv about how nice it would be to walk our Jessie here, especially since she had an instinctive dislike of most other dogs and would fight given half a chance. I explained that this spot was so remote that we would never run into anyone else. At that moment, we encountered a robust lady with two dogs running free. This was all I needed.

On the return journey to Javea, I tried to elicit some idea of how Viv felt about Casa Emelia.

'It's fine,' was the best I managed to extract.

Gloom descended, my confidence ebbed and I even began to think of the consequences of backing out.

It was not just the cost that concerned me. *What was I going to say to friends and people at work, some of whom were already thinking I was mad?*

We spent the next couple of days in and around Javea, but didn't return to Parcent. We talked about our plans to live in Spain, but without any real belief.

At one point, I sensed Viv was trying to spare my feelings by joining in the conversation at all. I was engulfed in an overpowering sense of guilt at having rushed ahead so impetuously.

Back in England that weekend, we walked Jessie in the Show Ground with no one else in sight. I looked upon our surroundings with a fondness I'd taken for granted. Conversation had not been easy and I'd given up trying to tease a positive response from Viv.

'There's one thing about Casa Emelia that I just can't stand,' she said suddenly, without any prompting from me.

Here's the crunch, I thought. Here's the bombshell.

'Those taps in the bathroom will have to go,' she demanded.

I made a solemn promise to replace them as a top priority. Our plans and dreams were back on track.

We had agreed to complete on Casa Emelia on 5th September and an appointment was arranged with the Notario in Javea for 12 o'clock on that day to sign the papers and hand over the money.

The owner had insisted that a large proportion of the sale price should be paid in cash, so our first call was to the Banco de Valencia. We left the bank with a cheque and a carrier bag stuffed with several million pesetas. We had to walk only about five hundred metres to the Notario's office, but I clung to that bag of cash as if my life depended on it, which in a way it did. Viv nervously rode shotgun, looking ahead and behind, viewing every strolling office worker with suspicion.

We'd arranged to meet our *asesor*, Colin Watson, in the coffee bar below the Notario's office, but we were early. I nursed a cup of coffee, the money never leaving my grip. I'd not met Colin, as all our dealings had been by phone, fax or e-mail, but I'd built up a mental image and I outlined him to Viv: Colin was middle-aged, portly, and judging by the slight slur in his speech and rasp in his voice, someone who enjoyed a drink and a smoke.

A Harley-Davidson rumbled to a halt outside, and a bearded, helmeted young man wearing jeans and a T-shirt dismounted.

'Mark?' he said to me as he walked in, probably because of the Banco de Valencia carrier bag I was clutching. I nodded.

Viv said cheerfully, 'Hello, Colin. Mark's told me all about you, and you're exactly as I expected.'

Inside the Notario's office we met the owner, Jon, his wife, his legal advisor, and his agent. The Notario entered, and after brief pleasantries, he departed and left us to get on with the business.

Confusion reigned.

There was a disagreement over the outstanding sum, mainly because the owners seemed unaware of the initial deposit I'd handed to their agent way back in March. Colin sorted things out, by writing down the sums on the back of an envelope. Eventually everyone was satisfied and I was relieved to slide the cheque and carrier bag full of cash across the table.

There was disbelief when Jon said he wanted to count it. We could have been there all day. Finally, it having been pointed out that the money was in sealed packets direct from the bank, he settled for counting the bundles.

Just as I thought we'd finished, his agent mentioned a few outstanding matters such as the apportionment of the year's rates and other local taxes. From handing over millions of pesetas we were now scrabbling around for small change and pushing hundred peseta coins around the table like a game of shove halfpenny. Still we were not finished. Jon chipped in.

'We have left five gas bottles at the house with some gas in, you must pay for this.'

Colin was astonished.

'This is unheard of,' he protested, but Jon was adamant. His legal advisor seemed to recoil with embarrassment, but the man stuck to his guns. A few more pesetas were passed around the table and at last everything was complete.

The Notario went through the formalities of reading the *escritura* before giving it the rubber stamp. He handed us a copy and offered his hand to congratulate us on becoming the new owners of Casa Emelia. Relieved it was all over, we retired with Colin to the coffee bar, this time for something a bit stronger.

Finally, we left Colin to pack his briefcase in the panniers of the Harley-Davidson and we headed to Parcent, to our new home.

Jon had been busy establishing his point about not being obliged to give us for free what we stingily refused to pay for. He'd removed every light fitting in the house, leaving bare wires dangling from the ceilings and walls. Only one light remained: a single light bulb in the small toilet, connected by means of twisted wires sheathed in insulating tape.

'At least the gas bottles are here!' I mentioned to Viv, adding that it was good to see that half of them were, indeed, full, perfectly in sync with her observation that half of them were empty.

But the weather was fine and the pool warm, so we took a dip and enjoyed a couple of hours in the garden, marvelling at the peace and tranquility.

Little did we know how transient and fragile this was.

We returned to the Parador in Javea, and home the next day to England. We were now just six weeks away from the start of our 'New Life.'

'... cooking was the one activity that utterly absorbed me and never became a chore.'

Rich Beef Stew
with tomato dumplings

You just can't beat a deeply rich, dark, warming stew on cold winter evenings. And you can't have stew without dumplings, can you? So for this one I dug out a trusted recipe for the dumplings and rummaged around the cupboard for the basic ingredients. Then I came across a pack of that trendy ingredient without which no meal was complete in the 1990's – sun-dried tomatoes. Now I know they're a bit passé these days, but I thought, why not? This was the result - dumplings with sun dried tomatoes – can you believe it? Try serving with a good helping of pickled red cabbage on the side. That's what I call real comfort food.

- *350g stewing steak, cut into chunks*
- *1 medium onion, peeled and roughly chopped*
- *3-4 carrots, peeled and cut into chunks*
- *150g mushrooms, quartered*
- *150ml red wine*
- *150ml beef stock*
- *1 tbls plain flour*
- *1tsp dried mixed herbs*
- *Black pepper*
- *A dash of Worcestershire sauce*

For the dumplings:

- *75g self-raising flour*
- *35g suet*
- *3-4 sun-dried tomatoes, roughly chopped*
- *3-4 tbls cold water*

1. Pre-heat the oven to 180° C.

2. Sear the beef in a large frying pan with a little oil over high heat until evenly brown (you may need to do this in batches). Place the beef in a large ovenproof casserole and stir in the flour. Next, fry the onions until soft and just beginning to brown at the edges, then add to the casserole with the carrots, mixed herbs and Worcestershire sauce. Add the wine to the frying pan and heat until bubbling, add the stock and bring to the boil, then pour into the casserole. Season with pepper then cover the casserole and place in the oven for 1 hour.

3. Meanwhile, make the dumplings. In a large bowl, mix the flour and suet then add the sun-dried tomatoes. Add the water and bring the mixture together to form a soft dough. Form the dough into 10 –12 small dumplings.

4. Remove the casserole from the oven and stir in the mushrooms. Place the dumplings on top of the bubbling liquid, then cover the casserole and return to the oven. After 20 minutes remove the lid and return to the oven for a further 20 minutes until the dumplings are just beginning to brown. Serve immediately.

Serves 2
Preparation time: 20 minutes
Cooking time: 2 hours

Pear and Kiwi Cheesecake

A riot of colour and flavour. How else could you describe this outrageously simple desert? It needs no cooking, and you can prepare it in advance. You will need a 3-inch metal pastry cutter (about 3ins long), and a blowtorch to help loosen the cheesecakes. Just don't set fire to the kitchen.

For the cheesecake:

- *4 pears, peeled, cored and cut into small cubes*
- *500g marscapone cheese (whipped cream would be just as nice)*
- *6-8 digestive biscuits*
- *50g soft brown sugar*

For the kiwi coulis:

- *4 ripe kiwifruit*
- *50g icing sugar*

1. Crush the digestive biscuits in a bowl and mix with the brown sugar.

2. In a separate bowl, mix together the marscapone and pear pieces.

3. Place a 3-inch metal pastry cutter in the middle of a serving plate and spoon in a quarter of the crumb mixture, pressing down. Add a quarter of the marscapone and pear mixture and press down firmly with a spoon or pallet knife. Using a blowtorch, gently heat the outside of the pastry cutter for no more than a few seconds, then slide off. Repeat for the remaining three cheesecakes, and chill.

4. Make the coulis.

Cut the tops and bottoms from the kiwifruit, and pare off the outer skin. Reserve four slices, and place on top of the cheesecakes.

Mash the remaining kiwifruit with a fork (you can use a blender), and add the icing sugar. Pass the mashed fruit through a fine sieve, discarding the black pips. Drizzle the coulis around the cheesecakes just before serving.

Serves 4
Preparation time: 20 minutes

Chapter Two

The New Life Begins

Friday 12th October that year will long remain in my memory.

It marked not only my 50th birthday, but my last day in work. My desk was as clear as it had ever been since 6th January 1986 when I first took up residence in room 313 at the Civic Offices.

There was an unfamiliar smell of lavender. Denise, the office cleaner, unhampered by the usual sea of paper, had been at work with the polish. The only things taking up space were the cards and gifts from colleagues and friends, many of whom popped in to remind me once more that they couldn't believe I was leaving.

Suddenly, I couldn't really believe it myself.

I was relieved to adjourn to the bar at lunchtime and take on some Dutch courage for the formal farewells later that afternoon. Then an old colleague, Roy Lewis, popped in with a bottle of Rioja Gran Reserva and it seemed sensible to try it out on the spot. After all, that would be one less bottle to carry home.

I was pretty well lubricated by the time it came to making my farewell speech, but I carried it off without offending too many people that I noticed.

I sobered up during the afternoon, and it was a strange feeling pulling out of the car park for the last time. I had expected I'd leap into the air and click my heels, but in the event, my final departure was tinged with sadness at the many friends I was leaving behind and not a little trepidation at the thought of burning my bridges at both work and at home.

The celebrations didn't end when I left the office. It was on to a meal at the Hare and Hounds, my local for the last seven years or so, with our good friends Martin and Alison Birt. True to form, Martin insisted on ordering champagne, and so it went on until around midnight when the landlord, Fergus, offered us all a free drink. I couldn't resist taking him up on a large calvados.

Sunday was the main event for friends and neighbours. The

party began at midday and by mid-afternoon Heath Lodge was bulging at the seams with sixty to seventy guests.

We all gathered on the drive for a group photograph. It was disconcerting to think we may never see some of these people again. Brian and Linda Parkes were there, and I couldn't help feeling a touch envious of their excitement at the prospect of moving in, tinged no doubt with a little concern at the antics of some of our more exuberant friends as the party wore on.

The following day was a write-off.

I was not too well (something I ate) so I had to leave Viv to do most of the clearing up while I drove slowly into Newbury to deliver her car to a dealer who was buying it.

Martin came along to give me a lift home and he'd obviously eaten the same thing I had.

The rest of the week was taken up with packing. We hadn't wanted to start the job until after the party, but this left only three days before the removers arrived. We'd seriously underestimated the time it would take and the amount of junk we'd accumulated over our ten years in Heath Lodge. I tried to be ruthless and throw out some of the bits and pieces I found in cupboards, had never seen before and did not wish to again. Viv was having none of it, and I had to resort to sneaking items into black bin liners when she wasn't looking. A serious argument broke out when I caught Viv packing two hot water bottles.

'What the hell do we need these for? We're going to live in Spain, for Christ's sake,' I said commandingly, trying to grab them, only to be overruled.

If I never see another packing case again it will be too soon.

We both worked flat out until late every evening wrapping, packing, labelling. As we slaved away, and it got later, I began to philosophise...We started married life with only a few sticks of furniture: bed, folding table, second-hand pots and pans. Like most people, we'd gradually acquired a full panoply of material possessions – umpteen dinner services, cutlery sets, crystal goblets and decanters, a range of kitchen implements and gadgets, and boxes of ornaments and souvenirs, most of which we had rarely used, or even seen for years. 'Now we can go right back to square one,' I said, to which Viv replied, '*What?*'

I had the greatest pleasure disposing of my working clothes – suits, double-cuffed shirts, and ties. I calculated, while packing, that in my working life I'd knotted and unknotted a tie more than 8,000 thousand times. I wasn't sorry to be relieved of this daily ritual. Then I thought about how I should dispose of the 30 or so pairs of black socks I'd acquired as part of my working uniform, and decided they might not have much second-hand value. So they came along to Spain to be relocated inside another wardrobe alongside three pairs of in-case-I-ever-need-them black brogues.

We were far from ready when the removal man, John Fowler, arrived on Thursday morning.

John and his two helpers started to empty the house, and at one stage everything we owned was strewn out for 30 yards along the drive. I seriously doubted it would all fit into the van, but John was a veteran, and gradually, with some trial and error, it all disappeared, with hardly a square inch of empty space.

By four o'clock, all our worldly goods were stacked in the back of the not-too-reliable-looking E-reg removal van. John stood over Viv as she vacuumed the empty house before he could put our hoover into the van.

John and his wife (another Viv) set off that evening to catch the Portsmouth ferry to southern France. The plan was, we'd all meet up at our house in Spain on Sunday evening. John and his wife were to travel on after that, heading for their house in Gibraltar where they'd stay for the winter. It was all set.

Viv and I had fish and chips in our empty house on Thursday evening, followed by a quick drink with Martin and Alison.

That night we slept in two sleeping bags on the floor of our empty bedroom with Jessie snuggling in between us. I lay awake, exhausted, thinking, 'What on earth have I done?'

At three o'clock we rose to a grey and drizzly morning, and set off for the Channel Tunnel.

I looked back fleetingly at Heath Lodge, knowing that from

twelve o'clock that day, it would no longer be ours. But there was no turning back, and so we were off.

We wanted urgently to be at the Channel Tunnel in good time so they could thoroughly inspect Jessie's certification, as we'd been warned they might. (In the event, they checked for weapons and drugs and never glanced at Jessie's scrupulously-prepared paperwork, *though I stood there holding it out plainly enough*.)

The 6.20am Shuttle was on schedule and we made excellent progress through France heading for Dijon and Beaune. From that point, the French motorways were almost deserted; a welcome contrast to my daily battles on the M25.

Our first stopover was at the Chateau Bellecroix in Chagny near Nuits St George. Wow – what a place. A picture postcard chateau complete with a long sweeping drive, twin round spires and its own winery and cellars at the rear. They were happy to accommodate dogs for eighty francs a night (without breakfast) although the receptionist raised both eyebrows as he looked across, rather than down, at Jessie.

We strolled round the grounds, then settled Jessie into the bedroom before going down to dinner.

As we left the room, perhaps made nervous by the receptionist, we worried about any damage she might cause, and for several minutes we stood silently outside the door. I was sure I could hear Jessie breathing on the other side, listening to us listening to her, but it was a game of patience, and when at last we heard her bones thumping down on the floor we sneaked away.

The dining room was a timber-panelled hall with an ornate vaulted ceiling supporting massive, glistening chandeliers. The walls dripped with oil paintings, seemingly faded family portraits of previous occupants of the chateau. Waiters were uniformed according to rank from the Maitre d' in a dinner jacket down to ordinary waiters in black waistcoats and white aprons. The sommelier wore a dark jacket and tie adorned with a silver wine cup.

They all clipped neatly across the polished oak floor and calmly executed well-rehearsed routines, delivering and removing plates. Crumbs were swept from the stiffly-starched, white tablecloth between every course, and the voluminous wine goblets, large enough to take half a bottle, were only fractionally filled, but topped up after every sip. A virtuoso performance.

We ate the most delicious meal, of 'the kind only the French do properly,' I told Viv; using simple fresh ingredients to produce a mouth-watering banquet. The cheese board was the size of the table and had a selection of over fifty cheeses – some 'Very sniffy, indeed,' I commented more than once, trying them out.

The whole evening was brilliant, and for a moment I wondered why we'd ruled out France so quickly. Then I asked for the bill and realised the meal had cost us a week's Spanish spending money. I reminded Viv to remind me to remind her, which I did at length, joining her in a few more sips, that this kind of extravagance – and I was pleased to see that she thoroughly agreed – would be hard to justify on our now limited budget.

Well satisfied with the money we'd saved at dinner, we made our way upstairs and found that Jessie had not trashed the room.

We were not in the least surprised. We had, it was clear, planned everything to perfection.

On the road at eight-thirty the next morning, however, battling heavy rain and heavy traffic, we were not so sanguine. As we skirted Lyon, we were belted by high winds and as we fringed the Massif Central coming over the mountains, we felt we'd be blown off the road.

Our second stopover was at the Villa Duflot in Perpignan, just north of the French/Spanish border. We were very tired when we arrived. The Villa was not as spectacular as Chateau Bellecroix but it was, we agreed, a fine place to stay – although if it had been a few miles further on, we'd have stopped to sleep in the car. The first thing we did was lie down and rest; Jessie, too.

And now, the first hiccups.

Our second hand LHD Landrover Freelander, imported from Germany, had performed wonderfully on the motorway, but early on Saturday evening I went to retrieve something from the car in the Hotel car park. I pressed the button for the central locking but nothing happened. I tried the spare.

Still nothing.

Panic! I could get into the car with the key but the immoboliser was on and the car wouldn't start. Fortunately, there was a very helpful man on reception who explained that he had come across this problem before. It was something in the vicinity of the hotel that interfered with the remote control. He rounded up a few reluctant hotel staff to push the car about fifty metres away, and after a little fiddling around, it started. The receptionist then recommended I park in a different part of the hotel car park for the night. I followed his suggestion and cautiously tested the remote button. Everything was fine.

At this point we dressed to have dinner in the hotel restaurant, and we were about to leave the room when Jessie, who had behaved impeccably up to then, made it clear that she was not going to be left alone. She barked and cried and scratched at the door when we tried to go out. Sensing that this time she was in the mood to do some serious damage, we gave in – well, Viv gave in and I was included in Viv's decision, and very sound it was, too – and stayed with her.

We ordered dinner to be served in our room and ate on the balcony, overlooking a palm-fringed courtyard and a fountain.

Dinner was excellent, but very slow, as each course arrived at half-hourly intervals, freshly cooked and served on dishes under domed silver covers. The first time they brought a course, the hotel staff were halted at the door by Jessie, who sniffed at, and wanted to inspect, every item of food and them as well. Jessie had already dined on her usual dry dog food, but by the time the main course arrived she was showing more than passing interest in our dinner. As we slowly dismantled the carefully presented meal, I noticed Viv push a piece of seared turbot to one side of her plate together with a soupsant of truffle sauce.

'You're *not seriously going to give that to the dog,*' I pronounced. To which, of course, there was only one reply. (I wondered, later, if anyone would notice just how highly polished the monogrammed plates were when they were returned to the kitchen, and I hoped they didn't think we'd washed up for them – but it was too late by that time, and if they did, well, if anyone was dog-poisoned, I didn't read about it.)

It was a great dinner, but – foolishly – I couldn't resist trying the car again just before going to bed. Nothing. Panic again, especially as the friendly receptionist had left for the night and was unlikely to be there on Sunday morning. I decided to sleep on it, but had a restless night imagining we would be stranded...for days...weeks, even...

Next morning, I got up early and ran down to the car.

Everything worked fine, except for my nerves, and I staggered back up to see Viv tucking into breakfast. 'Nice walk? Jessie and I had a lovely sleep-in. Your eggs are cold.'

Finally, then, we entered Spain. We crossed the border on the A7 on Sunday 21st October.

Heading south, we fringed Barcelona and bypassed Tarragona and Castello, and at last we caught caught sight of Valencia and the Mediterranean.

I'd been trying to contact John and Viv Fowler by mobile phone all day, without success. Thoughts that they might have broken down, crashed or got lost, were becoming convictions when Viv's mobile rang. John Fowler said they were at the house. At this point, we were fifteen minutes away ourselves; we grinned at each other – and Jessie barked: the timing was perfect.

We broke the back of the unloading that evening since we needed a bed to sleep on and, at my suggestion as Viv reminded us all, this had been the first item to be packed so it was crammed in 'behind everything else.' We got it out then put together a meal, cracking open a small bottle of Champagne to celebrate our safe arrival, another to toast all our precious possessions – and another to welcome the other Viv and John for the night – by which time they were asleep in the van.

Viv and John planned to leave mid-morning on Monday, but two workmen arrived to dig a large hole outside our house and cut off the water, while they repaired a leak. This meant that John couldn't turn the furniture van round.

This was my first encounter with real people in real Spain; as good a time as any to put my language skills to the test. It took about thirty seconds of blank, uncomprehending reactions before I resorted to sign language – and then, sin of sins, I found myself doing what I had vowed never to do: shouting louder, and ending every word in 'o,' as if that would help.

'*Cuando*,' (I got that far), 'you *finisho*. Mi amigo musto leavo soon-oh.'

With a bruised ego I returned and reported to John that the workmen simply shrugged their shoulders at me, as if that would help. 'Must be some Spanish thing.'

John went over and got it worked out in no time. He had to reverse down the narrow road for about seventy-five metres and the rest of us were to run round the van, shouting instructions.

Finally, he reached the road, he and the other Viv were waved into the distance; the workmen decided to leave five minutes later, job unfinished; and Viv and I were alone in our new home, starting our new life.

The hypnotic blue of the sky, langorously washed with green, lay reflected in our pool. The garden was glorious. Sunlight glowed softly gold on the hills. Life could not be more perfect.

Getting my priorities right, I left Viv to start unpacking and set out for the village in search of food. I like to call it a village, but it is, in fact, a small town. The Spanish call it a *pueblo*. Parcent *pueblo* was about a ten-minute walk away along a dusty old *camino* through the orange and olive groves.

We could see the church tower from our kitchen window and hear the bells chime every fifteen minutes. Curiously, the clock was an hour slow, though it caught up at the end of the week when local time was adjusted for the end of 'summertime.'

Parcent was known locally, somewhat grandly, as *Paraíso entre Montañas* – 'paradise between the mountains' – but one estate agent ad. described it as: 'a Provencal-style village with colour-washed houses,' and the combination, I thought, making my way through the picturesque town, was reasonably accurate.

I found the *panadería* and negotiated my way to a couple of loaves and half a dozen eggs, then turned the corner into the church square to find it was market day. The place was buzzing with activity.

At the first (and only) fruit and vegetable stall I bought large nobbly tomatoes, salad leaves, bright amber wild mushrooms, tiny young artichokes, potatoes still with dirt on them and a whole bag of oranges – all for next to nothing.

I was delighted, and thinking what Viv would say when I showed her, when I was suddenly joined by a foursome from Birmingham. Mr and Mrs Lime Green, and their friends Sky Blue and White, and all their friends, lined up next to me to remark on the variety and cheapness of the food. I shuffled away quickly, trying to recall some fluent-Spanish-sounding phrases.

My next stop was the large open-sided van selling a vast array of ham, salami, cheese, olives and lots of dried fish that looked to me like it'd be best suited to soling shoes. I decided I'd like to buy some of almost everything, but the van was surrounded by women jabbering away in Valenciano (they didn't speak 'Spanish,' I remembered, in this part of Spain). After about five minutes, noticing I seemed no further forward in the queue, I caught sight of a ticket system, a la Sainsbury's deli counter. I went over and took a ticket only to realise that the electronic number display wasn't working and a man was just calling out the numbers. Help!

The cluster of chattering women grew to a crowd, but still there was no semblance of a queue. The man called a number. I didn't think it was mine, but wasn't sure. I was trying desperately to recall the local lingo for numbers, when he seemed to take pity on me; looking towards the group of women he raised his eyes skyward. I went over and he took my order for some *jamón serran:* the local dry-cured ham, similar to Italian Parma ham.

'Here, look, this bloke's ordering bacon, I wouldn't mind some of that for breakfast.'

It was Mr and Mrs Lime Green, and I turned slightly and explained in my best civic meeting voice that this was 'not, in fact, bacon, but *cured ham.*'

'Oh, I've had that stuff before. It's horrible and salty – like eating raw ham,' said one of the friends.

Next I ordered some cheese, *queso de cabra.*

'You know that's made from goat's milk, don't you?' said Mr Lime. (This was very perceptive of him, I thought, since there was a picture of a goat on the outside of the cheese. I did not deign to reply.) 'I couldn't eat that stuff.'

'Indeed, you could not,' I said, adding something to the stall-holder which might or might not have been Spanish – anyway, he seemed to think it was funny – before I turned and left.

With my shoulders back and my nose still well in the air, I started briskly home.

But although it was only a short walk back from the village, laden with six or seven carrier bags and walking in the heat of the day along the dusty *camino,* I found it hard work. I was dripping with sweat and my arms were getting longer by the minute. Before leaving England, I had vowed never to push a supermarket trolley again, but already I was having second thoughts...and I began to think about 'home.'

The day we'd arrived at the house I'd found a torn-off slip of cardboard wedged in the door of the toolroom. There had been a message on it from Ted Marshall, my former boss, now retired. The note from Ted, delivered by himself (having somehow managed to mysteriously 'pass through Parcent') repeated that he expected a full report on our adventures in Spain. (It had been this demand, amongst other things, that had inspired me to start writing, even before we had left 'home.')

Ted had been Mr Stickler for grammar and punctuation in committee reports and would correct them in red ink. When he lost patience, he would just write 'ugh' in the margin; a sure and discouraging sign of his dissatisfaction.

I wondered now, as I walked home with my shopping, what he would think of Mr and Mrs Lime Green and their comments about the cheese – and what I should write about them, if I did, and what he'd think if my work were ever published and how many 'ughs' there would be in the margin, and whether he would give me a reference if our Spanish escapade turned to disaster…

By the time I got back to the house, I was totally exhausted.

That night, there was another reminder of work. At about one in the morning I heard a loud beeping sound: it angrily demanded my attention and repeated itself every thirty seconds. I tracked it down to our dining room, which was still full of packing cases.

Looking into the room, I realised my pager, which I had forgotten to hand back, was giving off its 'low battery signal.' The sound was coming from one of about twenty packing cases piled high in the corner. I put up with the noise all through a restless night and woke early next morning determined to track it down. The hunt was on. I listened every thirty seconds and gradually homed in on a group of cases right at the back of the room when, suddenly, it stopped altogether. I swear it knew I was after it.

Before the pager went off, I'd been reading the Costa Blanca News in bed and found out that Tuesday was market day in Jalon, the main town in the valley. I decided that we would give it a try the next day. I also read that Monday was a fiesta day in Jalon. There was a whole schedule of events listed, culminating in a fireworks display at eleven in the evening. About five minutes later I heard the fireworks at first hand.

Jalon is about six kilometres away but the noise of the explosions echoed around the mountains as if they were being detonated at the end of our road. Jessie started barking, then shivering, then trying desperately to hide in the shower. Finally, Viv woke up. I told her that I had just found another interesting market to visit. 'How does tomorrow sound?' We stayed up through the fireworks, planning what we'd buy.

The next day, after I'd not found the pager, we set off early for Jalon and the market, to find it was cancelled because of the fiesta, which was to continue all week, with fireworks every night. (This kind of thing happened all the time and we finally found out that we needed to get a calendar showing when each of the villages were having fiestas, to avoid going near them.)

We settled for a cup of coffee in Jalon at a little bar where the plastic tables took up half the narrow street and came in and out with the sun. I used my Spanish to order.

'*Un café solo y un cappuccino por favor,*' I said.

The waiter nodded. I knew cappuccino was Italian but I also knew that the word was universal, and I sat back to wait for my first Spanish cappuccino. The waiter returned with the *café solo* for Viv and a small glass of strong black coffee for me.

I accepted it out of curiosity – wondering if I'd encountered the most exotic version of cappuccino in the world – and found I rather liked it. It tasted slightly of alcohol. I later found out that the waiter must have mistaken *cappuccino* for *carajillo*: black coffee with a dash of brandy. I decided to order it often.

Our third day was glorious, with another clear blue sky; the temperature reached twenty-seven degrees by about two o'clock in the afternoon.

The pool looked inviting. I decided to give it a try.

Viv glanced at the water thermometer and said, 'Twenty degrees. The thermometer says *that's kalt.'* She marched inside. All I can say is that they were both right and I was definitely in need of a magnifying glass when I came straight out, shivering, shaking and bellowing about not having been clearly warned – although the dip had not been entirely wasted, I realised later, since Viv had been recording me with the new video camera.

Soon afterward, I enquired of our Dutch neighbour about the post, having suddenly twigged, after days of searching, that we didn't have a letterbox. He told me that we had to collect the mail from the *oficina de correos* in the village, which opened from half-past ten to half-past eleven each morning.

'Presumably,' I said to Viv, laughing, 'the postman goes off on the donkey to the next village, after that.'

I could not wait to get down there to have a look, to see if I was right, but my first visit was rewarded with nothing more than a modern little post office building and a sign saying: 'Closed for fiesta.' A passing English lady helpfully explained that the post-man lived in Jalon so he'd taken the week off.

The next week, I was finally able to pick up our mail, and found we had a bundle of cards from friends and former col-leagues welcoming us to our new home. I ran back to show them to Viv. We were going through them when she came across one Spanish letter in the bundle. I grabbed it and tore it open.

'It's the electricity company,' I told her. 'And...it informs us that...the previous owner...has *not paid the last bill.*' I held it up in triumph. '*They are threatening to cut us off!* but not until De-cember – HAH! – *that gives us a couple of months* to track – '

'Pay the bill,' Viv said.

'That *cunning basket, Jon*. He must be hiding out in Holland – '

'Just pay the bill.'

Ten days later, we realised that no one had phoned us. We had made lots of calls out, but nothing was coming in. Perhaps our friends were not missing us as much as we were missing them, we joked. Anxious to confirm that this could not be true, we began to investigate.

Eventually, we tracked the problem to the adapter we were us-ing on our English phone; it ensured that people phoning in got a ringing tone, but our phone stayed silent.

Off we went to Santos, the hardware shop in Jalon which we'd been told 'sells everything.' The very helpful proprietor, Pepe, spoke near-perfect English as well as a smattering of German, French and Dutch, so there was an international queue waiting to consult him and he was rushing around the shop, talking to several people at once.

I finally spoke to Pepe and he said that he could put a new plug on the end of our phone. We went back, got the phone, took it to the shop, and he cut off the old plug to find that our English cable had three wires, whereas the Spanish plug had four slots.

'It's a matter of guesswork,' he said.

We took the phone home to try it.

Attempt one: nothing. Back to Pepe. Attempt two: the phone rang and never stopped. Back to Pepe. Attempt three – the phone rang, but only when we picked it up, and only when there was no one on the line. We gave up and bought a Spanish phone.

On Thursday, a man arrived to install our satellite TV system. Four hours later, and with a dish that would not have looked out of place at Jodrell Bank, he reached the conclusion that our TV set was not working.

'Must have got damaged in the move,' he surmised.

The satellite system was installed, but we couldn't get a picture, though the system worked perfectly on his portable. Several phone calls later, and after sincere promises from a chap called Steve to come and fix it, our television set was in a repair shop run by a couple of Germans in Jalon. They promised to ring as soon as it had been fixed. I wasn't holding my breath. By this time it was almost two weeks since we'd seen television, listened to the radio or read a newspaper. What was happening in the world?

'Who cares?' I said to Viv. She pointed to the computer.

'We're better off not knowing,' I said.

Later that day I went to find an Internet Service Provider. I'd been advised that Wanadoo was the best free ISP in Spain. You wouldn't expect it in a small place like Jalon, but Pepe from the hardware shop told me that was easy to arrange, and directed me to a small internet café called 'Reig,' run by two attractive young women. They couldn't give me a CD for the computer, but they offered to register me with Wanadoo from their office.

Some fifteen minutes later it was done, and I came out of their office with an e-mail to *Estimado Mark* giving me all the details of my user name and password.

I couldn't wait to try it back home, but when I did, the system wouldn't let me log on and didn't accept my *contraseña* (password). I phoned the Wanadoo helpline and eventually got through to find the people more than helpful – especially the lovely-sounding Maria. She spoke perfect English and advised me at once to stop talking in Spanish. Then she slowly and carefully talked me through resetting the computer, entering parts I never knew existed. Eventually, success: we had lift-off. Maria sounded almost as pleased as I was when we finished.

I called Viv through. 'Great response for a change. I've been talking to the most wonderful young women all day,' I told her, 'and I've finally succeeded.'

She beamed at the computer. 'That's a first.'

But the phone connection to Wanadoo, we soon found out, was rather too expensive to use, especially during the day, so we agreed on a system whereby we logged on just once each evening to send and receive e-mails and use the Internet. After a few false starts, we set up an even better system that worked very well: a stop watch with an alarm to regulate each other's turn. Soon after that, we quit that system and used the computer whenever we liked, yelling if a spouse entered the room.

Friday was the big market day in Denia down on the coast, about twenty minutes away. The indoor food market was a cacophony of noise and colour, packed with butchers, bakers, fish stalls and tapas bars.

This market spilled over into the surrounding streets with hundreds of fruit and vegetable stalls noisily competing for business. I was in my element. This was what I came to Spain to see. A combination of over-enthusiasm and confusion with language (the words for a quarter kilo and four kilos are remarkably similar) left Viv and I to trudge our way back to the car laden with enough food to feed the five thousand, but at least I had *used my Spanish*, I said to Viv (who tended to ignore this point).

On the way back we found Amica: a large hypermarket. There, we bought all the mundane things like soap powder, detergents, toilet rolls – and beer: San Miguel. We were now pretty well organised, except for the wine.

This I bought at the local bodega, Riko's. The Jalon Tinto, straight from the barrel, cost an incredible 140 pesetas a litre – about sixty pence.

It's all in the mind, but there's something very special about drinking wine straight from the wood.

The big red fire hose trailing from one of the barrels and across the floor to the back room should have made me a bit suspicious of the origins of this particular vintage, and my scepticism should have been further aroused by four enormous stainless steel silos at the back of the bodega, looking more appropriate to an oil refinery than a purveyor of fine wine, and the fact that the Jalon Tinto was offered in sweet, medium, or dry might also have made me question the quality of the product – but who cared, it tasted fine and was dirt cheap. I couldn't care less where it came from, I thought, and I planned to say nothing.

Viv had noticed the same evidence, however, and she wasn't having any barrelled white, thanks. To be honest, it did taste like sherry, so I admitted the fact and although I was happy with my purchase I splashed out £1 a bottle for her, for some decent stuff. Then at last off we went home – to cook, eat, drink and be merry.

Our first weekend was making us tired, however, so we set out for an evening meal at one of the local restaurants in Alcalalí: Pepe's. Three courses each and a bottle of wine, all for £16.

The meal was nice enough, but – it was English. So were the customers.

'*I thought we had come to the real Spain, away from all the tourists,*' I hissed at Viv, and she smiled vaguely around the restaurant as if she fancied she heard a far-off voice (mind you, she does this so often I hardly notice it any more), though after we'd left, she admitted she agreed with me (and I have a theory that women do this *to prove they're dainty*).

Anyway, shocked and determined not to repeat the experience, we agreed on our way home, that no matter how hungry we were – within limits and depending on our mood – we would always, always search to find somewhere typically Spanish.

(Later, we decided we should ask our neighbours some questions about this strange restaurant, and how it had found its way into the real Spain. However, it was not the presence of the restaurant that they found strange, but that we should ask the question in the first place. The real Spain? Maybe ten years ago, but the Jalon Valley had gradually been colonised, and many of the restaurants in the area now catered for purely English customers. All these places had an identical menus, we were told – exactly like the one we had seen that night that had taken us back, weirdly, to the early 1970's, with its shrimp cocktail, steak and kidney pie, apple turnover and runny cream.)

Next morning was Sunday, and like every other day that first week, it was warm and sunny. Everything was quiet and peaceful, the silence punctuated only by the incessant twittering of birds and the occasional strangulated bark of a dog somewhere in the mountains. Then suddenly, a deafening roar of highly tuned engines interrupted the tranquillity.

A motor racing event had begun in Parcent and the cars were tearing up the mountain roads that overlooked our house.

Every 45 seconds another exhaustless Porche, Subaru or Mini Cooper gunned it up the hill at full throttle – doing a timed run up the winding road to the summit of the mountain. All we saw was a brief blur of red or blue or yellow between the trees as each competitor sped along the course. Every time the sound of a car faded into the distance, the next one revved up. After 90 minutes, much to our relief, it was quiet again, and we heard all the cars cruise quietly down the mountain in a procession.

Then they ran the race for a second time. Then a third. The third run was briefly halted by an ambulance tearing up the road as fast as the race cars – but after that, they were off again.

The event ran from 9am, to three in the afternoon.

'This is like living next to Brands Hatch,' I muttered, inside with all the windows closed, staring out.

'Worse,' Viv said, 'because the mountains amplify the sound. But I'm all right, I've got cotton wool in my ears. Want some?'

We found out later that this was a very popular sport in Spain and hundreds of spectators lined the route we were listening to. It was not unknown for racers or spectators to go over the edge.

Fortunately for us, we also found out, it took place only once a year, and the road was more often closed for cycle races than for motoring events.

Monday 29th October was Viv's birthday. I hadn't been able to find a card shop so I spent an afternoon creating one on the computer. I wanted to achieve a balance of rich irony, humour, affection and reassurance, and the message finally read: '*You're not getting old, just ripening in the Spanish sun.*'

Later, Viv was to point out there was a certain omen in the message, though she knew I couldn't have thought of it at the time of writing, having during my creative stint finished off the last bottle of Sancere wine she'd put aside for the birthday dinner.

I got out some champagne to make up for the loss.

While I was doing this, she pinned the card above the computer with a cunningly worded hint written on it that I should not make any more birthday cards ('Don't make birthday cards!'), although the thought was '*macho,* and almost but not quite *mucho,* appreciado,' which I still haven't been able to figure out.

And then came the saga of the gates. Our house was very private, with tall hedges all round the garden. But these were not Jessie-proof and there were no gates on the front of the drive. Gates and fencing had been ordered way back in September through a local English builder who lived in the next village, and everything was supposed to be done by the time we reached Spain on Monday 22nd October. On arrival, we'd found the fencing installed, but not the gates.

I phoned the builder on our first day and his wife said not to worry; 'The gates will arrive in two days.'

We left it for five days and phoned again.

There was a slight problem: the wrought iron gates we'd asked for were not to standard specifications, so the builder had placed an order for them to be specially made by a local Spanish blacksmith. They'd take about a week, the blacksmith had said.

A week later we heard, 'The blacksmith believes perhaps they will be ready in two weeks.'

In the meantime, we constructed a temporary barricade out of some chicken wire, an old garden table and a sunblind. It resembled something out of Les Miserables, and I took a few photographs, rather pleased, to send back to friends. The trouble was, it took ten minutes to dismantle this barricade every time we went out, and the same amount of time to resurrect it when we returned, and Viv was sure the neighbours were beginning to wonder what kind of people were holing themselves up inside Casa Emelia.

Three weeks, and still no progress on the television front, either. It remained with the repair shop in Jalon run by the two Germans.

'I had expected a bit of German efficiency from there,' I said to Viv, and I phoned them to say so.

They told me that their expert technician, who was Spanish, was very busy at the moment.

I reported this.

'Say no more,' was Viv's response. We were still on the repairmen's 'don't call us' list, and we hadn't seen television for nearly a month, she mused.

'Other than that,' I said, 'and the fact that one of the toilets keeps blocking, the water's been cut off twice and we've had daily power cuts, everything's going fine.'

Jessie barked, agreeing with both of us, and I took her outside for another photograph of 'Jessie Guarding the Miserables.'

One or two other things took a bit of getting used to.

Our gas, for cooking and water heating, was delivered by lorry every Monday morning. We just put the empty canister at the front of the house with 1450 pesetas (about £6) and he left a new one. The first two weeks went by without our having to replace a canister; all we had to do was organise a couple of spares.

Our refuse, *basura* – soon turned out to be another story. This we had to take to the main road just outside Parcent. I soon got sick of doing this alone, and one day Viv joined me, proving quite adept at forcing things into large bins.

We both detested the look of the two huge refuse containers that stood at the entrance to our development like a couple of ready-for-battle Giant Muffin Men, and wondered if there was anything we could do about them.

'At least they're emptied almost every day,' I said, watching Viv pull leaves and branches across the nearby old fridges, microwaves and toilets – which looked as if they'd been waiting round for years. She came with me once a week after that, and each time did a little more of this 'nature decorating.' I helped, once I cottoned on to her plan, and within a few months the old electrical goods had been all but swallowed up into the bushes.

Only the Muffin Men remained, and they were too big to do more with than point out to any visitors we had that these were a local negative attraction, like modern art sculpture back home.

A few more visits to Parcent revealed some hitherto unknown features. A second baker's shop produced light, delicious cakes, and a fish shop, open two mornings a week, sold the kind of tasty little sprats that would have been returned to the sea by English fisherman for fear of breaching EU conservation rules.

We also found a couple of bars and an attractive little cafe, next to a restaurant which seemed to open only at lunchtime, though not on Wednesdays, to serve only paella.

Nearby, a hairdressers, *peluquería*, had a sign saying, 'unisex.' I desperately needed a haircut, Viv said, but I explained that I'd have to check out the haircuts they did, first.

After that, I made it a practice, when I came into town alone, to drop in at the little café opposite. I sat near the window, and watched for haircuts. While waiting, I had one or two of the small black coffees I'd developed a taste for. Finally, one day after a few coffees I went over the road and got a cut, which turned out to be very nice, Viv said when I got home, though the rinse smelled awful, as if they'd smothered me in brandy.

By far the most famous thing about Parcent – well, it's mentioned in all the guidebooks; indeed it's the only thing mentioned in the guidebooks – is the Agricultural Co-op Bar, *Cooperativa*.

We discovered this on our way back from the post office one day. Outside it looked very grand, with a small terrace in the shade of some carefully pruned trees where all the old men of the village seemed to have congregated. There were a couple of vacant chairs on the terrace, but from the nervous looks of the old folk as we neared them, I got the impression they were reserved for people with a more historical-Spanish-terrace look about them. So we took ourselves inside for a coffee.

We'd never seen anything like it. It resembled a small wheel-tappers and shunters club. A large hall, it had a stage at the end and every wall was emblazoned with gaudy blue and yellow tiles. I could picture the local talent doing a 'turn' on Saturday nights. In years gone by, before the advent of political correctness, I'd taken part in the office Christmas Show, playing a north country comic complete with hob-nail boots, flat cap and a ferret down me trousers. The material was bawdy but not blue and I began to imagine a repeat performance here in La Cooperativa if I could only translate the jokes into Spanish. It would be something of a challenge I suggested to Viv, who had seen the video of the Christmas Show. After that, the thought never occurred to me again (though I still think she was WRONG).

The house speciality at La Coopertiva was Moroccan lamb, which you had to order a day in advance, and we decided we would try it, once we had eaten our way through some more of our last market purchases. In the meantime, the coffee was 'Very nice, indeed,'we told the staff as we left, shaking their hands one by one – and feeling, from the reaction to this praise, that we had made yet another set of new friends.

But soon it was Tuesday or Wednesday (by this time we weren't sure), and it was time for our biggest shock.

Our garden was raised slightly from the main terrace by an open, dry-stone wall. Standing in the *naya*, I suddenly noticed Jessie's ears prick up and I looked out to see a large black snake slithering, sidewinder-style, across the terrace. It appeared to have come from under one of the sun beds where I had been enjoying my afternoon siestas. Slowly it disappeared, all one metre of it, into one of the cracks in the retaining wall.

I didn't know whether *Señor Serpiente* lived there, and was just about to go in and ask Viv what she knew about snakes living in families, when she came out to see what I had shouted.

She immediately decided we must see a builder about having all the holes blocked up.

'*This despite your absolute assurances that there are no poisonous snakes in this part of Spain,*' she said. 'I would have had *serious misgivings*. And what about poor Jessie?'

'It must have come from somewhere,' I said, putting my shoes on. 'Hitched a lift. Definitely doesn't come from around here.'

I planted myself for a while by the hole into which the snake had disappeared, a raised mattock in my hands ready to pounce.

It was a gesture designed to assure Viv that fearless caveman would protect delicate maiden against most frightening of foes. I didn't really expect to see the beast again, and if I did, I planned to run for it.

The mattock grew heavier, and just as my patience began to expire, *Señor Serpiente* popped his head out of the rocks. My heart pounded. Luckily I saw no more of the snake than its nose and flickering tongue as it tasted the air and sensed my presence.

I held my ground, after all, and my grip on the mattock – until the snake retreated whence it came.

'I scared it off,' I reported to Viv. 'Terrified the poor thing.'

'Oh?' She stayed inside until I reported the find to the neighbours, and found out it had been a harmless grass snake.

So how was Jessie getting on? Well, the truth was that the woodlands and open countryside, which attracted us to the Jalon Valley in the first place, had attracted every other dog owner in this part of Spain. With a dog like Jessie, who likes to get her retaliation in first, this caused a few local difficulties. Fortunately, there were a great many different routes to take, so it was relatively easy to take avoiding action when confronted with a possible adversary.

Jessie didn't exactly hit it off with the old boxer-cross next door, Jason (Yason in Dutch), who seldom showed more of himself than a glimpse of cheerfully panting tongue between slats of a fence, after Jessie tried to bite his bum on their second meeting, but it seemed that Gerrard and Catharina were very understanding, or else Jason was old, wise and content enough with his lot to keep out of Jessie's way.

Then Jessie made one little friend: Sara, a young mongrel belonging to Henk – another Dutchman just down the road.

We all went for a walk together one morning and Henk took us up into the countryside – *campo* – at the back of our house. We walked for miles; first through orange, almond and olive groves carved into terraces centuries ago, and then into more open, treeless countryside with shrubs and bushes, including wild thyme, rosemary and lavender.

This was just what we were looking for, and luckily most of the other dog owners were too lazy or sensible to venture this far up, into the real countryside.

As ever, there was a drawback: on the weekends there were always several hunters in the *campo*. They usually hunted with a dog and a shotgun for rabbits and wildfowl, though I was told that wild boar were not uncommon.

Hunting, Henk explained, was not so much a hobby in Spain as a national obsession. 'They will shoot anything that walks or runs or hops or flies. If you run into a boar, run for your lives.'

Still, it was a lovely walk. The views were spectacular. I said we would be all right if we were brightly dressed, surely, and we began to make plans to roam around up there on a regular basis. But Viv pointed out, then, the obvious: it would only be safe if Jessie dressed brightly as well. The idea of attempting this put us off going back up the mountain for a while, until we learned boars were hard to run into. Henk liked a laugh.

Our other big challenge was to visit to the Banco de Valencia in Javea to collect credit and debit cards and withdraw some cash.

We set out on Thursday 1st November and were half-way there when Viv commented on how quiet it was, and how none of the shops seemed to be open. It turned out to be another fiesta day; All Souls, I think. We stopped for coffee and a waiter explained, 'We mourn the deaths of our fathers.' The bank was closed so we had to go back and return the next day.

Our bank was in the middle of Javea Old Town, with its narrow little streets, some just wide enough for two donkeys to pass. Now confident about driving on the wrong side of the road, I decided to drive into this old town to find our bank. It was a big mistake. Whenever we'd been there before it had been very quiet, but not this Friday. All hell had broken loose. The streets were choked with traffic and we were in the middle of it.

About a week earlier, an English friend had kindly sent us a newspaper cutting which reported that Landrover had recalled all Freelanders because of a fault with the handbrake...

And now, back to the traffic jam: we hadn't moved for quite a few minutes when I notice some of the cars in front beginning to peel-off up a road to the right. Ah! I decided to follow them.

We were now in another traffic jam, this time half-way up the kind of steep hill that, 'Wouldn't be allowed to exist in England,' I told Viv. I was sure it was about forty-five degrees – and us, I remembered suddenly, with an iffy handbrake. Then it began to slip.

I shouted, revved the engine hard and tugged on the handbrake, with Viv pulling the brake along with me, shouting with all her strength as well. By the time we reached the top and emerged from the queue we were both hot, tearful, distressed, short of breath and physically exhausted - and from the acrid smell I knew I had probably wiped three years' life off the clutch.

'I am *never* taking another short cut in Spain,' I said. 'It's too *hard* on my *blessed nerves* – pass me a tissue, will you?' and for once, Viv agreed.

'Not with me in the car,' she said.

A short time later, on a Tuesday after a stint of heavy gardening we were both taking a well deserved after-lunch siesta. The temperature was about 23 degrees and I'd stripped down to my shorts for a brief snooze on the sun bed. An hour or two later I awoke, dazed, to find Viv snoring softly away next to me.

We both looked a little sunburnt, I thought...Clearly, we were in for a run of warm weather.

By that Thursday, it hadn't stopped raining for two days. The log fire was burning in the lounge, the temperature had dropped to about five degrees (colder with the wind chill factor) and there was sprinkling of snow on the mountains.

'I didn't know we were coming to a ski resort,' I said to Viv. 'Where did you put those hot water bottles?'

'Those hot water bottles you didn't want me to pack?' She held one up from her lap and waved it. 'Yours is warming my side of the bed.'

I should have realised, I thought, that this cold weather could hit us when I'd come across a pretty postcard of Parcent in the tobacconists shop in the village – covered in heavy snow. The lady who sold it assured me it had been taken *many years ago*. Apparently, this kind of weather is *quite rare* and happens about *every ten years* – and it was 'just our luck,' everyone told us when we ventured out after the first two days of rain.

But now we were contemplating a white Christmas, something we hadn't seen in England for as long as I could remember. Secretly thrilled, I went round saying, 'I want my money back!' but wrote to describe our glorious winter weather to those friends who had booked to come and stay with us, and told them to bring 'hot water bottles and plenty of brandy.'

Meanwhile, there was progress at last on the television front, but not as we expected. I gave the German TV repair company in Jalon a further ten days, but still they hadn't phoned as they had promised they would. So I phoned again and said so, getting ready this time to bring up 'German efficiency,' once and for all.

'Ah,' the man interrupted, 'we wondered when you would call back.'

'Call back?' I enquired. What did they mean?

'We left a message on your answer-phone, the day before yesterday.'

'But I haven't got an answer-phone.'

'Oh, yes, you have,' was their response. They explained that the service was free with Telefonica, the Spanish phone service, and told me how to access my messages.

'Dumkopf,' I heard one of them say at the end of the phone.

I followed their instructions, pressing the correct buttons as instructed by the recorded Spanish voice. We had nine messages from people who had worked out that the recording, which interrupted if we didn't answer after four or five rings, was inviting them to leave a message after the beep.

This was a great novelty, and we listened to the messages several times – but back to the television.

After another two weeks the helpful German explainer of the answer-phone system explained that our old set was beyond economical repair and asked: would we like it back, or a new one? Well, what else could we do after more than five weeks without the moving wallpaper? Later that day we were the proud owners of a brand new Schneider television with instructions in Spanish and German, and we'd left the old set with the shop.

The BBC digital card had arrived from England, so I phoned the number for it to be activated – to be told it would take twenty-four hours. What's another day? The following day, Friday, I thought I would stock up for the weekend with another five litres of the dirt-cheap, sherry-like Jalon Tinto – so we could settle down to some serious television and catch up on what had been happening in the world. We tuned in that evening and, surprise, surprise, everything seemed to be working fine.

Then: 'Why is Sky News showing the wrong date? It says it's only Thursday,' said Viv.

I wondered if it was taking twenty-four hours for the satellite signal to reach Spain. We phoned back home to check the date and discovered it really was Thursday.

Somehow we had completely lost a day. How on earth was going I to make five litres of Jalon Tinto last until Monday, especially since Viv had started sampling mine, in order to criticise it, and taken a liking to the stuff?

That evening we settled down to watch a film on BBC Two: 'The Last Command,' made in black-and-white in 1955 and starring Sterling Hayden. It told of the fight for the independence of Texas from Mexico, and ended with the Battle of the Alamo.

Outside the house, the weather was just beginning to deteriorate as the film started. Very quickly the winds reached gale force. Thunder and lightning rattled the doors and soon rain was lashing against the windows.

The story of the Alamo is complicated enough, but interrupted by five power cuts it was even more difficult to follow.

Every time power was restored we had to wait for the digibox to reset itself, and then tune in to the right channel.

Just as Jim Bowie, Davy Crockett and co. began fending off another attack on the fort by the troops of General Santa Ana, the screen went blank again. The picture returned, only to show Colonel Sam Houston saying they had not all died in vain...

We were in for a long weekend.

After two weeks spent unpacking, we had a shopping list of essential items for the house and were pleased to find most of what we needed nearby. The garden centres, DIY superstores, furniture emporia and lighting shops displayed an enormous range.

This was just what we wanted, since we were still surviving with the bare wires inherited from the previous owner, Jon. He'd been kind enough to leave an extensive collection of outdoor lights dotted all around the house and garden, but as I pointed out to Viv, the bulbs in them were all the equivalent of about one candlepower so I suspected he'd bought them deliberately, in order to make us go round taking them all out and replacing them – but Viv said it showed a sense of humour. She directed me to stand to one side when we got back with the new bulbs.

When she had finished, the house and garden looked splendid in the evenings, though the previous owner obviously had also had a sense of humour when it came to installing the switches. One set of lights in the garden was switched on from the *naya*; another set was plugged in from the poolroom; two lights on the garden side of the house were switched on from the toolroom; for the patio it was to the hallway; for the front of the house it was to the dining room; and for the back of the house it was to the kitchen. For a while after the new bulbs arrived, it took us half an hour to get to bed at night.

But the garden really was wonderful; filled with all kinds of exotic plants such as yuccas, palms and prickly pear cacti, not to mention the oranges, almonds and olives. There was also that certain something in the garden that gave off the most wonderful heady scent in the evenings – jasmine.

Jon had left quite a large patch of bare earth around the fruit trees, and we decided that it would make a nice lawn.

'We are English, after all,' I said, and I had brought the lawn mower all the way to Spain.

So I bought the lawn seed, enough for a hundred square metres, and set about digging the patch.

It was going very well; the soil was red/brown in colour, and it was light and friable. Stripped to my waist and wearing my old gardening boots, I laboured away for a couple of hours each day: digging, raking and picking out hundreds of stones. I finished a little over half the area and thought about sowing the seed, but decided to wait until the whole area was prepared.

Then the rain came. The light, crumbly, red-brown soil soon resembled a soggy chocolate mousse, which Jessie delighted in walking into the house.

'Another good idea *bites the dust*,' Viv murmured, wiping off Jessie, and this time I agreed with her, I said, although I did point out, determined not to notice her little joke, that it was just as well we found out about it, 'sooner, rather than later.'

Some other little problems were becoming less amusing.

The toilet in the bathroom kept blocking, though it could easily be 'fixed' with the aid of a rubber plunger; but the problem became so frequent that I often thought of buying a couple of clips to screw to the wall so that a big rubber plunger would be ready for action whenever it was required. Always, though, I stopped myself, thinking that Viv would not go for a wall-screwed giant rubber plunger.

Our water supply was cut off several times, without notice. When normal service was resumed, the water, which was generally perfectly drinkable in theory, turned a pale red/brown colour, matching the colour of the chocolate mousse lawn site.

This was all too disgusting, and we became very attached to pure, imported bottled water, but after the next storm, with the garden tidied, the toilet fixed and the water running clear, we felt like trying out a few more local restaurants.

The first was a place called Los Achos. You can't get much more Spanish than that, I thought.

It turned out to be owned by a German who knew just enough funny English to try to amuse us, as if he had seen too many let's-be-a-stupid-German skits on TV.

'If your steak is no good I kilt ze chef,' he said.

As the evening wore on, his well-meaning attempts to make us feel welcome became increasingly irritating, but the food was excellent and the chef survived. I began to feel sleepy after dinner, though, and thought a little Jalon Tinto would wake me up. The owner had settled down a little, and I asked if he had any.

'Oh no,' he said, 'most of the restaurants won't sell it because it is too strong.' Then he remembered to be funny. 'It kilt ze gustomers.' It turned out that the light, fruity little number that came straight from the barrel in the bodega was 14.5%. No wonder I'd been sleeping better.

The following Sunday, we took our first trip out for Sunday lunch. We went to a little place up in the hills and found it packed with hoards of English folk; elderly men in trainers, slacks and acrylic pullovers; women in heavy skirts, knitted cardigans and sensible shoes. There were also a great many Spaniards out *en familia*.

I ordered the roast lamb, and Viv the pork escalope. Then she spotted a huge rib of beef on the carvery. We could have been in a 'Harvester' back in England, we said. The order was changed and Viv had the beef with a Yorkshire pudding that resembled a deflated football. They even had horseradish sauce – Coleman's. Not to be outdone, I just couldn't resist the *pudding de pan* when it was offered – and very good it was, too.

Although we would have enjoyed something a little more Spanish (to be fair, Spanish dishes were on the menu) we both enjoyed our 'traditional' Sunday lunch after so long doing without, and it was fun, in a strange way, to see the Spanish customers tucking into steak and kidney pie with such gusto, for all the world as if they were English and the pie was Indian.

Jessie turned obviously ill one day towards the end of the month and so we had to call on the local vet. We pulled up right outside the place on one of Jalon's side streets. No one was in the waiting room, so we went straight in.

We were greeted by not one, but by two vets. One wore a white coat and I was sure I saw a glint in his eye as he rubbed his Uriah Heep hands. The other was wearing a more elegant green jacket and he had a carefully trimmed goatee beard – perhaps, I thought, to complement the stubby little pony tail (I have a 'thing' about men's pony tails) protruding from the back of his otherwise bald bead (especially with bald heads). They both had a smattering of English, but fortunately the Spanish for diarrhoea is remarkably similar to the English. They were very thorough and after a full check up, involving a (gloved) finger, three injections and two packets of tablets, they were pleased to relieve us of the equivalent of £80.

'Why did you glare at them the whole time?' Viv asked when we came out. 'It's not your prejudice playing up again, is it?'

'Me?' I replied, catching sight of myself in a shop window. 'I'm just an Englishman who needs a haircut – and if you're thinking of the goatee and pony tail which I did NOT notice, you're quite wrong. I was *only interested* in the *fees* they charge. *That* little lot amounted to a *week's spending money.*'

'They didn't charge that much just because they've got pony tails, you know.'

'Did.'

'Didn't.'

But Jessie soon recovered, and all was calm for a while.

Then, just before the season for heavy rain, the official 'man from Del Monte' arrived to tell us, 'Yes,' to the oranges in the groves near our house. A lorry came soon afterward, to drop a mountain of interlocking, blue plastic crates at the side of the road, and that was closely followed by the 'crew bus.'

Within two days the trees had been stripped by hand by a band of swarthy-looking sorts who worked from dawn until dusk filling baskets of oranges then carrying them to be weighed and emptied into crates, before being loaded back onto the lorry as if they were packs of produce themselves. The main collector of the fruit was a company called 'Gragon' and 'Gragon Wagons,' as I christened them, began to appear all over the valley.

After they'd stripped the trees near our house, the road was strewn with rejected fruit and we found ourselves driving over oranges. I began to spot perfectly good oranges left amongst the trees and helped myself, when I was driving alone, to a few. I'd stop the car for a second, dodge in, grab the orange, dive out again, and drive on. I then found out that there's an old Spanish custom that anyone can take one orange from a tree for sustenance during their journey, so I thought that that could mean, 'each time, between when you start and stop – since that constitutes a journey in itself: starting and stopping.' It's complicated, but I love oranges and ended up with so many I had to take a lot home to eat later, in order not to waste them.

A bout of sunny weather at the end of November kept us in the garden, and my shorts, which had been put away for the winter, had another airing, giving a sad look to my now pink-again legs.

The break in the weather was followed by our first crop of visitors, three weekends on the trot. I rubbed some quick-bronzing lotion over my legs, pulled my best shirt on, and prepared to greet them.

But the Viv and Mark staff at Hotel Emelia soon found themselves too busy to spend time with the visitors – shopping, cooking, cleaning, washing up, making beds, doing the laundry.

It would make us think twice before saying to anyone in the future: 'Yes, we'd love to see you, stay for as long as you like.'

Another ex-pat said to me, 'Visitors are like fish, they go off after three days,' and I soon knew what he meant.

Just getting on with everyday things was also quite time consuming. We'd established a comfortable routine. By the time we dragged ourselves out of bed it was usually gone eight-thirty; not surprising as the sun didn't rise above the mountains until eight o'clock at this time of year. Then it was off for a long walk with Jessie, either in the hills or through the olive groves and vineyards. After that, breakfast. I usually pressed five or six oranges – at £1.25 for five kilos of oranges, it was cheaper than cartoned juice, I explained to Viv, when she asked why I needed so much).

After that, I brewed fresh coffee, using the trusty stove-top percolator I'd bought in Madrid many years ago. With bread or croissant, fresh from the *panadería* in the village – and a little local honey or marmalade, we were well set up for the day.

By this time it was often around half-past ten and we were saying: 'What shall we do today?' It was a lovely feeling, since this was often the most stressful decision we had to make. A trip to the post office or a bit of shopping around the market and it was time for lunch, usually at around two-thirty. We ate salads most days, with jamon serrano, mortadela, salami, chorizo or dry cured tuna, bread and freshly made alioli.

This was usually followed by a snooze in the sun and perhaps a little gardening; or time on the computer, or on trying to figure out how to use my digital camera. Then another walk with Jessie and, before we knew it, it was six in the evening – 'beer o'clock.'

Alcohol is very cheap in Spain and it would be all too easy (and affordable) to start drinking at ten in the morning and carry on until bedtime. This lifestyle could quite easily have appealed to me, so we adhered to a strict rule of no alcohol before six o'clock except, of course, if we had visitors or went out for lunch. (Then again, as a friend once said to me: 'It's always six o'clock somewhere in the world.')

At this time, evening, my frustrated chef persona took over and I spent much of my siesta trying to conjure up something to do with the wonderful fresh food we bought locally.

At six, I'd pour a beer and put my plans into practice. I spent hours preparing the kind of food I'd rarely had time to cook in England. Freshly-made and hand-rolled pasta, elaborate sauces, home-made pesto and dressings, rich and luscious casseroles. Nothing was too much trouble. I had a few minor culinary disasters but nothing really serious. The result of this lifestyle was that Viv had hardly cooked a meal since we came to Spain, and I'd lost weight – about a stone I thought. Put it this way: I had to cut two inches off one of my leather belts, and I was wearing trousers I hadn't been able to get into for years. So, 'the cooking and the weight are coming along well,' I said to Viv, parading past her in my old trews, giving the belt two or three snaps.

Progress at last on the gates, too. They finally arrived on 30th November, two months behind schedule.

They were magnificent.

With a coat of black paint and a touch of gold leaf, Buckingham Palace would spring to mind.

So we dismantled the Miserables barricade for the last time, and stood back in admiring anticipation for the builder to fix the gates.

He drilled four large holes in the concrete gateposts to take the hinges, then set them in quick drying cement. Once this had hardened, we were ready for the grand opening, but – oops, the builder had failed to realise there was a slight incline in the drive, with the result that the gates would only open half-way. Since the hinges couldn't be moved, we had to dig into the gravel drive to give sufficient clearance to open the gates fully. We set to work.

At this point the builder departed, promising to be back on Monday to fit a handle and lock. As a temporary measure, we tied the gates together with a piece of electrical cable.

A month later we were still fiddling with the cable each time we came in and out. We never saw the builder again, and I finally got round to doing the job myself.

'Look, this bloke's ordering bacon. I wouldn't mind some of that for breakfast...'

Leek and Cheese Tart
with *serrano* ham

This simple, but tasty tart is so easy to make, it almost feels like cheating. I used soft goat's cheese and serrano ham in this version, but you could use almost any crumbly cheese and boiled ham if you prefer. This recipe will serve two people as a main course, or four as a starter.

- *1 sheet of ready rolled puff pastry (approx, 10 x 8 inches)*
- *4 leeks, trimmed and sliced into 1cm rounds*
- *100g thinly sliced serrano or other ham*
- *250g soft goat's cheese or other crumbly cheese*

1. Pre-heat the oven to 180°C.

2. Boil or steam the sliced leeks for a few minutes until just cooked, but still firm. Drain and set aside to cool.

3. Meanwhile place the pastry on a greased and floured baking sheet (preferably non-stick). Using a sharp knife, lightly score the pastry about 2cms from the edge of all four sides. Place the sliced ham on the pastry, keeping it within the score lines. Arrange the leek slices on top of the ham and finish by crumbling the cheese over the leeks. Bake in the oven for 35-40 minutes until the pastry edges are brown and the cheese has melted.

Preparation time: 10 minutes
Cooking time: 35-40 minutes

Glazed Lamb
with a peach-honey syrup

This recipe is much simpler than it sounds and the result is an unusual, piquant sauce that really works well with roast lamb. I used a rack of lamb in this version and roasted it in one piece before cutting it into chops. If you cannot buy a rack of lamb, grilled or fried chops will work almost as well. You should be able to find peach confit or conserve for the syrup, but if not, try using apricot jam.

- *A rack of lamb about 500g or 6 loin chops*
- *2 fat cloves of garlic in their skins*
- *6 tbls white wine*
- *3 tbls peach confit or conserve*
- *1 tbls honey*
- *½ tsp minced or grated root ginger*

1. Pre-heat the oven to 180°C.

2. Brush a little of the peach confit over the skin of the lamb and place on a small roasting tray. Roast in the oven for 45 minutes (or grill the chops if using). This will give you slightly pink meat. Cook for a further 5-10 minutes for well done.

3. Meanwhile, in a small saucepan, heat the white wine and add the garlic cloves. Simmer for about 5 minutes then remove the garlic cloves, reserving the wine which should have reduced by half. Squeeze the flesh of the garlic from their skins and mash with the flat of a knife until you have a smooth pureé.

4. Return the garlic pureé to the pan with the reduced wine and add the peach confit, honey and ginger. Heat until the confit melts and combines with the other ingredients. The syrup is now ready to serve, and can be warmed through at the last moment.

5. Remove the rack of lamb from the oven and cut into chops. Place three chops on each serving plate and spoon over the warmed syrup.

Serves 2
Preparation time: 5 minutes
Cooking time: 45 minutes

Chapter Three

A Honeymoon Revisited

By early December the weather had improved enough for me to make progress on the planned new lawn. The chocolate mousse had dried out and I finished the digging and raking. I then sat back and waited for the grass to grow. The packet described the seed as *germinación rapido,* so I didn't expect to wait for long.

Over the next two weeks the weather turned cold again and rain flooded the lawn, creating pools of water with grass seed floating on top. The few sparrows that used to frequent our garden turned into a flock. They say there are no sparrows left in England anymore, and now I knew why. They had all migrated to Spain, like the rest of us, looking for the good life. They found it. The grass didn't grow, but the sparrows did. I swear that some of them had difficulty taking off.

After two weeks of this, I was convinced that all my efforts would be for nothing, even if I laid a new lawn once a month.

Then one sunny morning while our friends Alison and Martin were visiting, as we breakfasted on the terrace Alison remarked, 'What's that growing under the orange tree?'

It was the start of our new lawn, as a few expeditionary shoots forced their tips through the earth – which by now had set like concrete.

Though patchy, the barren brown wasteland gradually began to turn green. I still reckoned that the sparrows had eaten at least half the grass seed, but was wishing them good luck with it when a few days later I suddenly received the kind of advice a man really doesn't want to hear.

'You've obviously used the wrong kind of grass seed,' said a visitor to the house who professed to be an expert on the subject.

Apparently, I should have used something called *grama* which produces that coarse spiky grass from rhizomes, and is completely drought resistant. My grass would grow, but would need copious amounts of water unless I was content to watch it wither and scorch in the summer.

I wasn't in the mood to start all over again, so I said, 'Yes, but this is a new grass seed, for lawns near orange groves.'

The visitor drew back in his chair, getting red in the face.

'It's the oil in the ground that does it,' I told him. I was going to go on, but Viv, Alison and Martin had come into the room and we all had to go and see where the snake once lived.

During Alison and Martin's stay I drove them, very slowly, up the grand prix track where the boy racers had burnt up the tarmac a month earlier. The road is called Col de Rates and winds its way up and across Carrascal, the mountain range that all but encircles the horizon. Seeing the road, it was hard to believe the velocity at which some of the speedsters took on the sharp bends, with only a flimsy piece of metal armco and a few concrete blocks between them and a sheer drop of several hundred feet.

'How do these young Spanish men keep on target?' Alison asked. 'They must have pinpoint control.'

'It's the bull's eye mentality,' I said.

They both laughed. 'Bullfighter's, I mean,' I said quickly, determined not to make a joke by accident.

'Do you really think so?' Alison asked, and I slammed the car into third gear, revving so hard round the next bend the back of the car flung us all round in a semi-circle.

'Definitely,' I shouted as I shoved the gear back into second, not showing a flicker of panic. 'Put them behind the wheel of a car and it's like waving the proverbial red rag!'

Anyway, there was an observation point near the top with spectacular views of the whole of the valley. We could see the house as a tiny speck in the distance.

'Look,' I said. 'I can see Viv at the computer.'

This got another laugh. (Actually, Viv had said to us all she wanted to write some Christmas cards, to stop me writing any, but had then told *me* that the truth was, she didn't fancy going up the steep and twisty mountain roads, with my driving.)

Someone had thoughtfully laid in a large concrete plinth on the summit, and set up a sign pointing to it, saying it displayed a relief plan showing all the villages and towns stretching down to the coast some 25 kilometres away.

'Typical, an idea that hasn't been finished off,' I called out to the others, as we scrambled like mountain goats across slippery, jagged rocks to look at the plinth. 'This is broken ankle territory if ever I saw it,' I said, hobbling, 'ouch! – especially – because – look out!...most day-trippers are ill-equipped for rock climbing and won't have the sense not to try it.'

The three of us, after a rough scramble back, continued the drive over and beyond the summit of Col de Rates to reach, eventually, the tiny pueblo of Tarbena – just as the village band struck up and marched into the square.

It was Martin's birthday, and I tried to tell him that I had arranged the band especially to mark the occasion, and what was more, I went on – buoyed by the fact that they were laughing at a sort of joke I'd made, again – they were playing for us a slow, Spanish version of 'England's pleasant pastures green...' (Strangely, after I said it, it did sound a bit like that.)

The whole village had turned out in their Sunday best and the procession, led by two people in coloured sashes, disappeared into the Church. This was followed by enthusiastic bell ringing.

All the villages in the locality had their own brass bands and most played to a very high standard, I explained to Alison and Martin, although this was the first time I'd given it any thought.

Before heading home, however, we stood there marvelling for a while, that these small communities could produce sufficient musical talent to sustain a full complement of instruments.

The next day, Martin and I went out alone. Martin, who always packs his golf clubs before his suitcase, insisted we swung the bats at least once during his stay, and I had booked a tee time at La Sella Golf Club near Pedreguer...rather nervously, since I hadn't lifted a club for almost three months. We both played to the usual standard, however: Martin lost four balls, I lost five.

On the way back, I said I'd introduce Martin to a local tapas bar, forgetting it was a Monday so most would be closed. However, not to worry, I was sure one would be open.

We finally found ourselves in 'Bar Trami,' in one of the nearby villages; the only place we could find open. Judging by the looks that greeted our arrival, I doubted they saw many foreigners. It was full of local working folk, who were quite at home talking, drinking, eating – and dropping their empty sugar packets and fag ends on the floor, I noticed – presumably confident that someone would sweep up at the end of the week.

I managed to negotiate my way, elbowing delicately and with my head well raised, through the crowd at the bar and spent considerable time trying to order some tapas and a couple of beers. From the scowl on the barman's face as he looked at me, I suspected the kitchen was about to close.

The tapas took ages to arrive, one dish at a time, but was excellent. Martin suggested we have wine to wash it down, though I had my doubts about that, in this particular establishment. Not one to be put off wine, though, I went over and ordered '*una botella de vino tinto por favor.*' Despite raising eyebrows at this request, the barman disappeared willingly enough into the back of the bar, returning with a bottle of wine and two glasses.

'I may not be the world's greatest wine expert', I muttered to Martin, 'but even I know that red wine in a bottle labelled *rosado* is a bit dodgy.' And so it turned out to be. It was undrinkable.

'*Este vino no es muy bueno,*' I said. If I'd known the Spanish for, 'it tastes like gnat's pee,' I would have said it, I told Martin.

Finally, we settled for the only bottle that had a cork on it, and it had turned out to be a real *rosado*. So there we were, a couple of English tourists in a traditional Spanish bar, dressed in garish golfing gear, drinking rose wine together, noses up at the locals. I wondered, much later, what the locals had thought of us.

Shopping in the villages was an interesting experience which required the utmost patience, since it was usually done by the womenfolk, and the art of conversation, or should I say gossip, was far from dead. It didn't seem to matter how many people were in the queue, it was absolutely vital, from what I could gather, to ask how Tio Rodrigo was, or how Señora Santos was recovering from that nasty operation on her 'you know what.'

The frantic pace that typified life in much of Europe had yet to reach this part of Spain, and gradually I was beginning to appreciate the value and importance of spending time in conversation, rather than rushing in, buying something, and clearing out.

It was difficult to find these shops, since they were dotted throughout the villages; up narrow side streets and amongst the houses. No shopping precincts here. Added to that, they didn't exactly advertise their whereabouts. Take Jalon, for example. We walked round the town many times and each time we found another shop we wanted to visit – usually when we just happened to see someone coming out of an inconspicuous doorway covered with a chain mail flyscreen.

They also clung on to a very old-fashioned working practice in the retail trade, called 'service.'

Not long after we arrived, we were wandering around Jalon one afternoon when we happened across a wonderful butcher's shop, called Galan. A sizeable store, it had hundreds of hams, sausages and black pudding-type things hanging from the high, galleried ceiling. Some looked as if they'd been up there for decades, and many had little saucers beneath to catch the dripping fat.

Buying meat was not as simple as pointing at ready-cut joints. If you asked for lamb chops you were shown one of several complete loins and invited to choose which end you wanted, and how thick you wanted the chops cut.

I asked for four chicken breasts one day, so the butcher went out and came back with two chickens to show me, before he removed the breasts.

I was so struck by this that a little confusion ensued.

I asked him, stuttering, for *cuatro lechugas de pollo*. Spanish for breast is *pechuga* – *lechuga* means 'lettuce.' I got full marks for trying, from all the shoppers laughing in the queue.

Once cut, the meat was wrapped in greaseproof paper and presented in a number of neat little parcels. I hesitated before picking them up. It seemed they hadn't heard of polystyrene or cling film in these parts. Could this be hygenic? I wondered. But with all eyes upon me, I picked up my parcels and left the shop – to a cheery and noisy farewell. I went back home and told Viv how well I'd done at the butcher's, and she said, because impressed, or not liking the sound of the experience, 'Oh, that sounds nice, Mark. You can buy all the meat, then.'

I was in trouble with Viv one day in late December, though, for buying only a turkey breast at Christmas. As there would be only the two of us, and Jessie, I'd thought this would be a very sensible purchase. But *no*, Viv insisted we have a *proper* turkey.

On Christmas Eve, therefore, I set off for the butcher's in the hope of finding a bird. Despite an early start there were at least ten people ahead of me in the queue, so I knew I was in for a very long wait.

Just one forlorn turkey was left in the display cabinet and I was pessimistic about my chances. Luckily, it turned out that most people had pre-ordered their turkeys, so the lonely old thing could be ours. I wasn't sure we really needed a seven kilo bird, but I didn't dare go home without one, so bought it.

Stuck in the long queue, I began to think about the way the locals watched and listened to the other customers, and I started to get absorbed myself.

One had ordered a sixteen kilo turkey. The portly little lady butcher went out the back to catch it. The practice here was to leave the neck, head and feet of the turkey attached to the body, so she didn't take long. Back she came, holding the dead turkey upside down by the legs, with the huge body massively over her chest and stomach, turkey's head swinging between her knees, and the rest of herself invisible but for feet. It took two butchers and the customer to lift the thing onto the scales. No sheet of greaseproof paper would do for this bird, so they stuffed it into a giant white bin liner. Staff and customers joined to shove it over the counter. Everyone in the shop waited, as if to see how the customer would manage to carry the bird, and I might have been the only one technologically unchallenged when she unfolded a set of luggage wheels and strapped it on.

But even the most basic technology had failed to reach the market stalls in Parcent.

The lady at the fruit and vegetable stall that I passed that day, on my way home with the bird, would write down the price of each purchase on a scrap of cardboard, then add up using mental arithmetic (one down, carry four). When she arrived at a total she'd tear off the scrap of cardboard and hand it over by way of a receipt. So far (and I checked this every time I bought anything from her, using a calculator), she hadn't made a mistake.

I greeted the old woman as I rushed past with the turkey, anxious to get home out of a biting wind.

As the weather turned colder, we were pleased to make use of the fan-assisted log fire in the lounge. This was our only form of heating for the whole house, but it worked well.

We had been buying logs by the kilo and carting them home in the car a few at a time – until one morning, driving away from the house, we had to give way to a mini-tractor towing a trailer load of logs. I stopped to enquire if we could have a delivery and the ruddy-faced young man with a cheerful smile was only too happy to oblige. We haggled over the price of a mixed trailer load of orange, almond and olive wood, and struck a deal.

'*Hasta la una esta mañana,*' Miguel-Ángel called out as we parted.

With my limited Spanish, my ears only picked up on 'one o'clock' and '*mañana,*' so I expected to see him the next day. But '*esta mañana,*' I was soon to discover, means *this* morning. We returned to find the carport piled high with a thousand kilos of logs. We still had to pay for them, but I had no idea where to find Miguel-Ángel.

Dusk descended, and we were walking Jessie towards the village when I noticed a dim, flickering light in the distance, followed by the rasping sound of an ageing moped.

It was Miguel-Ángel coming for the log money. I paid on the spot and *asked if he also painted ceilings, haha,* but the joke was lost on him, though not on myself and Jessie. (We two, I often noticed, spoke the same language.)

December 11th marked our thirtieth wedding anniversary, and Viv and I planned a special day out. We had been married at Altrincham registry office in Cheshire in the company of a select band of friends and relatives, numbering fourteen in all.

After a reception at the Excelsior Hotel at Manchester Airport we walked across to the departure lounge bound for Alicante. We were booked on a three-week package tour in the two star Hotel Los Arcos on Benidorm's Levante beach. Out of season, we'd paid just £45 each for full board. I had in my possession the princely sum of £25 for spending money, and had managed to scrounge another fiver off my brother, Chas, at the airport.

Our status was announced to everyone in the hotel on our first evening. As we started our pre-dinner drinks, the waiter burst into the lounge with a tray and a bottle of Cava.

'*Which is the honeymoon couple?*' he enquired at the top of his voice.

Actually, it wasn't difficult to identify us, since we were about 40 years younger than everyone else. We sipped the Cava, and lingered in the lounge after dinner, conscious that everyone seemed to be keeping an eye out to see when we'd make our move. I took an intense dislike to all the guests that night.

In spite of the age differences and the dislike, however, we made some very good friends over the next three weeks. These were Dorothy and 'Auntie' Ray Levy, and Frank, a retired bank manager from the Isle of Man, and his wife Ann. We soon fell into the habit of taking after-dinner liqueurs with these people. Every night we laughed at Ann, who tried every colour and flavour of liqueur during our stay, always with the same response.

'You know, that's really rather nice.'

We couldn't find anything she didn't like.

The more we drank, the funnier she was.

Half-way through our last week at Los Arcos, our money was running out so we skipped the post-dinner ritual for a couple of evenings, and some of our new friends asked after us. Caught, I had to explain my embarrassment.

Frank approached me quietly the next evening and slipped the equivalent of £5 in my pocket. 'We had a whip round,' he said. 'It's your honeymoon, after all.'

At the end of our stay they presented us with a gift, a prettily decorated ceramic bell which found space in the packing cases and came with us back to Spain some 30 years later.

So we had very fond memories – almost tearfully fond – of Benidorm and of our stay at the Hotel Los Arcos. What better way to mark our anniversary than to pay a return visit? After all, it was only just down the road from our new home.

We turned off the A7 to be confronted by a panorama of immense, jagged skyscrapers.

Would we ever find our old hotel? We parked near the Levante beach and set off in search. Half an hour later, we were totally lost. We resorted to stopping people on the street, but even the taxi drivers had never heard of the Hotel Los Arcos.

We were just on the point of giving up, assuming that it must have been demolished, when Viv remembered that it was just around the corner from the Hotel Presidente. Armed with instructions on how to find to this much grander hotel, we continued with renewed optimism, followed the directions and found ourselves back at our parked car. Then we spotted the Hotel Presidente. But had our honeymoon hotel survived? We turned the corner and there it was, partly-clad in scaffolding, undergoing a much-needed facelift, and dwarfed by concrete monoliths. Our balcony with sea view now struggled to find sunlight in the shadow of these towering edifices to the ubiquitous package tour.

Worse was to come.

An illuminated plastic sign above the door announced the availability of 'John Smith's Smooth Bitter.' The 'Private Residents Bar' was now open to the public, and a blackboard by the side entrance declared: 'Tonight on Sky: Sunderland v Chelsea.'

We couldn't bring ourselves to go inside, but settled for a photograph taken by a wary Scottish couple, heedful no doubt of advice to be careful of strangers. Next, we went down to the deserted beach and took photos of each other standing in roughly the same spot where we had posed 30 years earlier.

Back home, I downloaded the pictures onto the computer and set them alongside the originals from 30 years ago. Apart from shorter hair (both of us) and a few added pounds, it was, 'Hard to spot the difference,' I called out to Viv. 'Look at this! – my shirt even blends into the background in the same way! I suppose I've always liked the same colours!'

'Little did we imagine in 1971, when we were just beginning our lives together, that we would find ourselves retiring just a short distance from where it all started,' I wrote to our friends, sending the sets of beach photographs and not mentioning the visit to the hotel.

By now we'd made several friends around the neighbourhood. Our first acquaintances were a 'young Dutch couple' in their mid-fifties, Leny (Lainy) and Wil (Vil). We invited them round for drinks and they both turned up in clogs. 'Honestly!' I said to Viv in the kitchen. 'I can't stop staring at them.'

What was more, they got me to try them on and walk round in them, which I couldn't manage. It was as if my feet were nailed to the floor. Viv took a photograph. (I thought later, after I had got to know them better, that they might have been trying out a joke on their new English neighbours, because I never saw them in clogs again – but at the time, this did not occur to me.)

They did some other interesting things I could not make out. For example, Wil rolled his own cigarettes from 'halfsware shag' but he was not allowed by his wife, he explained, to smoke indoors, and he popped out to the garden for a smoke every time I lit one of my usual Villiger cigars – which I smoked, of course, indoors, in front of his wife.

We were surprised to find that they were familiar with all the British television sit-com comedies and could rattle off details from episodes of *Fawlty Towers*, *Open All Hours* and *Keeping Up Appearances*. Leny did a screamingly funny impersonation of

Hyacinth Bucket, with all her affectations off to a tee. We invited them back often, never knowing what to expect but knowing we'd be entertained.

Christmas dinner, though, involved just the three of us: me, Viv and Jessie. We had a lovely day and spent ages on the phone (well, not Jessie so much, haha) talking to family and friends.

Boxing Day was quite different: we invited all the neighbours over for lunchtime drinks and tapas – the tapas consisting mainly of turkey sandwiches, since we had almost all of our seven-kilo elderly turkey to use up.

About 25 people turned up: English, Dutch, German, Spanish and Yorks. It was a bit like an EU summit, I remarked, passing out the drinks, except that everyone seemed to get along very well, even those who had never met each other before. We found ourselves using what bits of Spanish and German we knew, as well as English, in the same sentences, but nobody seemed to be listening in any case so the party was obviously going well.

Then came the drama of the mince pies. I was explaining to our Dutch neighbour, Gerrard, that the mincemeat in these pies was minced fruit, and not real meat. He seemed quite happy with my explanation as he munched away at his third helping, when Viv informed him that they also contained suet.

'What is suet?' Gerrard enquired.

'Shredded pig's fat,' explained Viv. Gerrard searched for a handkerchief in which to regurgitate the contents of his mouth.

'No!' I picked up another. 'Look! – it's not REAL PIG'S FAT! – look, I'll OPEN IT UP, SEE?' – but that was the end of the popularity of my mince pies.

It was at that Boxing Day event, when we began to learn a little more about the history of the area where we lived. There were many different versions, but it appeared that the whole development was 'irregular' because the roads and footpaths were never completed and didn't comply with current standards.

Some of the original residents had paid for these services in the price of their plots, but the money seemed to have disappeared. The Town Hall was pressing for something to be done, but according to folklore, the developer was divorced three times, had died intestate, and there was a quarrel over who was responsible for what. If the current impasse were ever to be resolved, the road was likely to be improved, but this would open up more plots for development.

As there were no undeveloped plots in the vicinity of our house, we were not too bothered, and most of the neighbours would have been happy if the status quo remained. Besides, given the speed at which things happened in Spain, I suspected it would be a long time before anything changed - though as things worked out, I was wrong.

Naively, I had assumed that our house was connected to main drains, but it was at the Boxing Day event that we discovered this was not the case. In fact, we were told, we had a septic tank somewhere in the garden. I couldn't find an inspection cover but Mick, who lived in the house at the back, told us not to worry as we would smell it when it needed attention. Viv and I looked at each other, and I decided to buy gallons of detergents and drain fluids and deodorisers as soon as the shops opened the next day. (Little did I know: my ignorance was at work.)

On Boxing Day, we were lucky. The day was quite warm and windless and the party was over before it changed; but during our first two months, the weather had been whipping from brilliant to ghastly – quite unpredictably.

According to everyone we met, this was the coldest, wettest autumn they could remember, and we had seen snow on the nearby mountains on two occasions, had several frosty mornings where ice had almost cracked the car windscreen, and downpours that lasted over forty-eight hours.

All this, of course, was minor compared to the blizzards that hit northern Spain and even Greece that winter, but we hadn't really appreciated just how far up in the mountains we were, nor the effect this would have on the weather and the sunlight. At this time of year, for a few weeks at least, the sun slipped behind

Carrascal at about a quarter to four in the afternoon – even though we could still see its reflective glow on the other side of the valley and darkness did not begin to close in until after six o'clock.

The instant the sun disappeared, it was as if someone had turned the heating off.

The temperature dropped by ten degrees in as many minutes, and sent us indoors to the warmth of the log fire.

After the winter solstice passed, the sun remained above the mountains for a few minutes longer each afternoon, but it felt just as cold.

Then suddenly, like a visit from another season, the cold, wet weather broke and we had a few days around Boxing Day when we were able to eat lunch on the terrace. The temperature rose to twenty-three degrees.

'Good old Sunny Spain,' I said to Viv, finishing off a sandwich. 'We could almost be in the Mediterranean.'

We drank to this, checked the temperature, shivered in our jackets, and hurried back inside to join Jessie by the fire.

'...a little confusion ensued and I asked for cuatro lechugas de pollo. The Spanish for breast is pechuga – lechuga means lettuce.'

Stuffed Chicken Escalopes

Traditional Christmas flavours are combined in this recipe to produce an impressive dish that makes a pleasant change from plain roast turkey.

- *4 chicken fillets*
- *4 pork sausages*
- *4 tbls cranberry sauce*
- *1 tbls fresh sage leaves, chopped (or 1 tsp dried sage)*
- *The grated rind of a lemon*
- *4 thin slices of Serrano ham*
- *For the sauce*
- *200 ml chicken stock*
- *200 ml dry white wine*
- *A knob of butter*

1. Pre-heat the oven to 180°C.

2 Place a chicken fillet on a board and carefully make a sideways cut three-quarters of the way through the flesh. Open out the fillet like a butterfly, then place between two sheets of clingfilm and beat with a rolling pin or meat mallet until you have an escalope about the size of a small tea plate. Repeat for the other three fillets.

3. Remove the meat from the sausages and mash this in a bowl with the cranberry sauce, sage and lemon rind. Divide the mixture into four and place a sausage-shaped portion at one end of each escalope. Roll each escalope to enclose the stuffing, then wrap a slice of Serrano ham around each piece of chicken. Place the chicken escalopes in an oven-proof dish and roast in the oven for 35-40 minutes. Allow the chicken to rest for a few minutes while you make the sauce.

4. Scrape up all the meat juices from the roasting dish and combine with the wine and stock. Boil until the liquid is reduced by half then stir in the knob of butter. Slice the escalopes if you wish and serve with the sauce poured over and around.

Serves 4
Preparation time: 25 minutes
Cooking time: 45 minutes

Christmas Fruits
with a toffee nut topping

Tangerines, bananas, dates and nuts – our house is always full of these for Christmas. Here's a recipe that will make sure there are none left over to New Year.

- *4 mandarin oranges or tangerines, peeled and separated into segments*
- *4 bananas, peeled and thinly sliced*
- *24 dates, halved and stones removed*
- *300 ml single cream*
- *40g soft brown sugar*
- *40g white sugar*
- *40g butter*
- *40g walnuts or pecans, shelled and roughly chopped*

1. First make the toffee topping. Melt the butter and sugars in a small saucepan over low heat and stir continuously until the sugar has dissolved and you have a smooth runny liquid (4-5 minutes). Allow the mixture to cool for 5 minutes then stir in 100 ml of the cream and add the chopped nuts. Set aside.

2. Arrange the banana slices in the bottom of a glass bowl or in individual sundae dishes. Add the mandarin segments and dates and top with another layer of bananas.

3. Just before serving, pour over the remaining cream then gently warm the toffee topping and spoon over.

Serves 4
Preparation time: 20 minutes
Cooking time: 5 minutes

Chapter Four

A New Year

The New Year began with a gala dinner at a Chinese restaurant near Moraira. We went along with some neighbours we'd met, Paula and Tom.

A dozen courses were served, together with as much Rioja wine as we could drink. There were brandies with the coffee, and Cava at midnight. The entertainment was provided by an excellent Spanish guitarist and singer. All for around £25 a head.

Just before midnight everyone was given 12 lucky grapes. In accordance with Spanish custom, we ate one at each stroke of the clock, to greet the New Year with a lucky mouthful of pips.

The party was a truly European affair with groups from Holland, Germany, Spain, France and Britain and there was some friendly rivalry between the tables, with 'Auld Lang Syne' competing with 'Tulips from Amsterdam' and the 'Marseillaise.'

I couldn't quite bring myself to start our dreary National Anthem, especially since the words: 'Send Her Victorious' seemed so inappropriate for the occasion, so I tried to arouse some interest in a chorus or two of 'Jerusalem,' but the Scots at the next table declined to join in with: 'England's green and pleasant land.' In the end, we all found common ground in the Hokey Cokey and the Conga.

Not long after New Year, it was getting a little warmer and we started going out again regularly.

One day we paid a visit to the Saturday Rastro Market in Jalon and found ourselves paddling in the mud amidst stalls selling what Viv called, 'A load of old tut. They call it a Rastro market, but this is just a glorified car boot sale.'

'I have a theory about people who buy this kind of junk,' I said. 'They gradually build up a collection of old rubbish until their garage is full, then they rent a pitch to dispose of it to fellow junk enthusiasts. The ultimate form of recycling.'

'Never mind that,' Viv said. 'Start on rubbish theories and we'll be talking about what you threw out when we left home.'

I saw where her logic led in that twisted argument, so let her take me in another direction.

We recovered from our critical tramp around town with coffees and brandies in a little bodega at about midday.

While there, I couldn't help rummaging around the interesting-looking, dusty wine shelves, in the name of replenishing our depleted stocks. We found a number of old wines at very reasonable prices, and that night tried out the prize of the collection, a Rioja Gran Reserva. It tasted odd. After a little of the other wines, it occurred to us that they could all have been stored in a cellar where the cooling system had broken down, and then the bodega owner had bought the lot, stuck it on the shelves, and waited for unsuspecting bargain hunters like ourselves.

'Or,' Viv added, 'It could have been sitting here for years, getting more heated and spoiled every summer, so nobody except us ever bought any. That would make us *really* naïve.'

Annoyed, we looked again at our finds.

Our search had also turned up a bottle of Cardenal Mendoza brandy. This is a Brandy de Jerez Solera Gran Reserva, one of the few I had not previously tried. The others – Carlos Primera, Independiencia, Lepanta and Gran Duque D'Alba – are all exceptionally good and, in my view, better than most Cognacs.

So we tried the Cardenal Mendoza. It was strange, to say the least, and had a lingering after-taste of liquorice. I carried it away, but we tried it again a couple of days later. It had completely changed into very smooth, mellow, caramelly brandy which years of holiday tasting in Madrid, Barcelona, Seville and other parts of Spain, had lead me to expect of Brandy de Jerez Solera Gran Reserva. We were back to congratulating ourselves, and put the other wines aside to see if something similar would happen. (We're still waiting, and test them every few weeks; some definitely do improve the more we drink of them.)

The New Year celebrations were still fresh in our minds when the subject of the septic tank returned. I remembered that Mick at the back had said not to worry, because I would locate it if ever a problem arose.

He was right. Our noses led us to a small, inconspicuous rock at the back of the carport. After lifting the rock and excavating several inches of gravel we found the inspection cover for what we later christened, 'the fossy.' Lifting it was a bit like entering a black hole and what we found was not pretty: a slithery, slimy, heaving black mass with an aroma to match.

In our naivety, as we called it – not minding being naïve about some matters – we'd not realised that we shouldn't be using the bleach and aroma-killers and strong detergents. We'd killed off all the friendly bacteria that made the thing work. As a last resort, we were told, we might need have it emptied by a sludge gulper – but two people told me we might be able to reactivate it by dropping something in to get it going again. Apparently a dead cat is best, but as I had 'sold my air rifle in England,' I said, I'd settle for a large piece of pig's liver.

'It looks quite appetising,' I told Viv when we bought it. 'If I was to sauté this in white wine, butter and shallots before dropping it in, I wonder what would happen.'

'That *might* defeat the object,' said Viv, with a glare normally reserved for vulgar comments, so it went in raw with a satisfying 'plop.' We had only the faintest of whiffs after that, so it probably worked. Anyway, 'I for one,' I told Viv, who said the same went for her, was 'never going to look into the abyss again.'

The Peseta-to-Euro transition came and went in early January, without too much fuss or confusion. We paid in pesetas and received change in Euros. There were a few long queues in the shops, but within three days all our pesetas had been spent. We reworked our budget in Euros and gradually found we no longer needed to think in pounds.

However, there was one casualty of the transition. Sadly, the little lady at Parcent market's only fruit and vegetable stall dispensed with the scrappy bits of cardboard which she had used to add up the bill.

She now had a set of electronic scales on which she added every thing up, though she still gave the total in pesetas before recalculating it in Euros.

We, also, changed tactics. Finally, we had worked out the queuing system at this stall, which was usually thronged with local women chatting and pushing in.

What we had to do was: *make for the produce immediately in front of the scales.* Whatever that was, we had to pick some up and plonk it on the scales the instant something else was taken off. In this way, we found, we'd stake our claim against all-comers. (Not that it really mattered, since the market was more of a social event than a shopping experience, but we only decided *that* after we'd conquered the system.)

Our weekly visit to the market was normally punctuated by a stop for 'coffee,' where we met many of our neighbours. (The job I really wanted was that held by the husband of the fruit and vegetable lady. He set up the stall early in the morning then spent the rest of the morning in Bar Moll in the village square, puffing his cigar, drinking wine and eating bread and olives with all his mates, while his wife worked her socks off serving the customers. He returned at the end of the morning to count the takings and pack up the produce.)

One day we decided to try one of the other village bars; one called Bar Guay. After a shock over our order for coffees and brandies when we saw the proprietor reach for a bottle of Bailey's (what *could* he have been thinking? *English* equals *BAILEY'S*?), we soon put him right, and settled in comfortably.

'We must come here again,' I said, thinking how deftly we were managing to make ourselves understood.

About to stand up and leave, I spotted one of the locals being served with a hearty bowl of some kind of steaming stew and I asked if I might have a small portion to try. Before we knew it, our table was being set for lunch and we had to extricate ourselves politely from another potentially embarrassing situation. I thought

I heard the proprietor mutter something like, 'bloody tourists,' but when we paid, he gave us a Bar Guay key ring and coin pouch.

The next day, back we were on his doorstep, this time to actually have lunch: I'd been thinking about the stew ever since missing my 'taste.' It turned out to be delicious, but elusive as to ingredients. The proprietor told me 'what was in it,' but I knew he was talking nonsense. 'Creamed Chicken in white wine,' he seemed to say – what kind of a simpleton did he think I was?

We went again several times, so I could figure out the ingredients, but I was never able to. 'Stew again,' said Viv, but she tagged along, and after a while she began to hum, every time I said something like, 'I think – this is *pork*.' I finally realised that she was humming, 'Oranges and Lemons,' to remind me of one of the greatest psychological-fixes I'd had since we arrived ...

Some time after we arrived at our house in October, I found that the lemon tree I'd seen growing on our property was an orange tree. I love oranges, but there were plenty of other orange trees, and I was disappointed to learn my dream of having a gin and tonic with 'ice and my very own slice' was going to have to be postponed. I didn't want to dig a good orange tree up just because it didn't grow lemons, but this particular tree had a problem with leaf curl, and that was affecting all the new growth.

I asked around and was told I could get advice on that, as well as about lemon trees – and order one if I wanted to – at the local agricultural cooperative in the next village of Alcalalí. Off I went, leaf in hand. Vicente was the man to see.

'Tengo un problema con mis naranjas,' I explained, tentatively showing him the affected leaf.

'No,' said Vicente, 'you *had* a problem – last year – when you should have sprayed the tree with insecticide. You have mixed your past with your present.'

'Sorry. I do that all the time.'

He looked unsurprised, sold me a bottle of the right chemical to use to prevent a recurrence of the problem, and when I came to pay asked where I lived.

'Ah, you are Parcentin,' he said. 'I can give you a discount.'

This was good news. I took the discount and, just as I was leaving, I spotted a couple of ancient cheeses on the counter. They had faded labels and mouldy crusts, and I remembered the 'very sniffy indeed' cheeses I'd tried on the night of the succulent feast, en route to Spain. Vicente was reluctant to sell these cheeses, he said, as they were *muy viejo* and he couldn't guarantee they were fit to eat – but he passed one over, told me it was a gift, and said he hoped I would enjoy it.

I dashed back to Viv and showed her the cheese. When she asked me what had happened to the lemon tree I was going to buy, I realised I'd forgotten all about it.

Vicente turned out to be a real character, with a modest grasp of English – much better than my Spanish – and I had difficulty, after that, going past the Coop Agricola without popping in for a chat. On a subsequent visit I did remember to enquire about the lemon tree, when I noticed that he had some in stock. I asked how long I would have to wait, before I had any lemons.

'How old are you?' Vicente said. 'Thirty-five or forty... Right, you are a young man, so you can afford to wait. You English are always so impatient. You buy this tree and you will have lemons in three years.'

Suspecting his flattery was a sales tactic, I immediately bought the tree, which, with the discount, was reduced from six Euros to five. He also threw in the last of the old cheeses, when I told him how much we had enjoyed the first one.

I dashed back to Viv and told her we had now had lemons, in three years.

Shortly after that, toward the end of January, our Dutch next-door neighbour, Gerrard, invited us out to lunch to celebrate his eighty-third birthday. He insisted he would book the restaurant and pick up the bill. Despite his advanced years, Gerrard had a strikingly cheerful disposition and nothing seemed to get him down; not even having his wallet lifted at a busy supermarket, which he told me about as if it was a joke. When I told him how upset I would be if such a thing ever happened to me, he laughed even harder.

Although he had two cars, Gerrard was most often seen on a little moped zooming, helmetless, along the bumpy road to the village to collect the post – ours as well as his, often. The moped was a marvellous idea and I toyed with buying one, but somehow just couldn't bring myself to be seen on this much-ridiculed mode of transport. Perhaps I needed to be in Spain a bit longer, Viv said, patting my hand, when I asked her advice.

The birthday lunch finally took place, with Gerrard, his partner Catharina, and some other Dutch friends. Most of us had the duck, which Gerrard recommended, and it was served with little sachets of 'home-made' orange sauce. All those oranges in the valley, and they used a packet, I thought. I supposed that's what you had to expect when the *menu del dia* cost just nine Euros. I shook my sachet and squeezed out the contents with tears in my eyes (though in fact, it didn't taste too bad, and I took Viv's home to see if I could work out the recipe).

A few days later, our other Dutch neighbours, Leny and Wil, invited us to a warm, sunny, Sunday lunchtime barbecue. We were introduced to friends of theirs, John and Margaret – the couple who had featured in the BBC series about life in Spain, 'Escape to the Sun.' This had been three years earlier, when John had done what I subsequently did: he'd come over and bought a house before his wife had seen it.

They appeared to be very happy and settled in Spain, and John said the only downside was the weight he had put on. This was, 'Contrary to my own experience,' I said quickly, 'as I continue to shrink to a shadow of my former self.' For some reason, this made everyone laugh, especially when I lifted my shirt, showed them my belt buckle and counted off the notches.

To keep up our good shape, and with the weather still warm and fine, Viv and I continued to explore the walks in the hills at the back of our house. One day we found a patch of the famous 'world's smallest wild daffodils' first pointed out to me by 'Barry Said' on my first visit to the Jalon Valley, almost a year before, and I took a photograph.

We also came across a public well on one of the paths.

There was a bucket on a chain, encased behind bars – to 'thwart would-be thieves,' I told Viv, reaching through the bars.

I dropped the bucket about seven metres into the water. After hoisting it up on a pulley, I poured the water into a trough inside the cage and it trickled through a spout set into the outside of the well. To my surprise, the water was clear and clean and perfectly drinkable – even delicious.

'Now I know what to do in the event of any lengthy interruptions to the water supply at home,' I told Viv, as she took a taste.

'You can,' she said, 'come up here with a bucket every half hour, if you like. But if there are any lengthy interruptions to our water supply, I'm off to a hotel.'

Apart from Viv's rapier-like wit, there were other hazards to look out for while walking in the Spanish countryside.

As well as the hunters with dogs and guns, we'd heard tales of snares, and poisoned bait, put down to kill the foxes.

There was also another danger for dogs, coming from an un-expected source: caterpillars – Thaumatopoea pityocampa. There is a species of moth that plagues the pine forests and produces these hairy caterpillars, the follicles of which, if sniffed or swal-lowed, can cause a swelling of the throat and result in asphyxia-tion if not treated immediately. Living on the edge of Parcent pine forest this was, potentially, a real problem.

The nests of the caterpillars hang like candyfloss from young pines and when ready, the caterpillars march off, nose to tail, in one long procession. Hence their common name – processional caterpillar.

We'd already spotted five or six nests on our walks. There is only one safe way, we were told, to destroy the nests: you had to burn them. Viv was frantic about the risk to Jessie so we made a plan to go out on a foray with a pair of secateurs, a metal bucket and some petrol, but we never quite got round to it, mainly be-cause we were distracted by a new danger.

This came in the form of poisonous toads. No sooner had we been discussing these (with me dismissing the threat, as I knew better) than we found a large, wart-covered specimen sunning itself at the bottom of a disused irrigation pipe.

Later, we discovered that there was an old, part-finished swimming pool just fifty metres from our house, and this was home to hundreds of these toads.

When the mating season arrived there was a continuous chorus of the things, all night long.

Some of them were so loud, they sounded more like – well, it suddenly struck me one night that they sounded *far more like a dog barking, than a toad trying to woo a mate.* To explain this, I thought for a while and came up with a theory.

'Listen, Viv...' I said. 'Lady frogs might be attracted to dogs.'

Viv looked up from her coffee, thought for a second, and said I could well be right, but never to present that theory to her in a birthday card.

'Fair enough,' I said (but who could resist?).

'I saw one of the locals being served with a hearty bowl of some kind of steaming stew...'

A Kind of Cassoulet

The French would have me shot, quite rightly, for calling this a cassoulet, especially as it contains chorizo, so put some Toulouse sausages in if it makes you feel better (after cooking them first).

- *1 medium onion, halved from top to bottom and sliced*
- *1 fat clove of garlic, peeled and chopped*
- *4 chicken thighs, boned and cut into bite sized chunks*
- *10 slices of chorizo sausage*
- *1 tsp mild paprika*
- *1 tsp mixed dried herbs*
- *2 glasses of dry white wine*
- *1 tbls tomato pureé*
- *2-3 medium carrots, peeled and sliced*
- *125g button mushrooms, quartered*
- *A 300g can of white beans (barlotti, canellini, or Spanish alubias)*
- *Olive oil for frying*

1. Pre-heat the oven to 180°C.
2. In a large flameproof casserole, fry the onions and the chicken thighs with a little olive oil over medium heat for 7-8 minutes until the chicken is browned.

3. Add the chopped garlic, paprika and herbs, stir and cook for a further 2-3 minutes. Add the carrots, chorizo and mushrooms, stir again then add the white wine and tomato pureé and bring to simmering point, scraping any burnt bits off the bottom of the casserole.

5. Cover the casserole, transfer to the oven and cook for 50 minutes.

6. Remove the casserole from the oven, strain the liquid from the beans and stir them into the dish. Return to the oven and cook for a further 15 minutes. Serve immediately with a jacket potato or plenty of crusty bread to mop up the juices.

Serves 2
Preparation time: 20 minutes
Cooking time: 1 hour 20 minutes

Steamed Sponge
with pear, dates and figs

So you've finished the cassoulet, now it's time for a little light pudding.

- *115g butter*
- *90g sugar*
- *The grated zest and juice of an orange*
- *2 eggs*
- *115g plain flour*
- *100g dried figs, coarsely chopped*
- *100g dates, stoned and coarsely chopped*
- *1 medium pear, peeled, cored and diced*
- *1 tsp ground cinnamon*

1. Grease and flour a two-litre pudding basin (plastic or pyrex is best) and set aside.

2. Weigh out and prepare all the ingredients, then mix the diced pear with the cinnamon.

3. In a large mixing bowl, cream together the butter and sugar using a wooden spoon until you have a smooth consistency (you will find this easier if the butter is at room temperature). Add the eggs, one at a time, and continue to beat, then add the orange juice and zest and beat some more (an electric mixer will help at this stage) until the mixture is light and fluffy.

4. Sift the flour into the mixture and beat again until you have a sloppy mix (it should just about cling to a spoon - add a little water if the mixture is too stiff or more flour if too soft).

5. Fold the pear, figs and dates into the sponge mix and spoon into the pudding basin. Cover loosely with foil and place in a large pan of boiling water so that the water comes half way up the basin (or use a steamer if you have one). Cover with a lid and steam the pudding over very low heat for 1½ - 2 hours until the sponge is set. Check occasionally and top up the water if necessary.

6. Turn out the pudding onto a large plate and serve with a blob of fresh cream or mascarpone.

Serves 4
Preparation time: 30 minutes
Cooking time: 2 hours

Chapter Five

Food, Glorious Food

According to local statistics, Parcent itself had an official population of just 779, so we were surprised when an elegant French restaurant opened in the village.

In return for recent hospitality, friends Peter and Yvonne had told us to book the most expensive restaurant we could find for their visit in February, so we booked El Raco del Carrascal.

What a find!

After an *amuse bouche* of little cod balls (or should I say little balls of cod? It seems politer) in pumpkin cream, there was a timbale of roasted vegetables with soft goat cheese, a soupsant of rosemary-flavoured sorbet, grilled monk fish in wild mushroom sauce. This was followed by an ever-so-light kind of bread pudding made from brioche, with a medley of fresh fruits, and a green and red coulis.

The pudding, served on a square white plate, looked so artistic that I told the waiter it must have been by Picasso (which he corrected, saying it was by Salvador Dali and pointing out the violin in one corner – though I couldn't make that out at all).

To top their brilliance off, they had my favourite Cardenal Mendoza brandy served in an enormous brandy snifter resting at an angle over a glass of hot water so that the luscious aroma wafted across the table.

I was in heaven.

The other meals looked just as good and, washed down with some excellent Rioja Gran Reserva, Peter was not too upset when the bill came to just over £100.

Sadly, but not unexpectedly, El Raco del Carrascal only survived for a couple of months before closing; a victim of the cheaper competition and most foreign residents' preference for apple turnover and sachet sauce.

For a while, I blamed the neighbours, but they didn't go out to restaurants often in any case, and didn't notice they were being boycotted, so I started mixing with them again.

Another Dutch couple we'd made friends with were Henk (who'd taken us up the mountain and told us about the hunters) and Gerry. They shared a grand passion for playing bridge – although they never partnered each other, they said, for fear of marital strife. (Everyone wanted to see something of this marital strife but nobody had, although they constantly tried to get the couple to partner each other at bridge.)

Henk was a keen sailor and in February he invited me for a day's sailing. He'd recently installed an automatic tiller and needed help with the English instructions, he said. In retaliation (we speculated), Gerry invited Viv to go shopping in Benidorm.

I'd never sailed in anything smaller than a North Sea ferry so I looked forward to the day's sailing with some trepidation, especially as the night before the wind had been howling through the mountains. I felt sure Henk would cancel the outing, but no, he arrived bright and early next morning ready for the trip.

Henk was seventy, but he drove like a lunatic. He told me that from the top of the mountain at Llossa it was possible to freewheel all the way down to Pedreguer some three or four kilometres away. Indeed it was, so long as he didn't touch the brakes as he swerved and screeched around hairpin bends. I was already a nervous wreck when we arrived at the port in Denia.

We boarded the tiny, 25 year-old, wooden yacht, bouncing up and down in the harbour as the wind continued to gust. After a challenging rigmarole that involved clambering through ropes and wires, I was shown into the cabin.

This was nothing like the luxury yacht quarters I'd envisioned. Henk had to clear away old papers, tins, boxes and bottles to find a narrow space for me to squirm into and sit.

Then it was time to get underway. Up top, he tried to start the outboard motor, pulling furiously on the cord over and over again. It gurgled and spluttered and even showed promise with a cough or two of blue exhaust smoke, but refused to spring into life. Now up top and watching, clinging to a rail, I thought I'd been reprieved, but Henk disappeared into the cabin and emerged with a box of spanners.

'Don't worry,' he said, 'This happens all the time.'

I *was* worried. Worried that he might fix it.

He fiddled and twiddled with the motor and after a quarter of an hour it did burst into life; hesitantly at first, but eventually reaching full revs with a level of vibration that thumped and shook the whole deck.

I 'weighed the anchor,' and, after some struggles, Henk untied us from the mooring and we put out to sea.

Less than half a mile out and still in the lee of the harbour, it was time to calibrate the tiller. This involved chugging round in circles for half an hour while Henk took compass readings and fed them into the computer.

Other than explaining a few words from a Spanish instruction book, I was not much help, because the other words were nautical expressions that meant nothing to me.

Eventually it was done, and the tiller seemed to work well, holding and adjusting to a fixed heading, compensating for the shifts in the stiffening wind and the increasing roll of the waves.

Much to my relief, Henk then decided it was too rough to put up the sails. He had probably noticed that my suntan had faded visibly in the last hour, I thought, giving him a smile.

'Yes, looks far too choppy for sails to me,' I said heartily. 'Perhaps it would be best to head back, now that we've had a good look around.'

Instead, he suggested it would be a good idea to drop anchor and make some coffee. There are plenty of coffee bars in Denia, I thought, but he was already filling the kettle.

Half an hour later, huddled in the cramped cabin, watching the kettle slide from side to side on the tiny cooker, I was feeling decidedly seasick. To avoid embarrassment, I went up on deck for air, and I just managed to hold myself up until Henk decided it was time to return to port.

Time to weigh anchor again.

Henk picked his way to the bow of the boat, balancing like a tightrope walker on the slender piece of deck at the side of the cabin. Then, on his hands and knees, he struggled for ten minutes to pull up the anchor against the ever-increasing wind, while I sat at the stern feeling sick and trying not to be and keeping my eyes fixed on an ever-changing horizon.

At this point Viv's last words before I left that morning, came back to me: 'Don't go diving overboard, we haven't made our Spanish wills yet,' and I began to think, staring out at the great white waves: *What if Henk – no, what if I – have a heart attack? Why aren't we wearing our life jackets? Where are our life jackets? Perhaps Henk doesn't have any. WHERE'S THE FLARE GUN?*

We made it back to Denia and he clambered while I staggered ashore, 'without further incident' as I would have diplomatically put it in a report, I decided, if I were back in the office. I thanked Henk for the day out, he promised to take me out again, at which time we would do some proper sailing, with all sheets to the wind, or words to that effect, and – I don't know, but this made me feel sicker than ever.

For three nights, whenever I closed my eyes to sleep I was back on the boat, swinging from side to side.

Not long after Christmas we had received a call from our old Cheshire friends, Sue and Peter, in response to our card. They were interested to know what we thought of Spain, as they had considered doing the same thing, they said.

Perhaps I enthused a bit too much in reply, because a couple of weeks later I received another call saying they were coming out to Spain to have a look, and had I heard of a place called the Jalon Valley?

They rented a villa in the nearby village of Lliber and spent their first night with us. I had put them in touch with our agent, Barry Said, and he had arranged to show them around a few houses over the next couple of days. They were, 'Only here to have a look round,' as they were about to embark on 'a six week round-the-world trip,' in about two months' time.

As an expert now on buying properties in Spain, I gave them the benefit of my advice. *DO NOT PURCHASE a property in a LARGE URBANISATION ON A HILLSIDE*, AND WHATEVER YOU DO, GIVE YOURSELF TIME TO THINK ABOUT IT.

Two days later Peter telephoned to say they'd bought a villa, outside Orba in the next valley. Absolutely beautiful property, with spectacular views down the valley to the coast at Denia, in a large urbanisation on a hillside. I just hoped, I muttered to Viv, that at sixty-eight, Peter could cope with the trillion bloody steps.

That was in early February, and much of the rest of that month was taken up with my own first major construction project – a pergola.

The lounge of the Casa Emelia formed a semicircle, and there was a quadrant-shaped terrace attached to one side. It faced due south and was an ideal place for summer eating, but it needed some shade. Hence the pergola; to be attached to the house on one side and to a series of graceful columns (yet to be constructed) at the outside edge of the terrace.

When finished, I planned it would be four metres wide at the house and eight metres at the circumference of the terrace. There would be thirteen heavy wooden beams forming a fan shape and that would stretch from the wall of the house to four supporting beams which would rest on top of the columns. I had been desk bound for more than thirty years, but it seemed simple enough.

I drew some elaborate plans to calculate all the angles and spacings for the beams and worked out the materials I would need. Then I set off in search. There was a *carpintería* on the outskirts of Parcent and I walked inside to a hive of industry. Heavy circular saws were buzzing, a planing machine was gouging its way through a massive plank of wood, and the workforce of four seemed oblivious to my arrival. It was as if I didn't exist.

The only one who saw me as something to look out for was a small tan terrier; tethered to a post in a corner, its stubby little legs skidding beneath it as it tried to break away, intent on sinking its teeth into my ankles.

I moved away. I coughed. Still no one looked up. I hopped from foot to foot trying to indicate my impatience, and eventually that, or something, worked. One of the men made a cursory gesture in the direction of an office in the corner and I marched over and stepped inside without knocking.

The chief carpenter was seated behind an expansive desk littered with scribbled drawings, notes and calculations. In the middle of a heated telephone conversation, he gesticulated frantically as he punched numbers on a calculator.

He seemed to be saying: 'How much? You must be joking.'

After a glance up at me, hovering beside the door, he quickly returned his attention back to the telephone. I sat down on the edge of a chair, my back rigid, until he slammed the phone down with an incomprehensible expletive, and a gesture that said: 'Stupid idiot,' or probably something even worse, I thought.

He glared at me. At last I had his attention, although by this time I was pessimistic about my prospects, and when I opened my mouth I found it was to ask for a glass of water. Suddenly, I could hardly breathe.

As it turned out, Jose-Luis could not have been more helpful. I had prepared for my visit by looking up a few words and phrases like wood, beams, pine, planed and cut; and after the water I strung them together, reading from my prepared script. I succeeded in provoking a quizzical look and a scratch of the head every few seconds, until Jose-Luis finally snatched the drawings from my hand and spread them on the desk.

He turned them this way and that as he rubbed the stubble on his chin, then he led me outside to the timber store where he pointed to a stack of timber that was exactly what I was looking for. A few more enquiries as to length, and a study of the template I had made for the curved ends I wanted for the beams, and there was complete understanding between us.

'*¿Es posible darme un precio?*' I enquired, anxious to know what I would have to pay.

'*Todo depende,*' he responded, as he explained it depended on the number of cuts he'd have to make, and the machine time.

'*No muy mucho,*' was as far as he was willing to commit himself.

We shook hands and I left with a promise that the beams would be ready within a week – '*mas o menos.*' Seven days later they were delivered, exactly to specification and at the right price. Jose-Luis even came round to the back of the house to see what I was up to.

When I explained that I intended to do the work myself, he rubbed his fingernails on the front of his cardigan before shaking his right hand up and down, then puffing up his cheeks to let out an elongated whistle. '*Mucho trabajo.*' (This man knew what he was talking about.)

With the timber organised, I set off to buy the materials for the columns. I'd made several reconnaissance trips to builders' yards beforehand, and had seen some concrete tubes that seemed as if they'd fit the purpose. So, off I went to Bloques in Jalon to be served by one of the girls in the office. I must confess to a bit of male chauvinism at this point as I was not at all confident the pretty young thing would be able to understand what I required. I'd previously measured the tubes I wanted: ones with a diameter of twenty-five centimetres. I took the office girl outside to show her and she returned to the counter to enter the details on the computer along with a cubic metre of sand/gravel and several bags of cement. I paid, and arranged delivery for the next day.

Just about to leave the office, I noticed that the invoice said: '*Tubos 18 cms.*' 'Stupid girl,' I muttered to myself before returning to the counter to point out her error. With a tut and a flourish she grabbed a tape measure and stormed out to the yard. I was almost running to keep up with her.

'Look,' I said, '*these* are the ones I want!'

'*Si señor,*' she responded. '*Dieciocho (18) centímetros.*'

'*No. Yo quiero veinticinco (25) centímetros.*' I insisted.

It was at this point that she produced the tape measure and placed it across the *internal* diameter of the tube.

'¡*Tu ves, dieciocho*!' She replied, pointing at the tape.

I'd been measuring the *external* diameter. We were talking about the same tubes. No number of apologies could make me feel less of a fool.

The materials were delivered the next day as promised, by a bright-looking young man who even had a smattering of English. Ah, I thought. No possibility of error, this time.

As he unloaded sixteen half-metre concrete tubes, curiosity got the better of him and he asked what I was building. I took him round the back to explain the project, and even displayed the plans, holding them up and telling him in Spanish that I had done it all myself.

'But why do you want the tubos?' he enquired.

'For the columns, of course.' *That* was perfectly obvious.

'But these tubos are for sewerage,' he explained with a look of incredulity on his face.

'*No pasa nada,*' I said with a shrug, desperately trying to hide my embarrassment.

He explained that the normal way to construct columns was to buy a cardboard tube with the required (internal) diameter, and fill it with concrete. Then you peeled off the cardboard.

'*Es facil.*'

Stubbornly, I resisted the temptation to ask whether the company would take the *tubos* back, since I didn't see how I could explain my error to the girl in the office.

He departed, saying, '*Tu tienes mucho trabajo.* '

Where had I heard that before?

Over the next few weeks I toiled away; mixing, drilling, banging, hammering, and constantly bobbing my head up to the open window to call out for another cup of tea. Viv gave me the nickname, 'Bob the Bobber.'

First off, I had to erect the columns. Right. I drilled the terrace and inserted four evenly spaced steel rods. Then I slipped four concrete sewerage tubes over each rod to form four columns, each two metres tall, before back-filling them with concrete. The tubes were designed to interlock, but being intended for underground use, they did not fit. The result was four slightly irregular columns that resembled an ancient ruin. After Viv caught sight of it, the pergola became the 'Acropolis.'

But the problem of the wobbly columns could, I suddenly realised, be easily fixed by a good coat of pebbledash to hide the joins. I bought a special tool for the purpose – one which I had seen in the hardware shop. This gadget comprised a round container with a handle which, when turned, rotated a series of sprung fins which 'spat' the pebbledash on to the surface to be treated. That was the theory.

My first attempt with a sand and cement mixture looked excellent, but fell off when it was dry. My second attempt, with a stronger mix and after wetting the columns first, looked even better, but still fell off when dry. By this stage I was getting desperate, especially when I saw all the teeth breaking off the fins in the pebbledash contraption.

I decided to seek expert advice from the builders' yard, but not from the pretty young office girl.

'Ah,' said the man I had waved over from a side counter, 'you need *mortera cola.*'

So I bought from him a bag of 'cement with glue' and obtained some further instructions, along with a new set of teeth in readiness for the third attempt. This had to be postponed because Viv was becoming impatient to see progress in the dining room, still full of packing cases, and the Acropolis was left in its ruinous state for the next few weeks. (But it was not to be the end of the pebbledashing saga.)

February brought the almond blossom to the Jalon Valley.

When we arrived, in October, the almond trees had lost their leaves. They looked bare and indistinct, like skeletons.

Now suddenly – almost overnight – they were awash with pink and white, and the whole valley took on an ethereal, gossamer hue, as if sprinkled with candyfloss and fairy lights.

We became aware that there were millions of almond trees, and we drove slowly up and down the road to Jalon, walked into our town, stunned; drank coffee in silence and walked back, stunned; all the while making a good attempt at taking a million photographs. For once, neither Viv nor I could find words to try to describe the view. The blossom lasted for only two or three weeks, and during that time the roads were full of coach tours of tourists, but for once we didn't care. It was as if they were our blossoms, ours as Parcentins, and we wanted everyone to see what we had.

The blossom faded, to be replaced by fresh, vibrant, green leaves which promised spring had arrived – and we could at last stop walking around in a trance, feeling guilty if we took a moment off from appreciating our pink and white paradise.

Then – checking the calendar – we remembered that March was the famous 'Month of the Orange Blossom.' Visually less spectacular, it was reputed to fill the whole valley with scent. We looked forward to this and, when it came, at first walked around breathing deeply and smiling in delight.

One surprise later in March was a mimosa tree in the garden that suddenly came out in a mass of yellow blossom. Unfortunately, when this disappeared, there was a yellow film of pollen on the pool and a sticky tide mark round the side that had to be scrubbed off.

We had initially agreed that a swimming pool was essential for living in Spain, but now we were beginning to think again. It was freezing cold still, and it would be some months before we could even dip a toe without getting frost-bite – and on top of that, we had, 'blasted blossoms.'

By now, we no longer even noticed the orange scent.

Spain had a wonderful array of regional foods which for some reason I had never seen in Britain. This was especially true of Spanish cheese. Spain produced some wonderful cheese, I found out, with a selection almost as varied as the French. There was Camerano from Rioja, Mato and Montsec from Catalonia, Roncal from Navarra, Idiazabal from the Basque Country, Quesucos from Cantabria, Tronchon from Valencia and Tetilla from Galicia. The list was almost endless.

I'd always been a fan of blue cheese and read about a rather special one called Cabrales from the Asturias region in the north of Spain. I made a mental note of the name and searched for it at a specialist cheese stall in the market hall in Denia.

The old man at the stall, whose white apron only just reached around his expansive waistline, seemed surprised, I thought, that I should ask for it by name, but nodded at once. He pointed it out, directing my attention to the front of the display. There was one tiny piece left for sale, and next to it stood a whole cheese, still wrapped in its original foil.

The small piece looked very green, dry, and well past its best. It would have been enough for my needs, but to avoid the shrivelled-up morsel, I said I wanted a larger piece.

'¿Es posible darme un trozo un poco mas grande por favor?'

'Si, no problema.'

He lifted out the whole cheese, cut it in half and then, taking me at my word, his knife hovered over a chunk weighing about half a kilo. I couldn't bring myself to ask for a puny, smaller piece so I nodded acceptance.

'Si, es bien.'

As he put the slab on the scales I suddenly realised it was every bit as green and mouldy as the tiny piece I was so anxious to avoid. I liked my cheese on the strong side, but this was a little too robust even for my dulled sense of taste – unless of course it was washed down with an equally robust vintage port...but then it would smell pretty high, and Viv would not necessarily go for that, although there was something about cheese that certain people found irresistible... In the car, I sniffed in the glorious aroma. When I passed through town I gave the cheese to Vicente.

By now we were going out and about much more often, and at the end of February it was time to pay a visit to the Town Hall in Parcent. In my final few months at work I had been involved in a long term plan to modernise services to the public by providing one-stop access to the Council through the Internet, via a call centre, twenty-four-seven, etc, etc. I was interested to find out how far our little town-village had progressed along this route.

You can spot the Town Hall in Parcent not because of the sign, there isn't one, but because it is the only building flying the Spanish, Valencian and EU flags. We popped along on market day at about half-past eleven to find all the doors locked and not a notice to be seen. We went into Bar Moll to ask some fellow Parcentins when it opened. They told us that Juan, the man from the town hall, had just finished his coffee and brandy and had gone back to work. We must have passed him on the way up. Sure enough, there he was at his desk.

We'd been told we needed a bonfire licence to burn garden rubbish. *'Una licencia para fogata por favor,'* I requested. What I really needed was *un permiso para fuego*, but he understood me perfectly and within one minute the document was completed and thumped with the official rubber stamp at no charge.

'Now that's what I call perfect one-stop service, that allows people time for a drink,' I joked to Viv, as we dropped in at a cafe for an 'only-one' brandy-coffee before going home. We were now officially licensed for the next month to have bonfires in our garden, before two in the afternoon and not on a Sunday or over the Easter holidays. I was quite proud of this and went over to tell the neighbours, who said we could also have our passports and driving licences photocopied and stamped so that we didn't have to carry the originals. Juan would be only too happy to oblige, again without charge. I rushed back to tell Viv and we tore in for another one-stop-and-drink visit to the Town Hall.

As February drew to a close, the evening sun lingered above the mountains for almost an hour longer than in the depths of December. Everyone kept telling us that this was the worst winter they could remember for years, but to us it was still a hundred times better than our last winter in England.

One cold wet day a neighbour remarked, 'In winter, Spain is a cold country with sun.'

At first this didn't make sense, but I later understood.

When the sun shines, which fortunately it does for a short while on most days, the weather is warm and pleasant. When it doesn't, it isn't.

'...we were surprised when an elegant French restaurant opened in the village.'

Cod
with cabbage and bacon

Since moving to Spain we've been eating almost as much fish as meat. It's cheap and it's healthy, but sometimes it can be a little bland so you need to give it a lift. This dish was inspired by our visit to *El Raco de Carrascal* and it's one of our favourite fish recipes – though Viv always wanted me to serve the cod with chips. Since I refused to cook chips she now settles for her favourite crispy mashed potatoes.

- *2 skin-on cod fillets*
- *¼ of a large white cabbage, finely shredded*
- *2-3 rashers of streaky bacon, cut into strips*
- *A handful of fresh parsley, roughly chopped*
- *A splash of white wine*
- *A knob of butter*
- *1 tbls thick cream or crème fraîche*
- *Rock salt*
- *Freshly ground black pepper*
- *Olive oil for frying*

1. Fry the bacon in a little oil until it is brown and slightly crispy. Set aside.

2. Boil the cabbage in a little water for 5-6 minutes until soft, but still slightly crunchy. Drain well and return to the pan with the butter and a splash of wine. Cook over gentle heat,

stirring occasionally until the butter has melted and most of the wine has evaporated. Add the bacon (and all its juices) together with the cream, parsley and a little black pepper. Heat gently until the cream is bubbling.

3. Meanwhile, cook the cod. Heat a little olive oil in a non-stick pan and fry the cod fillets skin-side-down over moderate heat for 7-8 minutes, depending on the thickness of the fish. Do not turn the fish over, but place a lid over the pan for the last two minutes of cooking. The fish should be just cooked and beginning to flake.

4. Spoon the cabbage onto warmed serving plates and place the cod fillets on top. Sprinkle with a little rock salt, and serve.

Serves 2
Preparation time: 10 minutes
Cooking time: 20 minutes

Crispy Mash

Mashed potatoes have made a comeback in recent years and most people have their own way of serving them so I thought I would have a go as well. This version is a little like baked colcannon and has the advantage that it can be prepared in advance and cooked when required. Viv says it's just as good as chips!

- *800g potatoes, peeled and cut into chunks*
- *¼ of a hard white or Savoy cabbage, very finely shredded*
- *1-2tbls olive oil*
- *150g Cheddar-type cheese, grated*
- *Salt*

1. Pre-heat the oven to 200°C.

2. Boil the potatoes in salted water until almost cooked (12-15 minutes). Add the sliced cabbage to the potatoes and boil for a further 2 minutes.

3. Drain the potatoes and cabbage, return to the pan with the olive oil and then mash thoroughly but don't worry if you leave a few lumps. Add most of the grated cheese and stir well. Season with a little salt.

4. Form the mash into 4 round patties. (I found it easier to press the mash into a round pastry cutter and then slide it out.) Place the patties on a non-stick baking tray and sprinkle with the remaining cheese. When required, bake in the oven for 25-30 minutes until brown and crispy.

Serves 4
Preparation time: 10 minutes
Cooking time: 45 minutes

Chapter Six

The Rain in Spain

The Jalon Valley is a wonderful place to live. It's green and it's fertile, and there's barely a square metre which is not cultivated for oranges, almonds, olives or grapes.

In early March I was driving through the Valley in clear blue sunlight saying to myself: 'Its good to be alive,' and thinking how lucky I was to live in such a beautiful place.

Of course some of the crops, especially the oranges, require copious quantities of water to survive. And that's why the valley is so productive. There's a river running right through the middle and over the centuries it has carved a ravine all the way from the mountains to the coast.

I always wondered – why then, even through one of the wettest winters in living memory, there was never more than a trickle of water to be seen in the riverbed?

And then it really rained.

More than 24 hours of non-stop torrential rain on Good Friday brought at least 12 centimetres of water, followed by a similar deluge four days later. The riverbed was a raging red/brown torrent. Driving down the valley brought back unhappy memories of the winter of 2000/01 in England when I was prevented from getting to work because of floods and fallen trees.

To think I came to Spain to get away from that kind of thing.

Worse still, I didn't have the consolation of retiring to the Hare and Hounds for a few beers by a warm fire in the company of other friends unable to get to their places of work. For the first time since we came to Spain I felt a little homesick as I trudged round Jalon wearing my wax jacket and wellington boots.

Some of the streets had turned into rivers and surprised and unprepared tourists looked like sorry little urchins, sheltering and shivering in doorways in their shorts and flip-flops.

Like so much of Spain, nothing ever seemed to be quite finished. More than a year earlier, I had first driven along the main road in Jalon that runs between the shops and the river. It was pretty enough, and there was obviously going to be some investment in this part of the town where most visitors first arrive. The kerbs had been raised and new footpaths laid, but the road surface itself was atrocious. When it rained, one part of the road disappeared under twenty centimetres of water and became impassable. Some twelve months on, nothing had changed. I began to wonder if it ever would.

(There was also a curious traffic system I had discovered on the bridge over the Rio Jalon. The single-track bridge was about seventy-five metres long and there were signs at each end saying, I think, 'give way to on-coming traffic.' This meant that on approaching the bridge you had to look across to the other side to see there was nothing coming, unless you were Spanish, in which case you just went straight ahead and nothing happened. I'm still trying to figure that one out.)

The rain brought a few other problems. Our bumpy camino became a little river and walking Jessie in the flooded olive and orange groves meant she got nice and muddy. The old towels were out in force to clean her up – something else we'd thought we would never have to do again.

I felt sorry for Jessie one day. Sitting on the bed, smelling damp and doggy, the fur on her head standing on end, she looked like a punk rocker. God knows what she must have thought of the changes we'd forced her to endure. Boiling hot one day, cold and damp the next. To top it all, the vet said she had to go on a diet, because she topped forty kilos when he weighed her.

Our pool was also taking a battering.

In mid-March, after a week of unseasonably hot weather – temperatures regularly hitting thirty degrees – the pool temperature rose from twelve to eighteen degrees.

It looked blue and inviting and I was tempted to follow the example of one neighbour and take a dip. Memories of last October when I shivered at twenty degrees persuaded me to resist, but by Easter Saturday the pool temperature had dropped back to twelve degrees, the water had turned a dirty brown colour and the bottom was covered with sand, bringing another problem.

With the waves lapping over the sides, I was forced to vacuum the bottom and pump some water out. This pained me no end since water is an expensive commodity in Spain and I knew that within a couple of months I would have to top up the pool to counteract the effects of evaporation. Despite this, three days later, the water level was again lapping close to the top and more pumping was required.

Once again we wondered if the pool was going to be worth all the effort, but in July and August, we were told, we could expect temperatures in excess of forty degrees, so we decided that next year we would think of some better way to cope with the off-season – perhaps invent some new kind of 'Miserables' pool cover – and wait for summer.

In between the storms I was able to make progress on the Acropolis, and in particular the pebbledashing.

Armed with my bag of *mortera cola*, my spitting contraption and more advice, all I needed were a few small stones to add to the mixture. I'd seen some of these outside a villa we passed on our walks, so off I went on the scrounge, bucket in hand. There were workmen at the site and I was greeted by Peter van Klaarwater, a barrel-chested young Dutchman who had just started his own construction business using Spanish labourers.

He was happy to give me some stones, and offered advice on the art of pebbledashing through his main man, Miguel.

With Peter translating, I explained to Miguel what I was attempting, motioning the winding of the spitting contraption.

A look of puzzlement changed his face, accompanied by a vigorous shaking of the head. His body language said, ' What is this English idiot trying to do?' He explained that my spitting contraption was intended for some completely different process and, as for *mortera cola*, this was totally the wrong material.

'Es muy dificil, tu necesitas un profesional.'

Sufficiently chastened by this stage, I decided to take his advice. Later that day Miguel arrived at our house wearing a smart checked shirt, suit trousers and polished brown brogues. Before he donned his torn green cotton overalls he looked every bit as if he was on his way to the office. His thick lensed spectacles hid the fact that he had only one eye, and his wiry frame disguised a well-honed set of muscles.

He got straight to work, mixing ordinary sand, cement and a few small stones with water to form a sloppy slurry. He poured the mixture into a rubber bucket and then, using a flat trowel, he literally threw the liquid onto the columns a bit at a time.

One hour and 40 Euros later, the job was done to perfection, and I was a very satisfied customer. Miguel allowed me to have a go myself, but wrenched the trowel from my hand after most of the mixture hit the patio instead of the surface of the columns.

Whilst Peter and Miguel were on site, I asked them about our plans to convert the toolroom into an en-suite bathroom to avoid the early morning queues when we had visitors.

'Itsa no problema,' was the initial response – followed by some hard thinking about how to connect to the existing fossy, over on the other side of the house and at a slightly higher level. Somehow I knew the fossy was going to feature in our lives again. The difficulty was that we couldn't find a way to see under the house to discover if it was possible to connect to the existing pipework.

Half an hour later, and after many *'Madre Mias,'* Miguel had bashed a hole in the side of the house and was peering underneath. He emerged with a dispirited look.

'Tu tienes un problema.'

There was insufficient space under the floor to make connections. The answer was to build another septic tank.

Not everyone can boast they are a two fossy family, but the potential cost filled me with dismay.

The only other estimate I had received for the bathroom was from a cheerful-looking Essex boy called Darren who failed to spot the potential problems, so I asked Peter to give us a detailed quote, fossy and all. Peter, who spoke fluent English, German and Spanish, as well as Dutch, arrived with a price the very next day and we started to haggle. To cut it short, we agreed on a deal, with Peter throwing in a new worktop for the kitchen as well as everything for the bathroom.

This was fine, but to reduce the price further (and to be included in the project), I offered to lend a hand with the construction work – since my time was my own, I explained, now that I had 'retired.'

Peter agreed to reduce the cost further, but explained he could only 'pay' me six Euros an hour, the going rate for an unqualified labourer in Spain. I said quickly, 'I wouldn't get out of bed for that in England,' but it was a take-it-or-leave-it offer so I agreed, even though Peter warned me the hours were eight to six and Miguel was a hard task master.

The very next day, a funny thing happened.

We were prevented from driving to the village by a large lorry, off-loading concrete *tubos* which looked suspiciously like the sewerage pipes I'd used to construct the Acropolis columns.

We'd heard rumours that there were plans to put in main drains, but they were just rumours. We presumed that, like so much else that was going to happen in Spain, it would not.

My Spanish was inadequate to approach the town hall bureaucracy, so Peter offered to come with us to find out what was happening.

We were indeed to have the benefit of new sewers – and a new road – all, if the man at the town hall was to be believed, *within the next three months*. We were promised there would be a letter to every resident and a meeting at the town hall to explain it all and how much we would have to pay. When Peter asked if connection to the new drains would be obligatory, the answer was a firm, *'Hombre, Si.'*

By the end of March the sewerage work had commenced with forty metres of pipes laid down the middle of the track, but still no letter or meeting.

As the rain fell and the work progressed the road became impassable, because of the deep trenches and piles of rocks. Everyone was forced to make a detour up into the mountains to find another way in and out of our small collection of houses.

Of course, there were no notices or diversion signs and every enquiry of the man wielding the JCB was met with that characteristic shrug of the shoulders that seemed to say: 'What's the rush? If you can't get out now, try again another day.'

Once, even the route up the mountains was also closed for sewer works, so there was no way in *or* out. Having popped down to the bank in Benissa, I returned to find the only way to get in was to weave through the olive groves at the top of our road. And we can just 'Thank God,' I reminded Jessie firmly, steering under the branches, 'We had the foresight – I had the foresight – to buy a four-wheel drive.'

Peter revised the price to exclude the septic tank and he arrived one Saturday afternoon with the contract.

He had obviously been working in property agent mode (one of a number of sidelines he pursued alongside his construction business), I thought, unless all this was for us: his normal working attire of jeans and T-shirt had been exchanged for smart trousers and a tailored jacket over a garish bright green, long-sleeved shirt made of shiny material which just about covered his ample frame. His blonde hair, normally arranged about his head as if he had just emerged from bed, was tidily combed back.

He looked very business-like, which looked promising to me, although judging from the sweat on his brow he was not very comfortable in the outfit. With the signed contract in his briefcase, he announced that work would start the following Tuesday which meant I *had to be 'on the tools' at eight o'clock sharp.*

I couldn't wait.

Then I found that after more than five months of getting up only when I was in the mood, it was agony to force myself from bed at seven o'clock on a damp, grey Tuesday morning.

Memories of hitting the M25 at that time every working day for over 16 years came flooding back.

My only consolation, I realised, half-asleep, was that the bath-room conversion should, in theory, be finished within two weeks, which meant...perhaps it wasn't worth getting out of bed for six Euros an hour and the experience, after all...

Then Peter phoned to say they couldn't start because of the weather and the mess they would make. I returned to our warm, cosy bed and didn't stir until nine-thirty, much later than I would normally have slept in.

Many years earlier, Viv had discovered a stray cat on a building site near our home in Surrey. She decided it deserved a better home and, thanks to her inexhaustible patience, *with animals*, Mac was finally persuaded to take up permanent residence; despite the unwelcome attention of the German shepherd we had at the time. Two weeks after his arrival, an outbreak of turf wars had left him battle-scarred with a nasty wound at the base of his tail. Several visits to the vet later, having run up a bill in excess of £200, I was beginning to voice my concern. By the time they started discuss-ing amputation, I had reached my limit. *'No more,"* I said to Viv, in my 'absolutely will not take no for an answer' tone. 'The cat will just have to take his chances.'

Mac survived for ten years after that. He was finally buried in the garden at Heath Lodge. Riddled with cancer, he'd struggled for every breath, like the fighter he was. He even summoned the energy to attack the vet as the lethal injection was being prepared. To calm him, the vet administered a large dose of morphine and he lapsed into oblivion with a contented look on his face. Small wonder, then, that I faced the next episode with a sense of *déjà vu*...

Ever since Mac departed, Viv had hankered after another cat. There are so many stray cats in Spain, it was perhaps inevitable that we would encounter one sooner or later. The trouble was that most of them were feral or diseased or both.

Out on our walk one peaceful Sunday morning, we spotted an emaciated white and ginger cat lurking in the olive groves. It was obviously unwell since it didn't even flinch in response to Jessie's frantic barking as I struggled to restrain her at the end of the lead. Viv had a brief conversation with the poor thing and decided it was a prime candidate for adoption. We returned home to collect the cat basket (something else I couldn't persuade Viv to leave in England) and a can of tuna.

As we returned to the spot where we had found the ailing cat, I was quietly hoping it had found the energy to run off, but I was not so lucky.

On the return journey home with cat in basket, my last words were, '*Don't* think I'm going to spend my Sunday morning at the emergency veterinary hospital in Denia.'

Half an hour later we were on our way, with the poor, flea- and tick-ridden little thing shivering in the basket under Jessie's watchful gaze.

I stayed in the car as I knew I hadn't the patience to wait around in the hospital. Viv returned after twenty minutes to say it was a tomcat, six to nine months, that seemed basically sound. The ticks and fleas were treatable but it may need an overnight stay. I saw the Euro signs pop up before my eyes. They just had to do a blood test before they could confirm it was well enough to be re-homed. This would take another twenty minutes or so. By this stage I was beginning to feel Viv was already firmly attached to the thing, confirmed when she suggested that we might call him Mac Two.

Sadly, this was not to be.

The vet called Viv back inside the hospital and she returned in tears after being told the cat had leukaemia and would have to be put down. It would take another twenty minutes and was to cost us thirty-three Euros. Conscious of our budget, to save the cost of a cremation Viv had agreed to bring the cat home so it could be buried. The rest of my peaceful Sunday morning was, it seemed, spoken for.

At this point I recalled the advice I had been given about the best way to reactivate the fossy, but Viv, amazingly, seemed to read my mind. '*Don't say a word*,' she got in, just as I opened my mouth and said, 'What about the foooo –'.

So I spent what was left of the morning conducting the committal, and both of us spent a gloomy afternoon with not much to say to each other.

Undeterred, Viv remained convinced that another Mac Two would adopt us before long, though with Jessie constantly on cat alert I was not so sure. We could easily have taken on one of the many cats looking for a home through the Costa Blanca News, but that was not the point somehow.

Things in the garden came on apace with the arrival of the warm weather.

Crocuses and daffodils came and went in February, followed by a riot of colour on the various succulents dotted around the garden, especially the osteospermum which came in and went out with the sun. We even had clumps of freesias, which filled the garden with scent. My father's fuchsias were doing well, but a second batch brought over by my brother, Chas, failed to survive (though I suspected that being stuck in a suitcase for the best part of a week had something to do with that lot).

The new lawn was looking much healthier and before the Easter rain arrived, I needed to use the sprinkler every day. I still had a feeling that this would prove to be an expensive folly, but Viv was adamant that Jessie 'needed somewhere soft to sit outside in the summer.'

All right, then.

I decided the lawn was in need of fertiliser, so off I went to my friend, Vicente, at the agricultural co-operative in Alcalalí. Not to be critical, but it seems I'd over-estimated his command of the English language. When I asked for fertiliser for the grass, finding water not enough to make it soft, he shook his head.

'It does not need fertiliser, or water. You will kill it.'

It took another five minutes of putting him right, and a search through his Spanish-English dictionary to *explain his mistake*, before I realised that with my much-improved Spanish I'd been asking for cactus fertiliser.

Viv had done little driving in Spain. Fear of the wrong side of the road and the narrow streets had made her nervous. This was not helped by the fact that the first time she drove the LHD Freelander in England, she'd mounted a traffic island at 40 mph.

I had my own problems, losing a wing mirror in an argument with a Transit van, so I was irritated. I pressed Viv just to get some more practice and get on with it, and she set off for the village one day. It was less than a kilometre away so I thought it was a relatively risk free adventure. Not fifty metres from the house, a giant cricket (Viv said the size of her fist) flew through the open car window and landed on her shoulder. Viv has a mortal fear of anything creepy-crawly and so she screamed, closed her eyes, and careered into the olive grove.

Two days later a giant kamikaze beetle made persistent, repeated attempts to break through the glass doors of the *naya*. This, together with the army of giant ants, and the gecko that lived in the poolroom, meant that Viv was very careful to keep the insect screens firmly in place at all times.

But then further information came to hand on the subject of the giant hairy caterpillars that pose a danger to dogs – and humans, for that matter. A chance discussion with a tattooed builder from Bolton further elaborated on the risks arising from processions of these nasty little beasts. According to our friend, the reason the caterpillars walk nose to tail in a procession is that, apart from the leader, who can spit venom up to one metre, the rest are all blind. Personally, I said, I doubted the veracity of this information. After all, everyone knows the real reason they follow the leader is that he is the one with the map.

As with so many odd things we heard in Spain, when no better story turned up we continued to repeat our own jokes.

We often heard conflicting accounts of local rules or practices, some of which would put the wind up people less sceptical than ourselves, we thought. In the end we learned to take much of what we heard with a large pinch of salt and put it down to the language barrier, missing a fair number of true stories in the process.

Our Spanish plumbing continued to amuse. The rubber plunger was still in use, and then the hot water pipes began to rattle when the tap was turned off. The sound was rather like a frustrated woodpecker, and continued for about five seconds. Curiously, the problem became worse after Miguel whacked the big hole in the side of the house. I suspected he'd dislodged a clip, so that the pipe was flapping around beneath the floor. Since I couldn't think of an easy solution, we lived with it 'for the time being' but banned the use of hot water during the night.

Power cuts were a regular feature of our lives, especially when it rained, the wind blew, or there was lightning in the sky. We once suffered 20 interruptions in one day, each lasting two or three minutes (and eight or nine as I started to type this chapter).

During more than five months in Spain, I ran into a number of British ex-pats in shops, bars and restaurants. One sad feature of some of them, was what I christened, 'Smug Syndrome.' Having chosen to live in Spain, many people could find nothing good to say about their home country. They acted as if everything was perfect in their adopted land, which, of course, it wasn't.

Within minutes of making my acquaintance, sufferers of Smug would make their views known. They always seemed to presume that I was of like mind. Perhaps from their experience, most people were – their friends, at least.

They thought Margaret Thatcher was the best thing that had ever happened to Britain, and their comments included, 'Enoch Powell was right'; 'Britain's going to the dogs'; 'Over-run by asylum seekers/illegal immigrants.' Or 'Tony Blair's ruining the country.' Anyone who questioned their wisdom was deemed to be a supporter of the 'Loony Left.'

These people couldn't understand why anyone would want to live in Britain, and some vowed never to return. I found this a bit rich, since most had made enough money in Britain to enable them to live a very comfortable lifestyle in Spain. I put it down to the fact that they all continued to read the Daily Mail, watch BBC news and East Enders, but couldn't or wouldn't learn enough Spanish to watch Spanish news programmes. If they did, they'd have realised that Spain had just as many problems as Britain, if not more.

'More than 24 hours of non-stop torrential rain...'

Tomato and Red Pepper Soup
with Garlic Croutons

This soup is perfect for those dull and dreary days when you think the sun has gone forever. The colour alone will make you feel warm. It's almost as if you can taste the sunshine, soaked up by the peppers and tomatoes as they ripened in the heat of summer.

- *750g of ripe tomatoes, roughly chopped*
- *1 medium red pepper, de-seeded and roughly chopped*
- *2 cloves of garlic, peeled and chopped*
- *1 tbls olive oil*
- *A pinch or two of chilli flakes (optional)*
- *Salt*

1. In a large saucepan, heat the oil and fry the peppers over gentle heat until they are soft (about 7-8 minutes). Add the chopped tomatoes, garlic and chilli flakes.

Cover with lid and cook over medium heat, stirring occasionally until tomatoes are soft and mushy (about 15 minutes).

2. Remove the soup from the heat then blitz in a liquidiser or with a hand-held blender for just a few seconds.

Strain the soup through a fine sieve, pressing with the back of a spoon to extract all the juices, then discard the left over pulp.

Reheat the strained soup and add salt to taste. Serve immediately, garnished with a few slices of red chilli, a little chopped parsley or snipped chives.

Serves 2
Preparation time: 10 minutes
Cooking time: 25 minutes

Garlic Croutons

In a large bowl, mix 2-3 tbls olive oil with a crushed clove of garlic. Stir in a handful or two of white bread, cut into small cubes. When all the oil has been absorbed, place the bread cubes on a non stick baking tray and heat in a hot over for 5 -10 minutes until the croutons are golden brown. Sprinkle into the soup just before serving.

Paprika Beef Casserole

The starting point for this recipe was a kind of beef goulash, but with a more Mediterranean flavour than the Hungarian original. The dominant flavour is paprika, though not the hot variety, and juniper berries give the dish an aromatic twist. If you can't find juniper berries, try adding a slug of gin instead. And if you can't find soured cream, just add a good splash of lemon juice to ordinary thick cream. Serve with plain boiled rice.

- *450g stewing steak, cut into small cubes*
- *1large red pepper, de-seeded and cut into strips*
- *1 mediun onion, cut in half and roughly sliced*
- *½ a small red chilli, de-seeded and finely sliced*
- *1 garlic clove, peeled and finely chopped*
- *2 tsps pimentón dulce or mild paprika*
- *1 tsp juniper berries, crushed*
- *1 tbls tomato pureé*
- *150 ml beef stock*
- *2 tbls soured cream or crème fraîche*
- *1 medium tomato, cut into small wedges*

1. Pre-heat the oven to 160°C.

2. In a large frying pan, sear the beef with a little oil until well browned. Transfer to an ovenproof casserole.

3. Add the strips of red pepper to the frying pan and heat with a little more oil until they have taken on a little colour. Transfer to the casserole. Repeat this process with the sliced onion.

4. Add the pimentón or paprika to the casserole together with the tomato pureé, chilli, garlic, juniper berries and beef stock. Stir well and place the covered casserole in the oven for 1½ hours.

5. Remove the casserole from the oven and stir in the tomato wedges and soured cream. Return to the oven and cook for a further 20 minutes. When ready to serve, top the dish with an extra blob of soured cream and garnish with a few slices of red chilli.

Serves 2
Preparation time: 15 minutes
Cooking time: 2 hours

Chapter Seven

One Swallow Doesn't Make it Summer

April, and the swallows arrived for the summer, swooping deftly over the garden and building nests in the eaves of some of the surrounding buildings.

One lunchtime, we were preparing to eat when we heard a crash from the *naya*. We rushed out to find a swallow sprawled on the floor, its wings splayed. It had obviously flown into one of the sliding glass doors. The poor thing looked so dazed you could almost see the stars circling its head.

I picked it up gently and could feel its tiny heart beat. It gripped my finger with its delicate feet and blinked rapidly, trying to work out what had happened. It remained perched on my finger long enough for Viv to get the camera and take a photo before I set it on the back of a garden chair. After a couple of minutes the swallow fluttered its wings and made a slightly ungainly take-off into the distance. I hoped there was no permanent damage, though its radar system obviously needed attention.

Other swallows (or were they house martins?) visited the garden, diving across the pool to gather water to make mud for their nests. Presumably they didn't mind the taste of chlorine, and perhaps it stopped their nests from going mouldy.

The swallows were also busy building nests in the village, weaving their way in and out of the narrow streets like guided missiles. 'I just counted fifteen on one old house alone, and I suspect,' I went back and told Viv, 'that these are the only things that hold the roof up.' (As usual, Jessie knew what I meant.)

Despite this portent of summer, early April had indifferent weather to say the least, with constant showers – not to mention the odd downpour. A cuckoo arrived, and something called a Hoopoe that looked like a crested Jay and delivered a song that sounded like its name, all day long.

The Campo was awash with wild flowers, and we saw something new every time we went for a walk. There were fields of poppies, hectares of wild garlic, several species of wild sweet peas and lavatera, clumps of wild antirrhinums and yellow gorse bushes as far as the eye could see. All this was interspersed with literally thousands of bushes bearing abundant white and yellow flowers. The scent of lavender and rosemary filled the air.

The blossom on the trees was replaced with fresh green leaves and small green, furry almonds. The vines, which up until then, had looked like stumps of dead wood, stretching out like rigid soldiers in perfectly straight lines, suddenly sprouted new shoots and flowers. Their growth rate was phenomenal, with one-metre fronds appearing within a month. Even the olives had small green buds turning into clusters of tiny yellow flowers, the embryos of the autumn's crop.

April also brought the long-awaited orange blossom of the Jalon Valley. This was about three weeks late because of the cold, wet winter and spring, but it was well worth the wait. The scent of orange blossom filled the air as we walked, or drove around, the valley. At times it was almost overpowering. It seemed strange that many of the trees still had last year's oranges on them as well as this year's blossom.

Our own orange trees blossomed, and we were now down to our final few oranges. It was rather sad to eat the last of them. The trees, though full of new green leaves, looked bare without their baubles – like a Christmas tree stripped of decorations.

Much to our surprise, our new lemon tree also blossomed, so, 'Maybe Vicente was wrong when he said I'd have to wait three years for fruit,' I said. (Who knows, I thought – by October I could be drinking a gin and tonic with ice and a slice of my own lemon – that promise I made to myself when I first saw the house more than a year ago.)

There was another fruit tree in the garden, one we couldn't identify. At first we thought it was an avocado, but it turned out to be a nisperus. The fruits were already coming ripe, and the markets were full of them. They looked like a small yellow plum but had skin like a pear, and polished brown pips inside. They tasted like a cross between an apricot and an apple. All around the countryside they were growing, and most seemed to be going to waste.

One consequence of all this blossom was bees. So many, in fact, that on still, sunny days the combined buzzing of the bees produced a background hum in the garden that sounded like someone using a power tool in the distance. Not that it was an aggravating noise: it was actually quite therapeutic.

One sunny afternoon I was lying on the patio listening to my Spanish lessons on the portable CD player (an eight-hour set by a French Canadian called Michel Thomas which I can thoroughly recommend).

As I concentrated, with my eyes closed, I heard a slightly louder buzzing noise. At first, I thought it was coming from the CD but when I opened my eyes, the whole garden was a mass of swarming bees – almost blotting the daylight out.

I ran indoors, fearful something had angered them, then watched as they moved together, close to our front hedge.

After a while, they seemed to disappear, so we ventured outside. A football-sized clump of bees had settled in the hedge.

Viv was not going to tolerate these unwelcome visitors and suggested I go and throw a bucket of water over them. I didn't think this was a good idea, and suggested we remain indoors. Viv was on the point of calling in pest removal experts next day when, exactly 24 hours after they arrived, they disappeared.

A few days after that, I saw a travel programme on television and it mentioned this particular phenomenon. Bee experts will probably correct me if I'm wrong, but it seems this happens when a queen bee is ready to mate. She leaves the hive, followed by up to two thousand male bees anxious to assist in prolonging the species. The queen settles in one spot and is surrounded by all the males. One male inserts its instrument into the queen's abdomen, leaves it there, and dies. Up to ten males follow the same procedure and make the ultimate sacrifice before the queen has enough semen to last for four years. She then returns to the hive. (Well, that story may or may not be true, but that's what I understood from the Spanish programme.)

In any case, with all the bees, it was not surprising that honey was very popular in this part of Spain, and that it came in 'flavours': rosemary, orange blossom, thyme and many others. One shop in Jalon turned out to specialise in honey, with huge stainless steel vats of the stuff, sold by the litre and poured into your own container – a kind of honey bodega.

Why is it that every book about people's adventures in a foreign country includes endless episodes about builders or plumbers?

I've no idea, but we were no exception.

I was still wiping the sleep from my eyes when Peter van Klaarwater and his crew eventually did arrive at eight o'clock one morning; five days late because of the weather. Within minutes there were power tools buzzing and sledge hammers thumping as they started to demolish the bedroom wall to create a new doorway in a former tool shed.

At one stage there were six workmen on site at the same time. The din was horrendous, and I was concerned for the neighbours, especially the visitors in the house across the road whose two-week stay was to coincide exactly with the start of our building work. We felt so sorry for them at one stage that we dropped in to hand over a bottle of wine as a peace offering (hurrying away before they could comment).

The new bathroom was, I thought, a simple, straightforward little job. After all, the room was just three by two metres. But I was surprised at the amount of building material off-loaded from a lorry. Two pallets of bricks, one pallet of breeze blocks, twelve bags of cement, two cubic metres of sand, twenty metres of plastic tubing, sixty roof tiles and four concrete beams. I tried to tell them that they had got the wrong specifications, but they went ahead. Eventually, it all came in together with thirty square metres of floor and wall tiles, bath, wash basin, shower, and toilet.

From all my experience of builders in England, I was just waiting for the problems to occur, but apart from the dust, which enveloped the whole house, and the dirt from the workmen's boots when it rained on a couple of days, the project started really well. The main problem was that our planned new dining room took a step backwards, this becoming home to all the tools and other bits and pieces from the old shed.

The work crew comprised, firstly, the previously mentioned Miguel, who always had a cheerful disposition. Despite complaining of painful elbow joints (later diagnosed as tennis elbow, though he assured me he had never in his life held a tennis racket, as if I'd made the term up), he managed to swing a lump hammer and shovel up the rubble like a teenager shrugging off his 48 years. He was meticulous, and after every task he swept up the mess before moving on to the next piece of work.

The second worker was Ecidro, a strong silent type who was a kind of superior master craftsman, constantly whistling the same few bars of an unidentifiable tune. He was quite happy laying bricks all day long, but thought it beneath him to mix or carry cement. For much of the time, that was my job, until I blew it one day by making the mixture a bit too sloppy and he seemed to lose faith in my ability. I was not too disappointed.

The remaining crew were Cheli (as in 'vermicelli'), and his son Chelitet. Cheli was in fact the foreman, the one with the knowledge of how things should be done, and I witnessed several heated discussions between him and Peter as the work progressed. Despite this, their attention to detail was fantastic.

One task was a small *casita* to house the new water heater and a gas bottle. I thought this would be fairly basic, but they constructed a miniature house, with matching roof tiles. They even pebble-dashed the inside of the *casita*, ready to be painted.

Throughout the first two-week period they stuck to a rigid work pattern. On arrival at eight each morning they got stuck in straightaway, stopping at half-past nine for breakfast, which lasted half an hour. They resumed work until one-thirty prompt. After eating, they sat talking or went for a walk, but never returned to work until three o'clock precisely; they then continued until six on the dot.

Ecidro knew the countryside, and often returned from after-lunch walks with bundles of leaves or wild asparagus.

Viv's job was to supply coffee at every meal break. Apparently we were quite honoured that they accepted this, since most English customers offered them instant coffee – which they wouldn't drink. Peter had assured them, however, that our coffee was good, though they looked amazed at Viv when she handed them her favourite brand, something called 'Morcilla.'

'*Mar*cilla,' Miguel said indignantly, staring into his cup as if daring it to turn into something undrinkable. (*Mor*cilla, it turned out, is black pudding).

By custom and practice, Spanish workers do not work without music. As Cheli was significantly deaf, we had the pleasure of listening to the radio at full volume all the time he was on site.

Much of the music was English and he sang along to whatever he knew some of the words to – his speciality being 'You'll Never Walk Alone.' The ring tone on his busy mobile phone was also set at full volume and played, 'The Mexican Danced on His Hat.' At one stage Cheli disappeared into the room with an angle grinder to cut out the grooves for the electrics. What looked like smoke poured out of the window and Cheli eventually emerged, white from head to toe, including his dyed black hair, and danced and grinned, in time to music.

One cold wet day, he ran out in the middle of a thunderstorm to cover the wet cement, wearing just a thin T-shirt and shorts. He returned soaked to the bone, but just carried on working, though he sneezed his head off for the next two days.

Viv took special pity on Cheli and Chelitet on another cold, damp day and invited them to have their lunch inside the naya rather than in the garden or in their old van.

Their lunch consisted of a tin of cold *calamares* and some of those very very dry bread rolls they call *bocadillos*. Experience had taught me that it was impossible to chew these rolls with any kind of dignity. You simply had to clasp the bread in your mouth and tear it away in a kind of tug-of-war between your teeth and your hands. Thoughtfully, Viv provided Cheli and his son with plates, and, to demonstrate that they were thoughtful, too, they declined to use them. The result was no crumbs on the plates – instead they landed on the table, on the floor, on the window ledge and in the pot plants. Viv was vacuuming crumbs up all afternoon, while I was busy 'working with the men' outside.

Well, I'd done that deal with Peter, I explained, which meant I was forced to lend a hand with the heavy work in return for the reduction in the price of the job.

But to be honest, with four people on site for much of the time, I'd soon realised I'd just be getting in the way, so I sat back and watched.

My major contribution was to dig the 20 metre long trench across the front of the garden to take the waste from the bathroom to the planned sewer pipes, soon to be installed in our road.

With a heavy-duty kango hammer to break up the rocky ground, I set about the task with a feeling I was being watched every step of the way to see if I would flag, but although after a couple of hours at full tilt I was dripping with sweat, something which never seemed to happen to any of the other workmen, I drove relentlessly on. At last I finished the final couple of metres of the twenty-five centimetre deep channel and I beckoned them over with a casual wave, feeling rather pleased with myself.

Miguel came up to inspect. Cheli, the foreman, was summoned for a conference. After a brief discussion the verdict was: 'Un poco mas profundo.' They wanted the channel ten centimetres deeper. Joke, right? I waited for a smile to crack their serious faces. When this failed to appear, I did as I was told. Despite my aching shoulders, I slept like a log that night. The next day the waste pipe was laid and I had the job of filling in the ditch. This was every bit as back-breaking as digging it in the first place.

So now we had the waste pipe laid beneath the front garden ready for connection to the new sewers. At least, that was the plan. By this stage, the concrete *tubos* were buried beneath the road from the village. An inspection chamber had been installed at the top of the road, just around the corner from our house.

Then we heard there had been a change of plan.

Our neighbours, Klaus and Marita, came round for lunch.

Klaus said he had it straight from the horse's mouth (the *gestoria* in the village) that the council was only installing drains in the *public* part of the road. Our stretch of road was private, so excluded. The new sewer finished about 75 metres from our house.

There appeared little prospect the new drains would extend to our house until the future of the whole area was determined.

This, we heard, was the subject of a wrangle between the local council and the authorities in Alicante. Even when this was resolved, it didn't mean anything would happen straight away. They'd still have to find an investor willing to take on the planned new development. The investor would then have to put in the infrastructure to the rest of the area, at a cost of millions of Euros, before any more plots could be sold for development.

I suspected this would all take years to sort out, and this, we decided, suited us fine. We rather liked things the way they were.

But it seemed we may have to be a two-fossy household after all, if we wanted to use the new toilet in the next couple of years.

We decided to wait until we had a clearer idea of what was going to happen before making our next move, and to help find out we retained the services of Margo, the *gestoria* in the village.

Margo was a kind of para-legal. She provided ex-pats with advice and translations. For a fee of 48 Euros a year we could seek her advice on any matter and consult her about any letters we received so she could tell us what to do. She knew her way pretty well around the town hall, or *ayuntamiento*.

Margo always had plenty of work as she provided a service to all the ex-pat communities in the area – German, Dutch and English. She never ceased to be amazed at the difficulties people managed to get themselves into.

'Why is it,' she said to me, 'that people moving to Spain so often seem to leave their brains at the border?'

Perhaps it was the sun or the scenery, or perhaps it was just that people were desperate to escape to a new life, but, as Margo explained, 'So many people buying property in Spain do things they wouldn't *dream* of doing back in their home countries. What's more, they pick up totally inaccurate information from unreliable sources, and bring it to me as if it's the Holy Grail.'

'I know exactly what you mean,' I said, and changed the subject to wine.

By the end of the sewer works, the bumpy *camino* had been slightly improved; though they stopped short of laying tarmac, giving us a thin layer of sand and gravel instead.

Not long after that newly-smoothed road had reopened, we were looking forward to a weekend without the builders.

Then, on the Friday afternoon, the sewer contractors returned to start digging up the road, again, this time to bury the water pipes. As a consequence, we were without water for Friday night and most of Saturday. As I said to Viv several times over the weekend, I suspected the workmen just went home and forgot to turn it on again.

'So phone up and complain,' she said, knowing that a heated conversation demanding and getting 'Action!' was well beyond my limited command of Spanish.

When, finally, the supply was restored we were treated to more pink/brown water for the first couple of hours, followed by our very own *agua con gas*, which spurted from the tap under such pressure that it sprayed all over the kitchen. In a glass, the aerated water gradually cleared from the bottom up, rather like a pint of Guinness. I held it up to the light wondering what this proved, but could think of nothing, except that it made me homesick.

Having learned from previous experience, we had an emergency supply of bottled water standing by for drinking, and some bottled tap water for washing. As for the toilet – we used bucketsful of water from the pool.

'You have to be able to improvise in Spain,' we said to each other, improvising madly.

(Despite this, when we talked to the neighbours about it later, everyone just shrugged their shoulders and said: 'This is Spain, what do you expect?' I could not believe how relaxed they were – they didn't even talk about how they had *had the foresight to improvise!* I strongly suspected, I told Viv, that the truth was that, like me, no one spoke enough Spanish to feel confident about complaining, otherwise someone would surely have been on to the *ayuntamiento*, playing merry hell. So there.)

The post office was in chaos for a few weeks when the cheerful and ever-so-efficient postman, Emilio, went on holidays and was replaced by a pleasant young woman who didn't have a clue.

Normally we went to the post office to collect our mail on weekdays between ten-thirty and eleven-thirty in the morning. Emilio would welcome us with a cheery *'Bon Dia Señor/Señora Harrison,'* pronounced 'arrisohhn' because the letter H is silent in Spanish (don't ask me, I'm only telling you). He'd then sort through the bundle for the odd numbers on our road and hand over the post for No.7.

This was well and good, but we also had to ask him to look through the *even* numbers because our electricity and telephone bills were addressed to No.12, not No.7. This was to do with the original plot numbers, whereas the actual house number depended on the order in which the houses were built. This was probably why, I explained to Viv, our neighbours on each side were No.4 and No.17. ('Spain!')

During Emilio's absence the young postmistress became overwhelmed. In an effort to speed things up, she resorted to handing over the bundles of post for people to sort through for themselves with the inevitable consequence that everything got mixed up. The usual two-minute visit could take anything up to three-quarters of an hour as the queue stretched out of the door and down the street.

It was just like being back in the post office in Lingfield, I said to Viv, except that everyone here was quite relaxed. They stood round chatting with neighbours and friends who, like them, had nothing better to do with their time.

The Church clock in the village, which had been silent since November, was restored to full working order in mid-April, chiming every quarter-hour. Like last year it was a full hour slow for the first week or so, but eventually caught up. This was not before it caused a panic one morning by ringing nine times just as I was waking up and making me think I would be late for the builders again. It was twenty to eight.

All this lead me to say to Viv that Parcent operated within its own time zone – 'Some time around 1938, I think.'

That got a merry laugh. 'A bit like you, then,' she said, unnecessarily recalling my inclination to hark back to the good old days when encountering conduct of which I disapproved.

Around this time, we discovered Parcent had a dark side to its history, one which did not appear in guidebooks. The village, like many in the northern Costa Blanca, was plagued with leprosy even up to the 20th Century. A sanatorium was built in nearby Fontilles and exists to this day, with a world-wide reputation for excellence in the care and treatment of leprosy sufferers.

Some other things in Spain, we found, were also impressive and were done outstandingly well.

By this time, our telephone and electricity bills came in English and the electricity bill even had a small graph showing monthly consumption.

Our bank, the Banco de Valencia gave us telephone-banking services, again in English, by ringing a special number.

Even our answer-phone service, which came courtesy of Telefonica, was translated into English.

All this seemed to suggest the Spanish authorities wanted us to be happy in their country, along with the Germans, Dutch, French and Portuguese, who all had similar facilities available.

Such praise could not, however, be lavished on the water company, which had a small office in the village that was open between four and eight on Tuesday and Thursday evenings.

We received a letter addressed to the former owner, asking for confirmation of our details. It took four visits over as many weeks before we were finally registered as the new owners, because on each visit they asked for something else.

First a copy of my passport, then my *Número de Identificación de Extranjeros*, then a copy of our *escritura* and finally a copy of a recent bank statement, presumably to prove we could pay. And we still hadn't had a water bill.

I explained that I was seriously concerned about 'This inefficiency, and its possible consequences,' to Margo the *gestoria*. She laughed and said the water company's new computer system had never worked properly and most people in the area hadn't paid for water for a couple of years.

'I thought as much,' I said, regretting our persistence.

The lunch with Klaus and Marita had lasted for nearly seven hours. Marita had a smattering of English, and she was keen to practice it, so she came armed with a German-English dictionary, which came in useful on a small number of occasions.

Klaus had very little English, but luckily Viv and I both did German 'O Level' at school (failed in my case).

'*Ich sprechen ein bischen Deutch*,' was about as much as I could remember, but this didn't prevent Klaus speaking to me in his native tongue as if I was fluent.

I managed to pick out the occasional word and, when all else failed, and we wanted to communicate something urgent, such as 'Pass the wine,' we resorted to Spanish where we were on roughly equal terms.

As lunched progressed, and another bottle or two opened, I began to chuckle to myself about the Basil Fawlty, 'Don't mention the War' sketch. I just couldn't get it out of my head. I can't recall how we got on to the subject, but I found myself explaining that my father-in-law had been in the British Luftwafe and my Dad was a Desert Rat. Viv was kicking me in the shins just as I was about to move on to the 1966 World Cup and England's most recent five-one victory, so I had to restrain myself, although I knew it would have gone down well.

Searching for a more meaningful topic of conversation, I just happened to mention that we had given Klaus the nickname Herman the German. By now my shins were really getting knocked about, and Viv was giving me that all too familiar 'deep-scowl

scowl' that said, 'You've overstepped the mark again.' I'd seen this look often enough before, usually as I stood on a chair to sing 'Jerusalem' at a dinner party or told my signature joke about a prawn and an undertaker, which requires a very broad-minded audience.

But it was too late. Marita explained the rhyme to Klaus, and they both roared with laughter.

'Who was it said that *German's don't have a sense of humour?*' I said loudly, beaming at Viv.

One of the nicest presents we received on leaving England was a card signed by all our neighbours on Tandridge Lane. It contained a couple of quotations written in perfect copperplate calligraphy by our next door neighbour, Martin Hardy. The quotations were by George Canning 1770-1827.

The first was: 'A sudden thought strikes me, let us swear an eternal friendship,' which we found quite moving.

Martin knew we had Dutch neighbours so the second quotation was: 'In matters of commerce, the fault of the Dutch is in offering too little and asking too much.'

I couldn't resist mentioning this to my neighbour, Wil, who acknowledged an element of 'Truth in Verse.' The next day, he sent me another quotation: 'In matters of behaviour, the English eat like groundhogs and drink like fish (Anon). Ouch! (But he added a note to say that, of course, he did not mean 'us,' so I scanned the message and sent it out to our friends.)

Martin's card was a signed print of a painting by Hilary Fett depicting a small group of people huddling under umbrellas at the seaside. It could depict nowhere but Britain.

This gave us great comfort whenever we felt homesick, so we decided to have it framed. We heard there was a *cristaleria* in Jalon and went in search. Eventually we found the place, tucked up a side street without a sign announcing its presence. It was, of course, closed. Luckily, as we turned away, the owner's wife and daughter returned from the market and opened the shop for us.

The dimly-lit workshop was like something left over from

Charles Dickens. There were cobwebs everywhere and off-cuts of wood, glass and mirrors occupying every corner. Racks of mouldings stretched up to the ceiling, offering a bewildering choice, and ancient tools were strewn haphazardly across a workbench covered in green baize.

It felt to me as if we were the first customers to enter the shop, in many a long year.

After browsing the selection for a while, we declined the gilt rococo and settled for something more restrained. Then we spent half an hour deciding exactly how we wanted the picture mounted, sorting through endless samples of card, and every imaginable style.

Our limited Spanish was, as ever, a barrier to clear communication. We left with Viv less than convinced that we had managed to make our wishes clear – and unable to get even a hint, *mas o menos*, of what it was likely to cost.

I assured her that all that had been dealt with by me – and assured the ladies that we were delighted to have met them, and looked forward to picking up the completed work.

As we departed, the rather attractive, well-proportioned young daughter explained that if the shop were closed we should ring the bell of No.47 next door.

'I'll go!' I said to Viv.

On Saturday morning at half-past ten, I went. I was greeted by the daughter, hanging over the upstairs balcony. Her hair was tousled and her skimpy nightie left little to the imagination.

'*¿Que quieres?*' she enquired abruptly – what did I want? Several things sprang to mind, but I settled, after a stutter, for asking if the picture was ready. After a ten-minute wait she emerged, hair brushed and smartly dressed, to hand over the picture and charge me 23 Euros, for which I thanked her politely, several times. They had done an excellent job, truly excellent, I said, not really looking at it.

I returned home with the picture to realise I'd not made a note of the quotations, now sealed in the frame. But all was not lost. Thinking quickly, and without saying anything to Viv, I set about carefully extracting the pins at the back of the frame, trying not to disturb the mounting. To my horror, I discovered that the picture framer had glued the card together so that all the messages and the quotations were sealed inside forever.

Fortunately, a desperate call to Martin Hardy back in England, mentioning *the difficulties one ran into in dealing with Spanish framers*, saved my skin before Viv found out.

The rain continued to fall and the garden continued to flourish. This, combined with the lawn fertiliser from Vicente, meant that by the end of April I was mowing twice a week. The lawn even had stripes and only a few bare patches. By the end of April, the weather finally came good, but ten days of sunshine and thirty degree temperatures turned the grass brown.

I was faced with a dilemma: pour on gallons of water, most of which would evaporate within a day, or watch it scorch.

After deciding on the water, I heard, a couple of days later while chatting at the gate with Klaus and Marita, that there was to be a hose-pipe ban in Parcent and that I should report any hose-watering plans to the *ayuntamiento*.

I didn't relish reporting that I wanted to use precious water to preserve my English lawn, so I explained to Viv that since, one, we were still awaiting a water bill, and, two, we had no idea what it was costing to sustain the small patch of green, it would be better, three, not to water in the meantime.

'Nothing to do with the hose-pipe ban, is it?' she said. 'Marita has a loud voice when she's speaking in English.'

Two weeks after they started, the builders were still on site.

One day I was helping with a small piece of carpentry when a screwdriver slipped off straight into my wedding ring finger. The result was a large hole, spurting blood in all directions. I became quite dizzy looking at it, and told the crew I had to go inside and sit down for a short while – as the whole finger numbed.

In the past, I'd always been quick to heal and an elastoplast stemmed the flow of blood. They say, however, that your blood thins in a warm climate, and I decided there was truth in this. 15

sheets of kitchen towel later, blood was still flowing profusely. Viv was out shopping. My mind wandered…Where's the nearest Accident and Emergency Hospital? What number do you dial for an ambulance? What's Spanish for, 'No, I don't need an anti-tetanus injection?' A couple of hours later, the throbbing was getting worse. I was about to crawl outside to ask for help from the crew when Viv returned earlier than expected. A little bit of sympathy, along with the bandage she was tying (TOO TIGHTLY), would be of some help, I told her, and my blood was definitely running thinner and that was potentially a very dangerous condition. How could she help?

YOU MIGHT THINK SHE TOOK ME TO THE HOSPITAL, BUT NOOOoooo…Perhaps I needed to drink more red wine, she suggested (and I definitely heard her say, '*Men!*' as she walked outside, leaving me and Jessie all alone at the kitchen bench with the empty wine bottle).

By the end of April, building work ground to a halt once more. They'd run out of tiles again. We were still awaiting the grand opening of the new en-suite bathroom with the wonderful tiles, though we wouldn't be able to flush the loo – yet. Despite the delays, however, we were delighted with the quality of the work.

We finished the month with a splendid BBQ with neighbours Pam and Tony, Tony's father Jack, and a few other neighbours.

It was one of those perfect Sunday afternoons, and we sat beneath the Acropolis to escape the heat of the sun. But the main topic of conversation was damp.

All the houses were miserably cold and damp in the winter. We all suffered from mould growth in the wardrobes and Pat said it had made her clothes shrink. Various remedies were discussed, including central heating, double-glazing, draught excluders and fungicide, but we finally agreed that all our houses were built for the heat, not for the cold, and who'd started all this, anyway? We'd been talking about damp for hours! I promised not to bring it up again, at least not on a sunny day at a BBQ, and changed the subject to plumbing.

'The blossom on the trees was replaced with fresh green leaves and small green, furry almonds.'

Mediterranean Curry

Can there be such a thing as a Mediterranean curry? Strictly speaking no, but then 'curry' tends to be used, incorrectly, as a generic term for spicy Indian food. So why not something spicy using Mediterranean ingredients? The inspiration for this recipe was Britain's most popular ready-made meal, chicken tikka masala.

The main hot ingredient is Spanish pimentón, a speciality of the Extremadura region, made from smoke-dried peppers which are then crushed to produce a form of paprika. Pimentón comes in mild (dulce), medium (agridulce) and hot (picante). I used the hot one here, but you could try the others for a milder taste. Serve with plain boiled rice.

- *4 chicken legs or 8 chicken thighs, boned and cut into chunks,*
- *2 medium onions, thinly sliced*
- *2 medium green peppers, de-seeded and cut into chunks*
- *1 clove of garlic, peeled and finely chopped*
- *1 tsp cumin seeds, crushed*
- *½ tsp turmeric*
- *1 tsp hot pimentón or paprika*
- *A half-inch piece of fresh ginger, peeled and finely sliced*
- *200ml single cream*
- *A handful of slivered almonds*
- *Chopped coriander or parsley*
- *Olive oil*

1. In a large frying pan, fry the chicken cubes over moderate heat in a little oil for about 5 minutes until lightly browned. Remove from the pan and set aside. In the same pan, with a little more oil, fry the onions and peppers until they begin to turn brown at the edges. Add the cumin, turmeric, and pimentón or paprika, together with the garlic and ginger and stir well.

2. Return the chicken pieces to the pan, add the cream, cover and simmer over minimum heat for about 20 minutes. (You may need to add a little water if the mixture becomes too dry). Add the slivered almonds for a couple of minutes just before serving and sprinkle with chopped coriander or parsley.

Serves 4
Preparation time: 10 minutes
Cooking time: 20-25 minutes

Croissant Pudding
with ginger and apricots

I stumbled onto this idea when I found a packet of dry croissant in the breadbin. Too crisp for breakfast, they were perfect for a kind of bread-and-butter pudding.

- *2 large or 4 small croissant*
- *75g crystallised ginger*
- *8-10 dried apricots, diced*
- *300ml milk*
- *100ml cream*
- *3 eggs*
- *Half a tsp ground nutmeg*
- *75g brown sugar*
- *A knob of butter*

1. Pre-heat the oven to 180°C

2. Use butter to grease a shallow 10-inch ovenproof dish.

3. Cut the croissant into thick slices and lay them on their sides. Spread the ginger and apricot pieces over the sliced croissant, pressing them in slightly, then sprinkle each slice with the brown sugar. Arrange the slices of croissant in the dish, leaning each one against the next until the dish is full. Don't be afraid to squash them up a little to fit them in.

4. In a separate bowl, beat the eggs with a fork to a uniform texture. Mix the milk and cream in a small saucepan and heat almost to boiling point. Slowly pour the milk into the eggs whisking all the time.

5. Pour the milk and egg mixture over the croissant, then sprinkle with the ground nutmeg. (The dish can be set aside for an hour or so until ready to cook).

6. Bake in the oven for 30-40 minutes until the top is golden brown and the custard is just beginning to set.

Serves 4-6
Preparation time: 15 minutes
Cooking time: 30-40 minutes

Chapter Eight

Cheli Comes and Goes

Wednesday, 1st May, was a public holiday, Labour Day; one of more than a dozen such holidays in Spain, excluding local fiestas. It peeved me that I was getting more public holidays than in England and I couldn't get the benefit since, in theory, every day was a holiday now.

As we walked in the hillside, the hazy early morning sun was already hinting at more piercing heat of later in the day.

It was always quiet and peaceful in the *campo* at this time, though there was usually a faint hint of activity in the village more than a kilometre away.

Normally we could hear the sound of metal beating from the blacksmith's or the clank of gas canisters on the back of the deliveryman's lorry. On this morning there was total silence. It was as if the whole world had decided to have a lie in.

We came across two old men from the village out walking, dressed as if it was winter in thick shirts and woollen cardigans; a sharp contrast to my shorts and T-shirt.

As ever, Jessie became the topic of conversation. I assured them she was *muy gentile,* as they crossed to the other side of the road fearful of an attack. I was pleased we'd at least been able to hold a conversation. It was a measure of the progress we were making with our Spanish, and generated a sense of belonging.

More tiles arrived at the beginning of May so we had high hopes of seeing the back of the builders at last. Cheli and Chelitet returned, with their radio, and pressed on with work. Peter assured us that two more days would see an end to the job.

It was not to be.

Halfway through the first afternoon I overheard a heated discussion on the phone between Cheli and someone, and realised all was not well. Peter arrived shortly afterwards to sort things out, but to no avail. There were too many floor tiles, not enough wall tiles. So work was adjourned once more.

More tiles were ordered. They were to arrive the following week. Deliveries to the shop in Benissa were on Tuesdays and Fridays, so we waited for news on each of those days.

'Sorry Mark, they weren't on the last delivery,' was Peter's first apologetic explanation, to be followed by, 'They're at the factory in Castello. If they're not on the next delivery I'll go and collect them myself.' Next it was, 'They haven't got any at the factory so they will have to make some more.'

I was beginning to ask myself why we needed a second bathroom, anyway.

Finally, as extreme exasperation set in: 'Mark, you won't believe this. The factory says the tiles have been made, but have to dry out for a few days before they can be transported. They promise they will be delivered by the end of this week.'

Only Viv's glance as I opened my mouth made me bite my tongue. I managed to choke out, 'Amazing, isn't it. Just as well we've got a good sense of humour.'

I went on to explain to Peter that he was lucky that I was so laid back in my new found way of life, too, otherwise I would have strangled him by this stage, haha. *As things stood*, I told him, there would be no more cups of coffee for the crew or supervisor – in fact, we would make extra special coffee for ourselves to drink in front of them, *one in each hand – with something in it –* until I saw the tiles at our house. Oddly, this seemed to do the trick, because two days later the tiles arrived, with Cheli and his radio; and with Peter looking round curiously for the extra special coffee – which I then had to invent by adding a dollop of brandy (and I could swear he knew this – he had a very funny look in his eye when he asked for a second cup).

During the adjournment the weather had improved and we were treated to the sight of Cheli in his shorts, his stubby legs, whiter than my own (hah!) and looking dainty in pale blue plastic sandals (haha!).

147

One last long – seemingly never-ending – day, and the job was finally, finally finished.

The results were splendid and Cheli's workmanship was first rate. We capitulated in the exuberance of the moment and gave a bottle of 'extra special' wine each to Cheli and his son.

Viv's last words on the subject were, 'If I ever suggest we should make any more changes to the house, shoot me, and if you do – don't look alarmed – I will shoot you.'

In between the last two phases of construction there were warnings that more rain was on the way.

After the horrendous Easter weekend, I thought we had seen the worst that Spain could come up with. I was wrong.

It started late on Tuesday evening, with a *real* deluge. The house, like most Spanish houses, had no gutters, so I lay awake most of the night listening to steady trickles of water splashing onto the path outside our bedroom window. By morning, the deluge had refused to abate and the garden was once again submerged in a layer of brown water, with larger pools beginning to appear. The swimming pool, which we had yet to use this year, was again full to the brim, the overflow unable to cope.

A bright patch of sky appeared briefly on Wednesday afternoon but it turned out to offer false hope.

We awoke on Thursday morning to find no change in the weather but considerable change in the landscape.

Water was cascading from the raised olive grove at the back of the house, a veritable waterfall, onto the gravel area that surrounded the terrace and the Acropolis. It was then flowing, like a wide, meandering river about five centimetres deep, through the carport, beneath the car, down the drive and out under the gate.

What made matters worse was that most of our precious gravel drive had been swept away.

We were not alone. Rivulets emerging from our neighbours' drives reached a confluence in the road, to form a torrent of rushing water some fifteen centimetres deep…one that carried gravel and small rocks in its wake.

And still it rained.

By mid-afternoon I was completely frustrated with being trapped indoors and decided to venture out. Jessie needed a walk even if she didn't know it. She hesitated on the threshold of the *naya*, reluctant to penetrate the curtain of water tumbling from the roof. She looked up at me – kitted out in my wellington boots, wax jacket and hood – as if to say, 'It's all right for you, but my fur's not waterproof.' I didn't care. I was getting out to see the action.

As we waded down the centre of the road, the water began to lap over the top of my boots and poor Jessie had trouble keeping her feet. Undaunted, I pressed on, my digital camera beginning to feel damp in my pocket. As we reached the sharp bend at the bottom of the road, the swerving swell of water gouged out a ravine that was threatening to undermine the foundations of a neighbour's garden wall.

We trudged on down the *camino* leading to the village, with me determined to see how the bridge was coping with the tide of water. Most of the gravel laid on the road by the drainage contractors had already been washed away, leaving one of the man-hole covers standing proud of the surface, ready to rip the sump off someone's car.

The bridge itself was impassable as the wall of water running down from the mountains cascaded over the top, carrying with it large boulders and trunks of fallen trees.

I wondered if the expensive electronics in the camera would withstand a bit of water, but decided to try it anyway, and managed to capture a couple of snaps to e-mail to friends to show them what a time we were having in Spain.

'*And at least,*' I bellowed to Jessie above the roar of water, '*we're not trapped in an office.*'

When the sky had finally emptied itself on Friday morning, it had deposited thirty centimetres of rain. Someone had once said to me that this part of Spain had the same amount of rainfall as the South of England, but that it came in 'big dollops.' They weren't kidding, I said to Viv, looking up 'dollops' in the dictionary with the idea that I could explain this to someone in Spanish.

24 hours later, barely a puddle could be seen, such was the capacity of the rocky soil to absorb whatever the weather brought.

I set out for Jalon keen to see what the river was like. Everything in the olive and orange groves seemed remarkably normal, but Jalon itself looked like a disaster area. The river, in full flood, carried all the litter and debris regularly dumped there after the weekly rastro market. The town centre, I discovered, had been cut off when a culvert, running beneath the road and carrying a tributary to the River Jalon, cracked and lifted, taking half the road with it.

For once the Spanish propensity for leaving things unfinished had backfired. A newly constructed riverside walkway had been left without a proper surface ever since I had first visited the town more than a year earlier. The retaining walls had been completed, street lighting columns had even been installed, but the overflowing river had washed away most of the foundations leaving sections of wall straddling thin air and lamp posts leaning at precarious angles.

The main event of the month was another espisode brought about by Viv's uncontrollable urge to rescue every waif and stray that came our way.

Jessie had been unusually quiet for a short while and Viv went to investigate, to find her nose-to-nose with a small dog at the gate. Given Jessie's normal response to anything with four legs, this in itself was remarkable, and made her just as culpable as Viv for subsequent events.

Taking pity on the poor thing, Viv offered it food and water outside the gate, but it showed no interest.

'*Leave it alone*,' I instructed. 'It will find its way home just as easily as it got here.'

I should have known better.

Viv fussed all day and theorised about where it might have come from.

At five in the afternoon we found it stubbornly seated in the road when we took Jessie for her walk. It decided to tag along as we followed our usual route up into the hills and I had high hopes that it would get lost or, better still, run off whence it came. It was having none of it. Every step of the way, it skipped jauntily along at Jessie's side.

At one point it darted up a side road as we turned back for home, then came skipping back to join us with a look that said, 'Hey, wait for me.'

Back at the house, Viv opened the gate and it shot straight into the garden as if it owned the place. We had a squatter.

Subsequent investigation proved *it* to be a *him*. My views on animal welfare differ considerably from Viv's, so I set aside my natural inclination to show him the gate with my toe up his derriere and reconciled myself to the fact that he would be staying the night. At this point I began to develop a theory about how this little chap had turned up on our doorstep. This is it:

A race of people from deep outer space were anxious to learn more about us earth dwellers, but being of such grotesque appearance themselves, they feared they would not be readily accepted on this planet.

So they decided to send one of their kind to earth, disguised in such a way as to avoid rejection. They researched long and hard to find two things. The first was all the most pleasing and appealing features of appearance, characteristics and behaviour that would ensure acceptance here on earth. The second was to find a simple human being with a soft heart and caring nature to take in their spy without question.

The little dog fulfilled the first criteria, and Viv fulfilled the second.

This was indeed the cutest dog ever to walk the earth.

His tiny, fluffy white legs were just a fraction too short for his body, causing him to kick his rear feet to one side as he scampered along. Other than that, he was just about perfectly made. His grey fur was the ideal contrast for his bristly white eyebrows and matching moustache. His bushy white tail stood rigid and vertical with the long fur fanning down so that it resembled one of those fly swishers favoured by African dictators when wearing their tribal costumes.

His willingness to jump on my knee and roll on his back for his tummy to be tickled must have been carefully programmed into his behaviour patterns to overcome my reluctance to let him stay. The same applied to his habit of stretching up to lick my face enthusiastically, despite my efforts at discouragement, and the way one of his long droopy ears flopped inside out when he shook his head and refused to right itself without outside intervention. But the *pieces de resistance* were his doleful big brown eyes and the way he cocked his head to one side when he looked at me as if to say, 'You can't resist me, can you?'

His creators had overlooked just one thing – ticks. He had several small specimens attached to his neck and underside, lurking in his matted fur. I glimpsed a reprieve. Surely, even Viv would reject him now for fear of cross contamination with Jessie. I should have known better. Half an hour later I was despatched to Jalon to buy 'Frontline' flea and tick treatment for dogs under ten kilos, and subsequently found myself holding his shivering body while Viv gave him a wash and blow dry with insecticidal shampoo. My last faint hope evaporated. There was no reason why he couldn't enter the house, was there?

He spent his first night in the *naya*, declining any interest in the bowl of water and dog food that Viv had provided in the hope of cementing the bond. At first light, I found him still there, looking up at me, head cocked to one side.

As I towered over him in my dressing gown he seemed to say, 'You won't get rid of me that easily.'

In a moment of weakness, I left the house door open and returned to bed, though he seemed reluctant to penetrate the chain-mail fly screen and it took five minutes for him to overcome his bashfulness. I was disturbed on the verge of returning to sleep by the weight of his body on my chest and the rasp of his tongue on my chin.

We had to decide on a name. Viv suggested Benji, but I insisted on Cheli. Why?

'Because lots of dogs are called Benji,' I said, 'and we need something new, and because Cheli will always remind me of what a nuisance he is.'

What was to be done with him? By this stage he had melted both our hearts and even Jessie seemed to want him to stay, showing not the slightest hint of jealousy at the attention he was demanding. But he obviously belonged to someone – the recently trimmed eyebrows were evidence of that – and they were bound to be missing him. We decided that we would be happy to keep him, but only after making efforts to trace his owners.

I took his photograph and ran off some posters in Spanish and English.

We walked him into the village, stopping people we passed to ask if they knew him.

Everyone made a fuss of him. He was that kind of dog.

We placed posters in the post office, the tobacconists, the bakery and the charity shop. We even stuck one up at the *basura*. The next day we took him to the vets in Jalon to see if he had a microchip but drew a blank. We left more posters in Jalon. Then we waited for the phone to ring.

Over the next seven days he gradually made himself at home and wormed himself even deeper into our affections. He began to eat, and soon picked up from Jessie that a raised paw was linked to a piece of food being popped in the mouth.

Jessie paid him very little attention other than a cursory glance in his food bowl just in case he'd left anything. She was usually disappointed. She gave him an occasional gentle growl when he picked up her toys, though she hadn't bothered with them for years.

We took him on our walks, but never on a lead. He grew in confidence, darting off out of sight always to return.

Someone said they thought they'd seen him at a small development of houses on the outskirts of the village so we walked him round, but he showed no signs of recognition.

One day Viv walked up the road to a neighbour's house, leaving him in the garden, but he managed to wriggle under the gate to follow. He was free to go any time but he chose to stay.

We decided that if his owners didn't appear on the scene we would keep him.

I e-mailed a photograph of Cheli in one of his cutest poses to Viv's father and he e-mailed back straight away to say, 'Quick, go and gather up the posters, this little fellow has got to stay.'

We thought about it. A week after he arrived, we left Cheli and Jessie in the house while we went to the market in Parcent. Viv was anxious that between them they might wreck the house, but we returned an hour or so later to find them both pushing to greet us, and not a sign of damage.

We checked the answer-phone for messages as usual. It said we had one new message but when we listened, there was just a click. I sensed immediately it was about Cheli.

Twenty minutes later, the phone rang again, and Viv answered. It was a foreign voice saying, 'You have my dog, I come to get him.'

A dark cloud descended.

'Perhaps he's not theirs,' we found ourselves saying, more in hope than expectation.

The lady had said she was coming from the mountains at the back of Jalon on the way to Bernia, some six kilometres away by road. We expected her to be with us in half an hour, but the directions Viv had given, I pointed out several times during the wait, were enough to have confused even the most proficient navigator.

Over the next hour and a half, we speculated about whether little Cheli could possibly have made the journey to Parcent.

In our hearts, we knew. I looked at Cheli in the garden with Jessie as you might look at a close friend you were about to lose. Viv put on a brave face, but I knew the anxiety she felt. The phone rang again. The lady was lost in Parcent. I gave her specific directions. I knew that these were Cheli's last few minutes with us and even I had to blink to hold back an involuntary tear.

As a precaution, we removed the thin red collar he was wearing when he arrived, so we could check and be sure that he really belonged to this lady. It was an unnecessary step. As soon as they met we could tell he was hers. Little Cheli was going home.

His owners were a German couple, Alexander and Edith Aretz, who ran a donkey sanctuary high in the mountains near Bernia. Although it was miles away by road, it was just on the other side of the peak that overlooked our house.

It was easy to see how the intrepid little explorer had found his way to Parcent. Edith, of course, was overjoyed. She told us he was two years old and had a little friend at home who had been pining for him for over a week.

'He was castrated four weeks ago,' said Edith.

'No wonder he ran away,' was my quick-fire, off-the-cuff response (ignored).

His proper name was 'Meni', which meant 'little man.' This described him perfectly, though he would always be Cheli to us.

Edith and Alexander ran a small tapas bar at the donkey sanctuary and Edith invited us to have lunch with them on the following Saturday. We accepted, thinking it would be nice to see Cheli (Meni) back in his familiar surroundings.

After Edith had left, we sat and talked for a while.

'We did the right thing,' we said.

'Wasn't it nice to see the joy and relief on Edith's face.'

'At least he will be back with his mate.'

'We would have wanted someone to try to find his owners if we had lost him.'

We consoled each other with these platitudes, but the truth was we were both broken-hearted. Even Jessie seemed subdued.

Our sorrow increased over the next few days as I went round the village taking down the posters, not helped by the fact that everyone enquired about him and said what a cute little chap he was.

Saturday came and I sensed that for Viv, the visit to the donkey sanctuary, Eselgestut Les Murtes, which had seemed like a good idea at the time, was now a less welcome prospect, but we were committed. As we drove up the narrow track in silence, to create a light atmosphere I once again reminded Jessie that I was glad I had decided on a four-wheel drive, which Viv would learn to handle sooner or later. Nobody laughed, though Viv spoke up to say that we seemed be on a road to nowhere, had I noticed? – and a minute later she pointed out some donkeys way off in the distance, even higher up the mountain.

Alex, whom we hadn't met before, greeted us; resplendent in ragged shorts and a rough white T-shirt stretching over his midriff. His unruly grey hair was the perfect match for a moustache that looked as if it would defeat even the sharpest razor, though the stubble on his chin had obviously succumbed in the last couple of days. They say that people grow to look like their dogs (or is that the other way round?), and the bright, friendly-looking Alex was the living proof of the truth in this observation. Edith joined us and was the perfect hostess, though she looked tired and we both sensed she was ill at ease.

Alex cleared off a plastic table and we sat down to a splendid lunch of never-ending tapas and a jug of rough red wine.

Alex explained how he and Edith came to be running a donkey sanctuary in the mountains of Sierra Bernia.

He had tired of life and work in Germany and had come to Spain fifteen years ago. He had fallen in love with the derelict old watchtower that was now his home – or would be, when it was finished. In the meantime, it remained a building site, with piles of bricks and rubble dotted around indiscriminately and various parts of the picturesque buildings shored up by scaffolding. The donkeys, now more than twenty in number, were an accident that had now become an obsession.

'And what about Cheli?' I asked. Edith said quickly that he was not himself.

I wondered for a second if it was something that we had done during his stay, but put it down to the fact that, understandably, he had been confined to quarters since his return.

She brought him out, but kept him on a lead. She appeared uneasy with the thought that he might be pleased to see us. He had run away before, it seemed, and, as he normally roamed with the donkeys, it was difficult to suppress his wanderlust.

'He may come to see you again,' she said at last, warmly, and apparently accepting that she could not confine him forever.

We left with mixed feelings. It had been wonderful to see Cheli again. He was pleased to see us, but Viv was convinced he wasn't – could not be – truly happy when we parted.

The uncertain hope that he might one day return was tempered by the realisation that we would only have to take him back again. Over the next few days and weeks we gained no consolation from looking up at Cheli's mountain and knowing he was just on the other side. Whether we would ever go back to Eselgestut Les Murtes remained to be seen.

Perhaps because of the Cheli incident, we came to be quite well known in the village.

People nodded and said good morning to us when we walked to the shops or the post office. I began to appreciate this sense of belonging, and to pay more attention the village way of life, noticing things I hadn't really seen before.

Old-fashioned values were clearly in evidence. Women could be seen every morning, not just sweeping the road outside their house, but mopping the pavement. Many of them seemed to be doing their neighbour's, as well.

The whole village was pleasantly graffiti-free, with the exception of a few political slogans and road signs with the Spanish town names blacked out and replaced with the Valenciano equivalent. This was reminiscent of the arguments that raged in Wales in the 1960's and 1970's and led some Welsh Nationalists to torch second homes owned by English people. It reminded me that though I was beginning to feel at home, I was still a foreigner, who barely spoke the language.

Apart from a few old men, the village was inhabited mainly by women during the daytime.

The younger wives gathered outside the school gate to watch over their offspring at playtime and collect them at the end of the day.

The men worked mainly on the land or in the building trade. The tradesmen gathered habitually in Bar Moll in the village square at around nine o'clock in the morning. Pedro the barman served them with what amounted to breakfast hereabouts – a large bottle of beer or a glass of wine, bread, olives, sliced serrano ham, chorizo sausage and pickled vegetables – all for one Euro. Many brought their own packed food as well.

I tried some of this fare one morning, just to show willing. It was robust, rustic food and all very enjoyable. I did hesitate over a pickled green chilli – *pimiento de padron* – convinced it would blow my head off, but Pedro assured me it was '*no muy caliente*' and urged me on. Not wishing to appear hesitant, I crunched the whole chilli in one, seeds and all. Either Spanish taste buds were less delicate than mine, or I was the victim of a joke, I realised quickly. It took all my powers of self-restraint to look as if I was enjoying it, grinning and nodding, but I could not disguise the sweat oozing from every pore in my body. Never, never again.

I was also persuaded to try a sample of shellfish that looked like spiny periwinkles. Pedro looked puzzled when I asked for a pin or something to extract the chewy flesh. I was given a lesson in how to use the long pointed spine at the top of the shell to re-move the flesh of these fascinating sea creatures, which turned out to be snails.

Fuelled by the influx of foreigners, there was no shortage of build-ing work in this part of Spain, especially those buying older houses and wanting to make alterations to suit their own particular needs.

There was also an influx of British tradesmen. Logos such as 'John Smith, Plumber,' or 'Steve Jones, Painter and Decorator,' were a common sight, not to mention the army of white van men, who would turn their hands to anything for cash, no questions asked, no VAT.

Like many other people, I'd often wandered through the streets of villages like Parcent in Spain and other parts of Mediter-ranean Europe, passing narrow houses with tiny doors and shut-tered windows opening directly onto the pavements.

It is rare to get so much as a glance inside these houses and, condescendingly, I'd assumed they must be dark and dingy little hovels. Not a bit of it. We were eventually invited inside a number of *casas del pueblo* and were surprised.

Dark and cool, yes, but many were palatial, with ornate moulded ceilings, magnificent tiling and furniture and fittings to match. Most had the benefit of an almost secret courtyard at the back, often home to a lemon tree or a few vines, and invariably dotted with carefully tended plants and flowers in ceramic pots and terracotta tubs.

They were all deceptively deep and spacious, often comprising five or six bedrooms on three or more levels, ending with a rooftop terrace.

Bar Moll became one of our favourite haunts on Monday mornings when we visited the village market. We didn't always need anything, but it was the foundation of village life and the bar became part of our life as well. We joined friends for coffee there after shopping and often lingered for the morning. I began to appreciate the finer details of this long-established institution.

The high plaster ceiling was a tobacco stained yellow and the cream and brown wall tiles blended beautifully, as did the brown plastic tables and chairs. A row of café nets covered the bottom half of the windows and almost, *almost,* reminded me of somewhere I had once been in Paris.

A set of ceiling fans disturbed the air and redistributed the smoke that swirled around a triangular, pseudo art deco wall lamp. As in most Spanish bars, a large television was perched high in one corner, though no one seemed to pay it much attention. The television's harsh tone bounced off the walls and forced customers to increase the volume of conversation to a loud hubbub that reverberated around the room.

The bar was dominated by a free-standing, cast iron log-burning stove; strategically placed to one side with a wobbly metal flue stretching, unsupported, up through the ceiling. Though nothing was ever said, we soon learnt that places near this fire were reserved for the elderly village folk.

Bar Moll was thriving, and in summer it expanded into the village square, Placa del Poble. It was the main source of catering for events at the neighbouring church when it was decked out in ribbons, with fresh flowers on white tablecloths in celebration of a wedding, a First Communion or some other important event in village life.

The atmosphere was superb. Nothing here had changed for decades.

Why should it? The place functioned perfectly.

The influx of visitors, and the village's new found wealth, had led to an increase in traffic in the narrow streets. Broken wing mirrors were a common sight.

Many of the more sensible villagers had opted to retain a more traditional mode of transport, the ride-on rotavator. The proper name for these ancient contraptions was *mula mecánica*, which literally translates to 'mechanical mule.' And that's exactly the function they performed.

These single-seater diesel engines with two small tractor wheels and easy rider-style handlebars, were perfect for negotiating the narrow streets and right-angle bends.

Some deluxe models had a steering wheel rising vertically, and potentially lethally, between the driver's legs, designed no doubt to discourage sharp braking in the absence of seat belts.

With a bench-seated trailer hitched behind there was room for the wife and kids as well as this year's olive crop.

They bore full vehicle registration plates and I wondered if they had been MOT'd. Another plate declared '20', which was presumably the maximum permitted speed in kilometres per hour. Many of them looked incapable of reaching even that.

They were not confined to the village streets. We frequently came across them on the open country roads, usually with a queue of horn-thumping drivers behind.

The increase in local traffic had forced the *ayuntamiento* to introduce a one way system in parts of the village, though no one seemed to take much notice of it.

Most of the road signs announcing, for example: 'No left turn,' were attached to the walls of houses, and many had been flattened by high-sided trucks, making them impossible to read.

One steep hill leading out of the village square had an unguarded sheer drop at one side, a danger to vehicles and pedestrians alike. (A 'Health and Safety Expert's Worst Nightmare' in England, and the kind of thing guaranteed to bring out mums with prams, blocking the road until something was done.)

I asked one of the passing locals if he didn't think it was dangerous.

He gave me a quizzical look then shrugged his shoulders.

'You can open a wine bottle with your teeth?' (At least, I think that's what he said.)

Parcent's other precious possession was the local co-op, Udaco. This august establishment fulfilled every possible requirement of local shoppers. Beer, wine, perfumes, medicines, cleaning tools and materials, groceries, and a collection of 'fresh' vegetables.

It reminded me of the Co-op in Handforth, Cheshire, where I was born. I was regularly sent off on my bicycle for a quarter of tea or some sugar, which they weighed out from large tins before packing it in neatly folded paper parcels.

'Don't forget to give the divi number,' Mum would always say as I raced off on my bike. On giving the divi number, I would obtain a small, hand-written receipt, a little larger than a postage stamp, which Mum would carefully stick on a gummed sheet. When the sheet was full it would be presented at the Co-op shop in return for a discount, or shares. Many a Christmas dinner was paid for in this way.

Udaco also featured an excellent butchery department run by an angel-faced, apron-clad, cleaver-wielding lady with rosy cheeks and a beguiling smile.

I found a good selection of meat could be had all week long so long as you understood the rules: lamb on Tuesdays, beef on Wednesdays and Saturdays, pork on Thursdays. Chicken and sausages? Available most days.

Shopping there was a daily event for many women and I often saw them taking one egg, three carrots and a couple of cabbage leaves to the till. They were often very kind to me, letting me go to the front of the queue, but only because they planned to spend most of the morning catching up on the gossip.

A row of chairs had been thoughtfully provided in front of the meat counter in anticipation of the waiting time while the chickens and rabbits were carefully prepared exactly to the customers' requirements.

There were two bread shops, *panaderías*, in the village, almost next door to each other. We preferred the bread from one shop but the cakes from the other, so in that way we were able to divide our custom more or less equally between them.

I was now quite familiar with most of the produce and found it much more satisfying to ask for what I wanted by name rather than simply pointing and saying '*dos por favor.*' I regularly asked for *pan rodondo, bocadillos, barras* (the Spanish equivalent of the French baguette) or *coca* – a kind of flat round pizza bread often topped with a few anchovies or tiny bits of sausage.

In the cake shop I asked for *caracola*; a pin-wheel cake made from soft pastry containing raisins and topped with a sweet glaze. *Caracola* means 'snail,' which described these buns precisely and I had a lot of fun with them at parties.

But I spotted something new one day: long thin buns about the size of a sausage and coated in sugar. Always ready to try something different, I asked for a couple then enquired what they were. A speciality of the Valencia region, I was told; typically dipped in coffee or chocolate. They were called '*Fartons.*' No difficulty remembering that one! I bought a dozen and rushed home to present them to the neighbours.

Agricultural momentum in the valley was now unstoppable. The small yellow flowers of the olive trees came and went in just a few short weeks, to be replaced by tiny green olives.

The velvet green almonds continued to swell and seemed already to be reaching maturity. The orange blossom had faded and next year's crop was already visible though hidden in the dense green foliage.

Sadly, my own orange trees seemed to have a very poor crop, largely due to a lack of expert pruning. A few small lemons had survived a natural culling as my newly planted tree seemed to be deciding how many fruits its fledgling branches could support. My one and only grape vine brought forth masses of fresh green leaves on metre-long tentacles, but only two tiny bunches of grapes could be found, in contrast to the abundant crops which were appearing in the nearby vineyards.

It was pruning season in the valley and the farmers were busy carrying out seemingly vicious attacks on the olive and almond trees and, to a lesser extent, the oranges as well. The preferred instrument of torture was the chain saw and these could be heard buzzing away from dawn until dusk.

One still, warm morning we stood and looked out over the full extent of the Jalon Valley. It seemed to be shrouded in layers of wispy white mist, giving a magical quality to the day.

But this was not a naturally occurring phenomenon, we found out. It was smoke rising from fires lit by the farmers as they disposed of the evidence of the torture they had inflicted so expertly on the fruit trees. The smoke billowed upwards to a single plateau-like layer which hung in the bottom of the valley until there was sufficient breeze to aid its dissipation.

As we were now beginning to sleep with the windows open in the house, it was not unusual to awake with the smell of wood smoke pervading our bedroom.

We were so at home in Parcent and the surrounding villages that we became reluctant to venture much further afield.

However, try as we might, it was impossible to avoid the occasional visit to a supermarket, if only because it was easier than carrying beer and wine from the village.

Benissa, a small town on the N332, was home to the nearest supermarket worthy of that description.

One day, we shoehorned our car into the badly designed underground car park (it seemed to have more concrete columns than parking spaces) and went in to shop. We had read about the dangers of bag snatchers in supermarket car parks and, though I dismissed the threat, Viv took it seriously. Later, as we emerged from the lift with our two trolleys wobbling onto the rough concrete surface, we spotted four smartly dressed young men – Spanish, we thought – hovering near the exit.

Viv was immediately suspicious.

She clasped her bag tightly and rushed towards our parked car. I stopped to look back and made the briefest of eye contact with one of the men who seemed to be following us.

He turned and walked back towards his gang. With Viv standing guard, her knuckles now white with the pressure of her grip on the bag, I unloaded the contents of the two trolleys into the back of the car.

I'd almost finished when a scream came from the far end of the car park – coinciding with a screech of tyres towards the exit.

The victim, a lone English woman, cried out, 'Help, they've snatched my bag.' Foolishly, she jumped into her car and raced out of the car park in an attempt to catch up with them. It was perhaps as well she failed, as the consequences may have been more serious than a lost purse.

She returned a few moments later to re-enter the supermarket and call the police. Apparently she'd done what many unwary women would do quite naturally in a seemingly safe environment. She'd placed her bag on the passenger seat of her car while loading her shopping into the boot. As she did so one of the men had distracted her while another quietly open the passenger door and lifted the bag. Only when she returned to the car, after replacing the trolley, did she realise what had happened, leaving the well-practised thieves plenty of time to shoot out of the car park.

Despite complying with every request from the water company to register our names, we were *still* awaiting our first bill.

Now living on a limited budget, water was the only commodity we had yet to pay for, and I was very anxious to know what it was costing me so that I could decide whether I could afford to sustain the now luxuriant, and very thirsty, new lawn. I'd heard no more about water bans but had come to genuinely fear the cost of water.

Hopes of action were raised one day when a man from the water company arrived in our road and replaced all the meters positioned outside the houses.

All the new meters were set at zero and I started peeking at some of them as we walked round the development, to compare our consumption with others. We were just about average.

One day, we noticed a damp patch outside a house owned by some Dutch people who hadn't been in residence since the new meters were installed.

I glanced round then quickly flipped the lid of their meter out of curiosity – only to find a reading of one hundred and fifty cubic metres: enough to twice fill our swimming pool. Something was obviously wrong.

The gates to the house were locked so Viv climbed over the wall (I remained, in charge of Jessie). At the back of the house Viv found a running hose-pipe and a pleasant new water feature in the garden – a small lake. She let me in and we turned off the flood that must have been running for two or three weeks. Through another neighbour, we managed to get a message to the owners in Holland.

It appeared that the visiting gardener was the culprit and I wondered how many week's wages it would take to make recompense, not knowing the cost of water...and my calculations succeeded almost every night in sending me off to sleep.

Our links with the village were becoming ever stronger.

We became attached to a restaurant on the outskirts of Parcent called La Tasca, which had the advantage that it was within staggering distance of home.

As frequent diners on our own, as well as with all the visitors we took there, we were becoming well known to the owner, Pepe, and his *delightful* (business) partner, Celine. The food was described as Mediterranean but regional specialities were on offer according to the season.

Most of the menu changed daily and Celine would explain in Spanish, what they had. We sometimes had difficulty understanding the Spanish, so Celine would patiently try again in French, her native tongue, and between the two versions we usually managed to make a selection based on guesswork. We spent many pleasant evenings at La Tasca, often running into friends, though things did not always run smoothly.

'*Soo sorry*, Mark, we have no musssels tonight,' Celine explained in her soft, delightfully insinuating voice one evening, knowing my penchant for *mejillones* whenever they were on the menu.

'That's okay,' I replied heartily. 'I'll have the sardines.'

'Ahhhh…' she said, before turning to Viv. 'And we have just run out of pork fillet in mustard sauce. I'm so sorrrry, Vivien, because I know it is your favourite.'

I paused to think of the best way to express my violent annoyance. Trying to come up with a biting and pointed phrase that was mild and subtle, yet sarcastic enough to communicate severe displeasure, pleasantly, I stared into space.

'It is such a pity you came today, Mark,' she went on. 'If you were here tomorrow night we would have everything, because we stock up for Saturdays.'

'*No – no, that's no good at all, I'm here right now, and...*'

'Then you can come again, tomorrow!' said Celine, directing her most delightful smile at me. 'Tomorrow, I promise I will do something special … just for you alone.'

'So – what's the soup today?' I enquired.

A chance meeting with our only Spanish neighbour gave us an unexpected opportunity.

Rosa, who lived nearby with her husband and small baby, Usue, said she was anxious to improve her English and asked if we'd be interested in spending a couple of hours a week together so she could help us with our Spanish at the same time. We jumped at the chance.

Over the next weeks we shared many discussions concerning the ultimate logic of our respective languages, and exchanged and laughed about quite a few colloquial phrases.

Rosa already spoke excellent English, but struggled with some of the pronunciations, and at one of our weekly sessions she said she wanted help with that.

Viv started in, and had got to a demonstration of the pronunciation of 'poor,' when she had to go and fetch the coffee. I quickly explained that as well as various meanings, there were *four words* in English all spelt differently but pronounced in exactly the same way – *poor, pour, pore and paw*. These she had to know, as she may be called upon to use them all in the same sentence (which I was just thinking up).

'How can this be?' said Rosa, 'I will never learn to speak English properly, there are no consistent rules.'

'Oh, yes, there are.' I explained: 'A paw is the foot of a dog or a cat, but not a person, unless unruly – you see?'

Rosa asked, 'This is the same for a horse?'

'Oh *no*,' I said, 'that's a *hoof*, as in '*roof*.' But you *must* pronounce 'h' like 'happy,' not apple. 'Poor' has two meanings.'

'English is impossible!'

'The poorly horse, pawing the ground in the pouring rain –' I began, 'had a pore – no, wait a minute, a dog's paw – '

Viv came back, and my teaching career tailed off.

By the end of May, we were both feeling and looking quite rosy. The builders were a distant, and now less painful, memory.

The weather at last improved to what we expected of late spring in Spain.

We were even making use of the pool at last, as the surface glistened invitingly and the water temperature moved into the twenties.

For most of our seven months in Casa Emelia we'd enjoyed blissful peace and quiet, often with the birdsong and croaking frogs providing the only distractions.

Klaus and Marita had returned to Germany for four months, soon to be followed by our other next door neighbours, Gerrard and Catharina, who escaped from the summer heat by returning to Holland.

Silence reigned – for a short while at least – until slowly, almost imperceptibly, we began to notice changes in Parcent, in Jalon, and in the all the local shops and restaurants.

An early morning traffic jam en route to the market confirmed our suspicions. English (and German, Dutch and French) voices dominated conversations.

Parking spaces – a rarity at the best of times – were becoming impossible to find.

Pool maintenance chemicals were selling almost as fast as sunburn cream, and the bodegas in Jalon were struggling to cope with the demand for flagons of vino tinto.

The tourist season had started.

'...I thought we'd seen the worst that Spain could come up with. I was wrong. It started late on Tuesday evening. A real deluge...'

Bacon and Mushroom Pots

Bacon and mushrooms are a classic combination, but with thyme, garlic, and plenty of sun-dried tomatoes, they are even more delicious. This quick and easy starter takes only a few minutes to prepare and can be warmed through just before serving. Serve with plenty of crusty bread to mop up the juices.

- *6-8 rashers of streaky bacon, diced*
- *200 g button mushrooms, quartered*
- *2 onions, peeled and diced*
- *2 garlic cloves, peeled and finely chopped*
- *6-8 sun-dried tomatoes, roughly chopped*
- *1 tsp fresh thyme, stalks removed (or ½ tsp dried thyme)*
- *Freshly ground black pepper*
- *4-6 tbls single cream*
- *Oil and butter for frying*

1. Using a non-stick frying pan, fry the bacon in a little oil over moderate heat until lightly browned. Remove from the pan and set aside.

2. Add the onion and garlic to the pan and fry gently until the onions are soft, but not brown.

3. Return the bacon to the pan and add the thyme, mushrooms and tomatoes with a good knob of butter and season with pepper. Continue to fry gently until the mushrooms are cooked.

4. Just before serving, add the cream and warm through until the mixture is bubbling. Spoon into warmed ramekins and garnish with a sprig of thyme or parsley.

Serves 4
Preparation time: 15 minutes
Cooking time: 15 minutes

Beef San Miguel

I used to make a casserole like this on cold winter nights in England, and I never thought I'd need to cook this kind of food in Spain. It just goes to show how naïve I was.

The original recipe was made with brown ale, but I only had a can of San Miguel in the fridge so I used that instead – hence the name. By all means use brown ale if you can find it, but this version was just as good, though a little paler in colour.

- *750g stewing steak cut into bite-sized chunks*
- *1 large onion, roughly sliced*
- *2 fat cloves of garlic, peeled and chopped*
- *3 tbls plain flour mixed with a little salt and pepper*
- *6 medium carrots, peeled and thickly sliced*
- *300ml San Miguel cerveza*
- *300ml beef stock*
- *2 tbls tomato pureé*
- *200g mushrooms, quartered*
- *2 tsps vinegar*
- *2 tbls French mustard*
- *1 tbls brown sugar*
- *1 baguette (or similar loaf) sliced into rounds*
- *1 tbls chopped parsley*
- *Olive oil for frying*

1. Pre-heat the oven to 160°C.

2. Toss the meat in the seasoned flour to coat evenly then fry in a little hot oil until browned. Place in an ovenproof casserole and set aside.

3. Fry the onion and garlic until soft then stir in the remainder of the seasoned flour. Gradually stir in the San Miguel and beef stock then add the tomato pureé, sugar, vinegar and 1tbls of the mustard. Heat until boiling then add to the casserole with the carrots and stir well. Cover the casserole and place in the oven for 1½ hours.

4. Meanwhile spread the remaining mustard on both sides of the sliced bread. Remove the casserole from the oven and stir in the mushrooms. Place the bread slices on top and press them gently into the cooking juices then return the casserole, uncovered, to the oven for a further ½ hour. Serve immediately, garnished with the chopped parsley.

Serves 4
Preparation time: 15 minutes
Cooking time: 2 hours

Chapter Nine

Searching for Shade

The vagaries of the weather in May were replaced with the monotonous predictability of June. As the sun climbed high in the sky, casting only minimal shadows in the middle of the day, we awoke each morning to clear blue skies and warm sunlight.

Our bedroom faced due east and even with the *persianas* pulled down, strands of sunlight penetrated the tiny gaps between the shutters to create a checkerboard effect on the wall. We would lie and watch the pattern move slowly along the wall as we contemplated getting out of bed to face the increasingly arduous tasks of daily life in our first Spanish summer.

On many mornings it was only the necessity of taking Jessie for a walk that prompted us to get out of bed at all. Our morning walks were curtailed when Jessie slowed to snail's pace, panting to cool herself, though we usually returned before eight o'clock.

At least we had the benefit of an after-walk plunge in the pool, something not available to Jessie; she'd had an aversion to being immersed in water ever since she'd slipped and fallen into a pond in England.

Suddenly we found ourselves reminiscing fondly about the gentle warmth of the winter sun and the joy of the log fire, as the evenings chilled. It was only June, and we knew that worse was to come in July and August, always the hottest months in the Costa Blanca.

We'd not appreciated just how the summer heat and the power of the sun would influence our well-established routines.

Doing anything the least bit energetic brought instant beads of sweat, so we confined any efforts to early in the morning and later in the evening.

Afternoons were spent in the shade by the pool, reading, snoozing or, in my case, composing the next few 'Now That All the Excitement's Over' chapters of my 'Magnum Opus' in my head.

As the sun moved inexorably along its high summer arc, so we moved round the house opening and closing the windows and *persianas* in an effort to keep it out. For the most part this worked, though by the end of the day the air itself had absorbed the solar heat and it was impossible to escape. Even the tiled floors, which had frozen our feet in the winter, gave precious little in the way of relief. We contemplated installing air conditioning in the bedrooms but stuck to our original intention of experiencing our first summer without it, muttering that it would not be long before we changed our minds.

My culinary endeavours became less adventurous. Even slicing a tomato was an effort. We nibbled on salads and cold meats or fish, or something thrown on the gas barbecue and that didn't require much attention. Gradually, I found more inventive ways of presenting lettuce – adding orange, grapefruit, avocado, or my favourite, watermelon. We rarely ate before nine o'clock in the evening and even beer o'clock was often put back past seven, in deference to the heat.

Through all of this we noticed small changes in our surroundings. Though still predominantly agricultural, the Jalon Valley is pepper-potted with collections of villas, many clinging to the steep-sided slopes, and we couldn't help thinking that there was a danger of over development, especially when we saw several prospective new urbanisations with roads already gouged from the virgin hillsides ready for the next influx of holiday-makers or permanent residents from cooler parts of Europe.

I wrote to my friends back home that I was '…resisting the temptation to wish they would put a stop to any more development that could further erode the valley's natural beauty. After all, I was first attracted to the area by the pleasant surroundings and cheap property prices, so there is no reason why others should not want to follow suit. The demand seems insatiable and the authorities seem anxious to take advantage of the investment that comes with it. There is no real evidence of pressure on the local infrastructure, except perhaps that the bodegas are having difficulty coping with the demand for Jalon Tinto.'

The truth was, each time Viv and I saw another giant earth-moving machine or heard another JCB pecking away at the mountainside we had but two thoughts on our minds: *'CLEAR OFF!'* and *'THIS IS OURS!'*

One cool evening in mid-June we decided to take a drive to see what was to be found if we travelled further inland to the head of the Jalon Valley. The village of Castell de Castells was our destination as this was the home of Barry Said, the agent who had introduced me to Casa Emelia. Although the village of Castells was only fourteen kilometres away, the narrow, windy road meant the journey time was always longer than expected. Once through Murla and Benichembla, the mini urbanisations disappeared – as did the orange groves and vineyards, which required a frost-free environment. Almonds and olives prevailed, alongside an occasional pine tree.

The clear blue sky which we left behind in Parcent soon disappeared to be replaced with dark, thunderous clouds. By the time we reached Castells it was pouring with rain. We abandoned our plans to walk round the village and stayed in the car, following the signs for *Centro Urba*.

We reached the small village square, found it choc-a-bloc with parked cars, and followed a direction sign that pointed to what seemed to be the only way out. The road narrowed and became steeper as we approached a right angle bend and we found ourselves peering over a precipice.

Viv began to panic, I shouted, 'Don't panic!' and we both panicked. We would have jumped out of the car except that we were wedged between two houses and it was impossible to open the doors more than just a few centimetres. An old man emerged from one of the houses, obviously used to the sight of shrieking motorists, and waved us on.

'*Poco a poco*' he said – 'Little by little' – so I obeyed.

As I inched the car very carefully down the steep slope and round the corner, I was able to inspect at close quarters the gouge marks in the walls where other lost motorists had failed to negotiate the bend. Several forward and reverse movements later we scraped through, only to be confronted by another, equally daunting, manoeuvre before we were able to extricate ourselves from the perils of the one-way traffic system and exit the village.

'Never again,' Viv whispered.

I nodded, unable to utter a word.

Purely by coincidence, Barry Said telephoned a few days later. He'd finally bought his dream property, 'A small *casita* and 14,000 square metres of mainly almond trees on the edge of Castells.' Would we like to come over and see it and share a paella at his house in the village?

'With pleasure,' I said. 'So long as we don't have to drive into the centre. It took us a week to get out last time. We are not, not – not to put too fine a point on it, words fail me.'

Barry laughed. 'Not that many cars go over the side,' he said, 'but I have heard of a few people, so I'll meet you at the edge of Castells, and show you what you're missing.'

When he did meet us outside the village, he guided us quickly to park in a lay-by just a few minutes away.

Barry, we could see, was bubbling with excitement.

'It's quite small, and a bit basic,' he said from the back seat as we parked, 'but the views are spectacular. We'll have to get out and walk from here.'

We zig-zagged our way down a narrow cart track that was gradually being reclaimed by native vegetation and finally glimpsed a tiny tiled roof nestling on top of crooked walls, and a hut, or house, constructed, it seemed, of stones picked up from the surrounding land.

As we reached the house, we saw a small plot, the only piece of level ground for miles.

Standing in front of the ramshackle structure the view appeared endless, first over vast tracts of almond groves and eventually, in the far distance, the actual castle perched on a mountaintop from which Castell de Castells took its name. There were just two other properties in sight. So this was real Spain.

'It needs a little work, it's a bit basic inside,' Barry repeated.

He wasn't kidding. As the heavy metal door creaked open on its rusting hinges, a family of bats fluttered round the room, startled by the sudden ingress of light. Viv screamed and ducked as they circled overhead, despite Barry's hand-waving, and my shouts of assurance as I hid behind her, that they would not collide with anyone at all so long as she remained still. The bats settled back in their upside-down positions between the wooden beams of the low ceiling. We crept into the only other room.

This room was home to half a dozen old mattresses and Barry explained that the *casita* had been used by local hunters out for the night. Obviously this was not a recent occurrence as the mattresses had been attacked by rats and the foam stuffing was littered all over the earth floor. A collection of old beer bottles and a few dusty drinking vessels were the only evidence of recent occupation.

Barry announced his plans with convincing enthusiasm, explaining where he would put the kitchen and bathroom and how he would lay out the space.

Outside, he asked us to imagine the raised *naya* and ground floor terrace he had already created in his mind. I could imagine nothing, but Viv stared with enthusiasm at wherever he pointed, and I tried to nod endorsement.

Finally, I asked about the availability of basic services.

For water there was a bottle-shaped stone well at the back of the building, though a more reliable source would be created by installing a water deposit half way down the track and accessible to a tanker for delivery, Barry explained, gesturing as he drove an imaginary tanker uphill. The lack of mains electricity was easily overcome by solar panels with a small generator for back up, he added. Telephones? – hah! He would rely on his mobile.

He seemed to have it all worked out, but for two problems – time and money. He spent all of his time earning the money, so he planned to retire from the property agent's business just as soon as he had raised enough cash to live off for the rest of his days. The trouble was, he was already fifty-eight and time was running out.

The place was idyllic, the views were spectacular and you would certainly get peace and quiet in this little corner of Spain. Barry assured us that there were other, similar retreats hidden away in the mountains, but Viv and I looked at each other. Perhaps, I thought, we were not quite ready for real Spain, or possibly real Spain was not quite ready for us. We weren't sure we were ready for such a challenging, hermit-like existence...

The arrival of summer brought with it the first keen onslaught of holidaymakers heading for the mountains in search of steak and kidney pie.

They were easily recognisable by the shade of their skin. Most permanent residents of the Costa Blanca develop a soft, weather-beaten brown tan, achieved without really trying: simply by living outdoors for most of the time. Most holidaymakers arrive with pasty white flesh tones, again achieved without trying: by months of confinement in centrally heated homes and offices.

As if to emphasise the difference in skin coloration, many of the men, giving their shorts a first outing of the year, insist on wearing black socks to create the maximum contrast with their sun-starved legs. They are just as easily recognisable at the end of their two-week pilgrimage, their pallor replaced by shades varying from sore pink to overdone purple.

Viv and I marvelled at the ability of some of these people to stake themselves out in the sun from dawn until dusk, trusting that a thin layer of sun block would save them from soreness and sleepless nights. For our part, Viv and I spent every hour of daylight searching for shade. The Acropolis came into its own, the brushwood roof providing a pleasant dappled shade in the middle of the day. There was no escape for the lawn as the soil set like cracked concrete and the patchy blades of grass withered and shrivelled under the sun's incessant power. More water was called for...though we were still awaiting that famous first bill.

'...the summer heat and the power of the sun would
influence our well-established routines.'

Chicken Tagine

Spanish cooking has lots of African influences, not surprising really since the Moors ruled parts of Spain on and off for around 400 years.

This variation on a typical Moroccan tagine combines succulent chicken with subtle spices and dried fruits.

Ideally it should be served with cous cous, but plain boiled rice would be almost as good.

- *4 skinless chicken thighs, boned and cut into bite sized chunks*
- *1 medium onion, roughly chopped*
- *8 dried apricots, quartered*
- *A handful of seedless raisins*
- *1 large tomato cut into wedges*
- *½ tsp cumin seeds, crushed*
- *1 tsp mild paprika*
- *½ tsp turmeric*
- *150ml chicken stock*
- *Olive oil*

For the cous cous:

- *125g cous cous*
- *125ml chicken stock*
- *About 1 tbls each of finely diced onion, red pepper and green pepper*
- *1 tbls chopped parsley*
- *A knob of butter*

1. Pre-heat the oven to 180°C.

2. Heat a little oil in a frying pan and fry the chicken and onion together over medium heat for 5-6 minutes. Stir in the cumin, paprika and turmeric then add the apricots and raisins together with the chicken stock. Transfer to an ovenproof casserole, cover and place in the oven for 30 minutes.

3. Remove the casserole from the oven and stir in the tomato pieces. Return the casserole to the oven, uncovered, and cook for a further 15 minutes.

4. As the casserole is cooking, prepare the cous cous. Gently fry the diced onion and pepper until soft then set aside. In a large saucepan, bring the stock to a rapid boil then add cous cous, butter, diced vegetables and parsley. Remove from the heat, cover with a lid and leave to stand for about 5 minutes then gently reheat, stirring constantly until steaming. Serve immediately with the tagine.

Serves 2
Preparation time: 10 minutes
Cooking time: 45 minutes

Hot Cherries
with ice cream

The neighbouring valley, the Val de Laguart, is famed for its cherries and renowned for the pink and white blossom in early March. By June, the markets are awash with the fruit. I first tasted this dish in Manchester in 1975 and I had forgotten all about it until I saw piles of fresh cherries in my local market. I can't claim it's an original recipe, but it's one of my favourites. Don't try to remove the pips, just leave a spare plate on the table.

- *750g fresh cherries (choose the ripe ones that are deep purple in colour)*
- *3-4 tbls white sugar*
- *Vanilla ice cream (or whatever flavour you prefer)*
- *Mint tips to garnish*

1. Remove the stalks from the cherries and wash thoroughly. Place the still wet cherries and sugar in a medium sized pan and bring slowly to a boil. Continue to cook over medium heat, stirring gently until the cherries start to go soft and the liquid turns syrupy (about 10 minutes).

2. Spoon the cherries into serving dishes and top with a blob of ice cream. Pour over the syrup and garnish with mint tips.

Serves 4-6
Preparation time: 5 minutes
Cooking time: 10 minutes

Chapter Ten

And the Band Played On

Ever since we'd arrived in Spain the previous October, Viv had been asking everyone what we might expect of the weather in July and August. The answers varied, but the overwhelming consensus of opinion was 'hot.' This was usually followed by, 'What did you expect?' So it came as a pleasant surprise when the early part of July brought cloudy skies and stiff breezes to freshen the air after June's intensive grilling. It was not to last.

By the end of the month the heat seemed like a permanent fixture. There was a brief opportunity early each morning when we took Jessie on a truncated route, usually through the olive groves, to enjoy some shade. By the time we returned to the house, the beads of sweat were already forming and would remain for most of the day. The slightest exertion turned us into soggy, withering jellies. Lethargy reigned. Or at least it would have done if I hadn't offered to do a bit of building work as a favour to Klaus and Marita next door during their sojourn in the pleasantly mild summer warmth of Schleswig Holstein.

I'd foolishly agreed to raise the height of the boundary wall between our respective gardens – which involved humping fifty or so large breeze blocks up to a height of almost three metres. I took some consolation from the fact that the weight of two of these blocks was roughly equivalent to the weight I had shed since arriving in Spain some nine months earlier, and at first I looked forward to this as an interesting experiment.

I worked in short bursts of an hour or so each day, mixing a batch of mortar and continuing until it was used up. In just shorts and sandals, I toiled away, after a few days cursing my impulsive generosity in volunteering to do the job.

Perspiration oozed from every pore as the sun beat down on my back and shoulders; my shorts needed wringing out once an hour. It's hard to describe the sheer exhilaration of jumping straight into the pool at the end of each shift.

When the blockwork was finished and the wall had been roughly rendered it was time, once again, to try my hand at the art of pebbledashing. This time I was going to get it right. I remembered everything I had learnt from the Master Craftsman, Miguel, as I set about the task.

The sand, stone, and cement was mixed to a sloppy slurry, then carried to the far end of the garden in one of those two-handled rubber buckets which the Spanish seem to use for everything, and which I had bought expressly for the purpose.

Trowel in hand, I recalled exactly how Miguel had deftly flicked the mixture onto the wall with unerring accuracy so that it stuck immediately and gradually formed a uniform finish. Strangely enough, my brief tutelage under The Master proved to have been insufficient, because the mixture clung in blobs or dribbled down the wall to splatter on the ground.

Spurred on, I persevered and eventually it came 'good,' though I noticed a marked difference between the beginning of the work and the end. I scraped off the first batch and went over it again. Eventually, I was able to stand back and admire my pebbledashing with the kind of self-satisfaction that I'd rarely felt in my last few years in the office. Finally, it was time to shovel up the material that had splattered on the ground. There was at least as much here as on the wall itself, but the job got done.

A couple of coats of paint, and I was able to e-mail a photograph of the finished job to my friends back at the office, and finally, after adding a few nice flowers to the picture, to Klaus. He replied to say it looked perfect, almost as good as the sketch he had left with me, but the true test would come when he returned to Spain in September, and what were those things that looked a bit like dead flowers?

I was gradually becoming accustomed to living in the intense heat and for me the hardest part was forcing myself to be inactive between midday and seven in the evening when the sun slowly eased down behind the large carob tree at the end of the garden. It was only then that we emerged from our enforced hibernation to resume our nocturnal existence.

Viv was not faring so well. Her menopausal hot flushes were only exacerbating her discomfort. One minute she would be sitting comfortably in the shade even as the temperature rose towards thirty-five degrees. The next minute she would be drenched in a sweat as her hormones played up.

'Not again,' I mentioned more than once, cheerfully glancing at her distress. 'Perhaps you'll get used to it.'

I was glad I was the male of the species, I explained, not least because my cooling system seemed to work more efficiently than Viv's.

'I've so far escaped symptoms of male menopause,' I told her.

'Perhaps they're yet to come,' she said wearily. 'Or perhaps they're destined to pass, like so much else, without your noticing.'

I kindly sloshed her another glass of iced water, and she tossed some at me in return.

Then there was Jessie. At the height of July, Viv coped for most of the time by keeping out of the sun, sitting in the shade of the olive tree by the pool or retreating indoors, but at least she had Jessie for company. She, too, searched out the coolest spots in the house and garden. When the dog ventured out into direct sunlight it would take between twenty and thirty seconds, but then she began to pant rapidly. Naturally, Viv regarded Jessie's panting as symptomatic of distress, despite my emphatic assurances that it was merely the natural way for a dog to cool down.

'People sweat, dogs pant,' I said severely. 'It's time to worry when she stops panting.'

This made matters worse. From then on, whenever Jessie was lying still and comfortably (usually when she clung to the cool tiled floor in the north facing bedroom), she stopped panting – causing Viv to run up, hot and panting, to check that she was still breathing.

The fact was that Jessie coped better than both of us – at least, for most of the time.

'No need to worry,' I said to Viv, fed up with the whole thing. 'Let's not fuss. Look at me, I'm not worried. Only for a couple more months, and if you don't make it, there's the fossy.' A fresh dollop of iced water landed on my head.

Then, in the middle of July, poor Jessie contracted gastroenteritis and we were both in a panic. It was back to Doctor Jekyll and Mr Hyde at the veterinary surgery in Jalon. Nine injections later and she was still under the weather.

After the final trio of injections early one Sunday morning we returned home and this time Jessie was seriously distressed. She paced from room to room, unable to settle for more than a minute or so. Her pulse was racing and she was panting frantically. We called the vet and he offered to come out to the surgery later in the day – which meant we had to wait for two and a half hours.

It was the longest two hours of our lives. We both knew she was desperately ill – then just as we were getting ready to leave for the vets, Jessie raised her head. By the time we arrived in Jalon, she was fine, and I felt like an over-anxious father as we tried to explain just how terribly ill she had been an hour or so earlier.

'You should have seen her,' I said. 'She – didn't she, Viv?'

'Better safe than sorry,' said the vet, shrugging. 'But probably it was just a reaction to the injections. No need to worry.'

At that second, *I swear I saw the Euro signs pop up in his eyes* as he added a few more notes to Jessie's ever-expanding file (although Viv nudged me after we got outside, to say – ridiculously – that she had seen them in mine – as if *I* would be that obvious).

This was not the only discomfort suffered by our beloved hound. There was also that aversion to fireworks.

This became an all-too-frequent problem as the local villagers needed very little excuse to celebrate with pyrotechnics.

A wedding, a confirmation, Uncle Angelo's birthday, F C Valencia winning the Spanish Premier League – all these events sparked off noisy celebrations.

The fireworks they used were not the colourful spectacle we were used to seeing in England on bonfire night.

They were mainly home-made, sub-atomic missiles, launched

with a high pitched whistle: they soared high into the stratosphere before exploding with an ear-drum-splitting bang which echoed and resonated all the way around the valley.

Jessie's response was to dash indoors and we still found her curling up, cowering in the base of the shower.

No amount of consolation or reassurance on our part would induce her to emerge, so in the end we simply left her to it, with me – aided by Viv grabbing my arm – resisting the temptation to turn the tap on.

Life in Parcent continued unaffected by the summer heat. The schools had long since closed, though the local young people showed little difficulty amusing themselves in and around the village. Many spent their days at the outdoor municipal swimming pool on the edge of the village.

I marvelled at how this tiny pueblo could afford a facility of almost Olympic proportions. My old London Borough, with a population of close to a quarter of a million, had spent years arguing over whether to refurbish a decaying swimming centre which nobody seemed to want to use.

In the evenings, many of the villagers were involved in the local band, which practised most nights of the week on a piece of ground at the back of the town hall. Practice sessions started at around eleven in the evening and continued until well past midnight. They were obviously limbering up for fiesta week in August when, we were told, they would often play into the early hours of the morning. Again I wondered how this small community could support a full brass band. From my experience in England most young people were more interested in listening to music than learning to play. And most small bands needed to beg, steal or borrow (or organise jumble sales) to pay for instruments.

Strolling through the village early one Saturday evening, I stumbled across another local recreation – pilota. The more sophisticated pilota, practised in the Basque Country, involves men strapping a basket to their arms and flinging a small ball at a wall in what is reputed to be the world's fastest ball game. Parcent had its own, slightly more genteel, version.

As I turned the corner off one of the village's many steep climbing streets, I found my usual route blocked by rows of wooden chairs brought out of the houses; these were occupied mainly by older men.

The street was similarly blocked at the far end and my destination, Bar Guay, was in between. I decided to postpone my visit, reluctant to invade the pitch where a form of four-a-side pilota was in progress.

Two teams, one in blue, the other in white, confronted each other between the rows of houses that seemed to delineate the court. The team members, it seemed to me, ranged in age from sixteen to sixty. Their hands, which they used to 'bat' a bouncy ball from one end of the street to the other, were heavily taped with Elastoplast.

I had great difficulty *understanding the rules*. More often than not, play was interrupted when the ball became lodged in a doorway or on one of the balconies where privileged spectators enjoyed a grandstand view.

Perhaps, I thought, the umpire called a 'let,' though I could never see an umpire, and I never did find anyone who could explain those rules (and I had great difficulty understanding how anyone could enjoy *a game without rules)*.

We heard that Bar Moll had put out tables and chairs in the evenings and was presenting a summer menu.

In need of some Dutch courage, we said, laughing at our own little joke, we invited Leny and Wil to join us there for dinner one evening. Pedro the barman looked puzzled when I popped in a few days beforehand and asked to reserve a table – judging from the fact that he made no attempt to write down my request, or to ask what time we wanted to be there, I gathered a reservation was not essential – but I went back and reported that it was all arranged; and hoped for the best.

When we arrived in the village square we found one of the red plastic tables set with a paper cloth, which we assumed was for us.

The rest of the tables were unoccupied and we thought we might be the only diners, but we'd forgotten that the practice in

Spain is to eat late, and our arrival at eight-thirty placed us at least an hour ahead of the locals. We were well into our meal by the time the other tables came into use.

Here was village life in microcosm, I thought, looking excitedly at Viv. She got out her small camera and I pretended to drop things or pour more wine so that she could get clicking under cover of the action.

Old men returning from work on the land stopped off for a drink and some tapas.

Younger men did the same; still dressed in their working clothes after a day in the building trade.

Stooped old women, usually dressed in black, entered the church with dignified demeanour, declining the opportunity of a post-confession drink.

Later on in the evening, some of the local boys cruised through the square in shiny cars – elbows hanging casually out of the windows, stopping at the side of the tables to show off mobile phones and eye the female talent. They moved on only reluctantly, when an old man on a *mula mecánica* revved an ageing diesel engine behind them, filling the square with fumes.

The limited female talent illustrated the dichotomy between modern and traditional Spain.

Wil and I couldn't help staring as one group of young women entered the square, led by a slender, bleached-blonde teenager wearing a pair of denim hot pants that barely covered the cheeks of her bum.

They reminded me of a bright red leather pair that Viv had worn in 1968, I said, nudging her and trying to explain to everyone how it was, while keeping my eyes on the girl. Elaborate makeup and a broad hipster belt, worn purely for decoration, enhanced this girl's outfit. A tight-fitting top with the zip pulled down to show just the right amount of cleavage completed the ensemble.

I stared, everyone at the table stared; first at the girl and then at Viv, as she insisted that she had never looked in the least like that and what's more I had looked a right clown in 1968, too.

This quartet of girls contrasted sharply with another group, more modestly dressed and chaperoned by their mothers. As the boys cruised past, their attention focused on the first group who preened themselves like exotic parakeets and flirted outrageously in search of attention. By contrast, the second group seemed to attract few approaches from the boys – who, as they cast admiring glances towards the pouting prima donna girls, were glanced at disapprovingly by the other girls' mothers.

The meal was very pleasant and efficiently served, but the locals seemed to be eating food that I hadn't seen on the menu.

Some of it looked much more interesting than the meal I'd just eaten and I assumed this must be available only to those in the know. Viv was cheerfully tucking into chips for the first time in months, since I'd removed them from the menu at Casa Emelia, but I was not satisfied and took a few walks between the tables, trying and not succeeding in figuring out what we were missing.

We lingered over coffee, then – enthralled with the atmosphere – and called it a day at about midnight, just as the bin men arrived in the square. They parked the refuse truck next to us, and popped over to Bar Moll for a beer before resuming their garbage collection round.

'That's what I call the end of a perfect day,' I said, and for once *everyone* seemed to think I'd come up with something funny.

As the days grew warmer we began to adjust to an enforced new regime. We ate later in the evenings, long after the sun had disappeared. The most oppressive part of the day was late afternoon, by which time everything around us had absorbed the radiant heat of ten hours of unbroken sunshine. Everything was hot: the terrace, the poolside patio, the walls of the house. Even the rocks in the garden were too hot to handle.

After dark, the warmth began to dissipate, and so we lingered after dinner under the Acropolis, often until midnight.

The new climbing plants were growing at a phenomenal rate, already beginning to engulf the pillars. Our favourite was the night-scented jasmine that released its heady perfume into the still, evening air.

We were fascinated by the family of geckoes that had taken up residence in the new timbers; attracted no doubt, by the insects and moths that were drawn to the newly installed lights. We decided we liked the geckoes, as they were voracious eaters of creepy crawly things that might otherwise have pestered us... but it was sometimes a little disconcerting to be eating our meal to the accompaniment of a gecko crunching on a grasshopper half its size – still struggling and wriggling its legs in a vain attempt to resist being swallowed.

Then Viv was not too amused when she awoke one morning to find a gecko clinging, limpet-like, to our bedroom ceiling. She demanded immediate action, but it took a few minutes to engage my brain.

'It's good to have a gecko in the house,' I said. 'They eat your moths, so then your moths can't eat your clothes. I read about it.'

I was hoping that my inventive suggestion had bought me a few more minutes in bed, but Viv was not convinced and so, eventually, I came up with a plan.

I stood on a stool and managed to trap the little creature with one of the dome shaped nets we used to keep the flies off food in the kitchen.

So far, so good, but with my arm stretched to the limit and beginning to ache, what was I supposed to do next? I sent Viv to bring in the stepladders and transferred from the stool before sliding a piece of card between the ceiling and the dome, trapping the little fellow to be released in the garden.

Viv took a photograph of this part of the operation, and it was Mission Accomplished.

There was also an enforced change in our well-established breakfast routine.

Ever since we arrived in Spain, I had taken time each morning to squeeze five or six oranges for juice. But they were at last coming to an end and were difficult to find. I came across a gypsy lady selling oranges in a lay-by just off the N332 near Gata de Gorgos, one day. They were not the best oranges I had seen, but good enough, I thought, for juice. I bought ten kilos.

Next morning I pressed the first batch and placed the juice in the fridge while we took Jessie for a walk. The breakfast preparations were completed with croissant and freshly brewed coffee.

I was just about to sip the juice, by now poured into a glass, when Viv noticed some white particles floating on the surface. They were tiny maggots, about twenty, some still wriggling.

We consigned the rest of the ten kilos to the bin. I discovered later that maggots from fruit flies are often found in older fruit, especially fruit that has fallen to the ground, so it is best to buy from a reputable source.

Fortunately, by now the markets were awash with small pink grapefruit, *pomelos*, so we switched our allegiance to secure a continued source of vitamin C.

I was beginning to understand the rudiments of the Spanish rural economy, helped by regular, though stilted, conversations with an old man from the village who tended an allotment, some olive groves and a small vineyard we passed on our walks. His name was Jose-Maria, though he was known as Pepito, for reasons we couldn't quite understand. Technically we were trespassing, but he always seemed pleased to see us and happy to let me strike up a conversation of sorts.

When we first encountered Pepito, he was kneeling, shirtless, beneath an olive tree, six inches of underpants exposed above his trousers. He was a large man with a cheerful face, broad shoulders and a paunch that suggested he enjoyed his food. His complexion was ruddy, though this may have been the effect of his labours; the rest of his exposed torso was surprisingly pale.

To begin with, he was hacking away with a mattock at the small shoots growing from the base of the trunks of the olive trees. Then he raked the area beneath each tree to clear it of weeds and rocks and form a circle of clean dry earth ready for the nets which would later be laid to catch the fallen olives. There were about fifty olive trees on the plot and I didn't envy him the task of clearing each and every one of them in the heat of summer. Sensibly, he worked just a few hours in the early morning and late in the day, returning in between to his house in the village.

I asked if the olives were for oil, or for eating, or for sale; and he embarked on a long and detailed explanation on the state of olive production in this part of Spain.

His olives had almost no value. His plot was too small and the olives were not of good enough quality to command the premium paid for fashionable Extra Virgin oil. He needed 100 kilos of olives to make 25 litres of oil, and he had to pay for them to be milled. He'd have some olives pressed by the local co-operative; some he preserved for eating, for his family, and the rest he would sell. The whole crop was worth only a few thousand pesetas (he hadn't made the transition to Euros).

He explained that he only persevered on the land because it was the old way and he knew nothing else. His whole existence on the land had been reduced to a hobby in the autumn of his life.

It was a sad and depressing tale, which, I suspected, applied to much of the less productive land in the valley. I saw very few young men tending the olive groves and wondered what would happen when the present generation eventually petered out. There were already several abandoned and overgrown olive groves to be found dotted around the village. They were easy to spot. Without proper husbandry an olive tree, perhaps hundreds of years old, will soon regress to its wild bush-like state, overgrown and bearing only tiny, worthless fruits.

Pepito was equally disparaging about his small allotment, only a fraction of which was now being cultivated. It seemed to be flourishing with giant beef tomatoes, plum tomatoes, bulbous aubergines, enormous marrows, slender courgettes, rows of onions and a variety of beans, all sown in rotation to produce throughout the season with the aid of a piped irrigation system.

He explained that in years gone by, he would have cultivated the whole plot and sold some of the produce in the village.

But his age, and the introduction of industrialised farming, left him to grow just enough for his needs.

He was scathing about the vast areas of poly-tunnels in Almeria and Andalucia which were gradually putting small growers out of business.

'*Soy un pescado pequeño en un mar grande,*' he explained.

I was anxious to impress Pepito with my knowledge of the Spanish names for some of his crops, so I stood at the side of his plot reeling them off as I pointed.

'*Guisantes, calabazas, zanahorias, pimientos, espinaca, calabacines, berenjenas,*' I said, hoping the words sounded as if they just happened to trip off my tongue.

'*Y onions,*' he replied pointing to a newly planted patch of sprouting green leaves.

I knew that the Spanish for onions was *cebollas*. '*¿Onions es Valenciano?*' I surmised, pronouncing the word 'onion' in a Spanish accent.

'*No. ¡Es Inglés!*' he replied, with a huge grin on his ever-cheerful face.

Not for the first time, I was guilty of patronising one of my Spanish neighbours.

I felt privileged to know Pepito. Despite the slow demise in his way of life he was always polite and cheerful and I looked forward to our brief conversations about the weather, the state of his crops and events in village life.

'*El tiempo esta un poco loco este año,*' he said one day in reference to the weather.

It had been cooler with more cloud than usual, though to us it was hotter than we would have liked.

My only regret was that my limited grasp of the Spanish language prevented me from getting to know Pepito better. He must have many a story to tell about his life and the changes he'd seen.

I determined to try harder, realising that I would never get the best from my new life in Spain until I could hold my own in more than just a basic conversation.

At the tip of the summit of Col de Rates, the road that weaves it way to the top of Carrascal and overlooks our house, there was a German restaurant that specialised in ham hocks and sauerkraut. We'd been there a couple of times, but only for a drink on the terrace, which had spectacular panoramic views over the whole of the valley.

One bright, sunny afternoon in mid-July, we noticed a small plume of smoke rising, almost vertically, and hovering above the restaurant in the still, cloudless sky. At first we thought someone had burnt the bratwurst or perhaps a Volkswagon Beetle had expired at the top of the climb and caught fire in the car park.

It turned out to be the first forest fire of the season, a common occurrence at this time of year. It was quickly extinguished by fire fighters with the aid of a couple of helicopters ferrying water in large buckets trailing from cables. The buckets were replenished from a reservoir, built for the purpose on the outskirts of Parcent.

By late afternoon, the helicopters were busy again, this time disappearing over the back of the mountain range to the west of our house which forms a backdrop to our garden.

Again, we could see a few wisps of smoke, seemingly in the far distance.

We thought little of it, assuming that like the earlier incident, it would soon be brought under control.

The helicopters buzzed away, their flight path crossing our garden as they circled in rotation to scoop up more water. As dusk fell, the helicopters were grounded, for fear of entanglement in the many over-ground cables in the vicinity of the reservoir.

It soon became clear that the fire was out of control.

As I started to prepare our evening meal, the night sky glowed amber, flames illuminating vast, billowing clouds of smoke that began to drift in our direction.

It looked like a brilliant red sunset.

Shepherds' delight, I thought, confident the heart of the fire was some distance away.

Twenty minutes later, we were not so light-hearted.

The fire had reached the summit of the mountain and was beginning to creep down the other side towards our house.

A line of flames, stretching for at least five hundred metres, fringed the wavering line of the mountain-top creating a giant silhouette like the outer surface of the sun during an eclipse.

Occasionally there was an explosive burst as one of the few remaining pine trees became engulfed in the fire.

By now we could hear the crackle of flames amidst the wailing of sirens as the whole of Alicante Province's fire fighting contingent converged on the scene.

Neighbours were emerging onto the road to stand around discussing the situation.

The consensus of opinion was that it was not yet serious, but some sensible precautions would not be inappropriate, especially as the wind was strengthening and swirling in all directions.

Everyone has their own idea of what amounts to sensible precautions in such circumstances. I ignored one piece of advice from a neighbour who suggested we should dump all the gas cylinders in the swimming pool, and did the most obvious thing I could think of on the spur of the moment. I packed an overnight bag with a few clothes and a change of underwear, remembering my mother's usual concern whenever I left the house as a youngster. ('You don't want to be admitted to hospital with dirty underpants,' she would say, in concern over what the nurses might think (I should be so lucky.)).

I then gathered our passports and the document folder containing all our paperwork, checking that the deeds to the house were there and, importantly, the insurance policies.

Viv had her own ideas and priorities in the event that our house was reduced to a pile of smouldering ashes.

First, her jewellery was gathered together from a variety of secret hiding places around the house.

There was a brief panic when she couldn't remember where she had hidden a couple of pieces, but a search through dozens of shoeboxes that were being used for knick-knacks and doo-dads in the wardrobe finally revealed the missing articles.

Then it was time to worry about Jessie.

'Have you packed the pet passport?' she queried as I racked my brains trying to think of more serious contingency plans.

'We need to pack some dog food and Jessie's bed, oh, and her lead, and her toys and some water,' she urged.

'All right.' In my new laid back, de-stressed lifestyle I made a point of never getting angry, so I complied 'meekly.'

195

This was definitely not the time to raise, yet again, the issue of Viv's disproportionate concerns for the welfare of the whole of the animal kingdom, I thought – ready to scream.

'My *God*,' Viv shrieked, just when I thought we had finished loading the car. 'The *cats!*'

'*What?*'

Viv had been left in charge of two cats belonging to neighbours next door and further down the road. Then there was a third cat, which Viv coveted, but who belonged to another neighbour who did not quite live up to Viv's expectations of a pet lover.

'Where did you put the cat basket?' she demanded.

'You must be *joking.*'

'I'm not joking - quick, and we have to find some boxes for the other two cats.'

'Look, the house is about to burn down and all you can think about is *sodding cats*. Let's get a sense of proportion here.' I started the car and backed sharply. 'The cats will have legged it long before the fire gets here.'

'*That* is my *point*,' replied Viv.

Two minutes later I was balanced precariously at the top of the step ladder trying to unhook the cat basket from the ceiling of the storeroom, uttering foul expletives under my breath. (At one point while we packed our belongings before leaving England I had consigned the frayed old basket to a skip, but it was no surprise that it emerged from the furniture van when we arrived in Spain.)

Just as I reached full swearing mode, Maurice, our neighbour opposite, arrived.

'We're having a fire party!' he said. 'Come and join us for a drink. We can't go to bed so we might as well enjoy ourselves, and we can watch the fire from our patio.'

He beamed up at me.

'I'm saving the *bloody cats!* ' I shouted. 'I haven't even had my *bloody dinner*, and – '

'They took off hours ago. Come over, and have a bite.'

'Oh?' I climbed down.

'I'd love to,' I heard Viv say, 'though *he* might prefer to stay here, where he's got the car handy.'

'Hahaha, your wife's quite a –'

'Yes, she is, isn't she,' I said. 'But do you really think – ?'

The way Maurice explained it, a party did suddenly seem to be the sensible, British, thing to do, and there would be food.

'Can I bring something? A bottle of wine, some beers?'

'Might as well,' said Maurice. 'Only be wasted, if the place goes up.'

So at one in the morning we were sitting on Maurice's patio with his family and the neighbours, enjoying a glass of wine and watching the distant flames raging down the mountainside. There was a lull in conversation and suddenly we heard the muffled tones of the village band…practising at the back of the town hall.

'Listen,' I said. 'The fire can't be that serious! – the band's playing, as usual.'

'That's what they said on the Titanic,' said Jean, Maurice's wife.

'Anyone for a dip?' Viv added, passing around the chips and still showing *amazing good humour*, I thought, considering we had only just escaped with our lives. Women!

By four in the morning the fire had spread sideways across the mountain, but never looked as if it would really threaten our house. The wind abated and the flames dimmed until there were just a few small pockets giving off a faint glow.

We finally decided it was safe to go to bed, but we put our bedding in the lounge from where we could keep an eye on the still smouldering hillside. We fell asleep at once.

Next morning, we were disturbed at seven when the helicopters resumed their water-bombing runs, circling above the house on their way to the reservoir. They continued for most of the day. I considered phoning to complain about the noise, but thought better of it when Viv pointed out how absurd that would be.

We began to talk about the helicopters, and I mentioned that I had heard that they had the right to scoop water from swimming pools if the need arose.

I recalled a story some years ago when, in the charred aftermath of a forest fire, a body had been found clad in a full wet suit, snorkel and flippers. The poor man had been scooped up from the sea by one of those open-bellied planes used for fire fighting in Australia. Viv laughed, and I laughed even louder, assuring her that I had never believed it, I wasn't that much of an idiot. Neither of us used the pool that day.

Later, we heard the fire was started deliberately, and a man had been arrested. There were rumours he was a local landowner aggrieved by a decision to declare his small area of pine forest a, 'conservation area.' He'd hoped that destroying the trees would mean he'd be able to sell the land at an inflated price for development. The local Mayor was quoted saying, 'It doesn't matter if there are fourteen fires, that land will never be developed.'

'No wonder our bonfire licence expired in May and can't be renewed until October,' I said over a leisurely breakfast next morning as Viv and I went over the events.

'You know I wouldn't have gone without the cats,' she said.

'*Of course you wouldn't,*' I said. 'And I would never have driven off without you, either. That was all said in the heat of the moment.' Then I heard what I'd just said. 'Hah! I made a joke! – heat of the moment!'

Viv's eyes remained firmly fixed upon a piece of toast she was measuring up for dissection.

Back in May I had received a phone call from my old boss, Alan Bowness, who'd finally set a date for his retirement: the 31st July. He was planning to convene the usual small contingent of colleagues for a long liquid lunch at Davey's Wine Vaults in Greenwich – and with me, if I could make it.

My flight was booked the next day and my good friend Martin had agreed to meet me and put me up for a couple of nights.

'Lunch at Davey's,' a real spit and sawdust place, had become something of an 'institutional event.'

The idea had been instigated by my old colleague, Leyland Birch, who was Chief Solicitor at the London Borough where I worked. (He was a good friend and mentor, from whom I learned much about the subtleties of working with, or against, politicians and, more importantly, about life in general. Sadly, Leyland died prematurely, just a few months after retiring on the grounds of ill health. He left behind a lovely young wife, Shirley and two fine teenage children.)

After that first time, everyone had wanted it to continue.

In fact, a visit to Davey's had become de rigueur whenever there was something to celebrate or commemorate, and my own departure from the world of work had been marked in just this way. In any event, we held an annual 'Leyland Day' in February each year to remember and celebrate an extraordinary man.

So it was that I made my first return trip to the UK since leaving for Spain some nine months earlier.

On my first night I sat up with Alan until three in the morning catching up on news and office gossip. The next day I re-entered the Civic Offices for probably the last time. It was a strange situation, and already I felt like an outsider; out of touch and a little uncomfortable. It was a warm day and the offices were hot and stuffy, just as I remembered them to be from sixteen summers spent in the same eight square metres of municipal magnolia.

I was, by now, used to much higher temperatures, but for some reason I felt the return of the stomach-churning anxiety that I had suffered at some stage during most working days in my last few years of work. I began to sweat, not helped by the fact that I was wearing long trousers and socks for the first time in almost four months. Luckily, I was armed with a shopping list, drawn up by Viv, of items unavailable in Spain, and this gave me the excuse to extricate myself.

Lunch at Davey's that day was a jolly, but relatively sober affair (I know, 'jolly, but sober' – ugh – but that makes sense when you consider that it would probably be the last such occasion for *me*, so I was bound to feel I was missing out on something, while the jolly English resident contingent would continue to get together once a month).

On the way back to the Civic Offices I contacted Martin on his mobile phone to establish his ETA. He was stuck in traffic about twelve miles away on the M25 and had moved only a few yards in the last half an hour. For a moment I felt a twinge of Smug Syndrome, in place of my 'missing out sobriety' (as above) when I remembered what had prompted my decision to give up work and move to Spain. Then it occurred to me that this was serious. The pubs were open and I was missing valuable drinking time.

Back in the Hare and Hounds for early doors, nothing much had changed, except that warm Greene King IPA was no longer to my taste. I switched to lager but even that tasted lifeless compared to San Miguel. I struggled, my shrunken belly lacking its previous capacity to hold several Friday night pints.

All the regulars were in their usual places, letting off steam at the end of another week in the pressure cooker world of work.

Saturday came.

To save me visiting all my ex-neighbours, Martin and Alison had kindly arranged a lunchtime barbecue and invited everyone round – and everyone did come. Martin said I had to earn my corn by acting as barman for the day, but I failed miserably, distracted by every new arrival demanding answers to the same questions. What about Jessie (always the first enquiry)?

Were we happy, how was Viv getting on, were we coping with the heat, how did we fill our time, what was the secret of my weight loss, and what did we miss most?

It was a splendid day, made better by the weather, which was almost as good as in Spain. Corks were drawn at midday and the barbecued lamb was devoured by mid-afternoon. A few stragglers, with myself included, were enticed back to the Hare and Hounds where, this time, the Greene King IPA slipped down more easily; just as I could have easily slipped back into this comfortable, cosy way of life.

We returned to find Alison frying bacon on the barbecue. A small group of incorrigibles with the staying power to keep up with Martin's generous hospitality remained in the garden until late in the evening. It was only the chill and damp in the air which finally brought proceedings to a close. It was the first time I had felt dew for months.

Martin and I rose at five-thirty the next morning for the

bleary-eyed return journey to Stansted and on to Alicante.

My brief return to England had been an enjoyable interlude. It would have been more pleasurable if Viv had been with me, but Jessie could not be left, could she? Home was now Spain and Casa Emelia, and I was glad to be back. I think Viv was pleased to see me return.

'I've really missed you,' she said as soon as I walked through the door. 'What's for dinner?'

'...we lingered after dinner under the Acropolis, often until midnight.'

Carpaccio
of cheese, ham and pineapple

Carpaccio is an Italian term that refers to something that is thinly sliced and usually raw. And that's the secret in putting this dish together. You will need a good sharp knife and a steady hand.

- *1 small ripe fresh pineapple*
- *1 medium red pepper*
- *8 very thin slices of jamon serrano or palma ham*
- *75g of fresh parmesan cheese, finely shaved*
- *Freshly ground black pepper (optional)*

1. Cut the top and bottom off the pineapple then pare off the outer skin and remove the centre core. Slice the pineapple as thinly as you can into rings and place four or five slices on each of four serving plates, overlapping them slightly. Sprinkle with a little black pepper.

2. Cut the bottom off the pepper, then slice into very thin rings removing any pith. Arrange these on top of the pineapple.

3. Cut the serrano or Palma ham into wide strips and pile these in the centre of the pineapple rings.

4. Sprinkle the parmesan shavings over the top and serve.

Serves 4
Preparation time: 20 minutes

Chicken Liver Salad

Chicken livers are one of the tastiest and cheapest foods you can buy and yet they are often overlooked or simply used to make pâté. Their delicate texture and flavour make them ideal for a quick and tasty salad. The secret is not to overcook them, but to leave them slightly pink in the middle. Try serving with a crisp green salad.

- *250g fresh or frozen chicken livers (thawed if frozen)*
- *A knob of butter*
- *1 tbls olive oil*
- *1 tbls balsamic vinegar*
- *Salt and pepper*

Remove any fatty bits from the chicken livers and cut into chunks. Melt the butter in a frying pan and fry the livers over medium heat for 4-5 minutes, turning occasionally. Season with salt and pepper. Pile the salad in the centre of a serving plate and spoon the livers over the top. Add the oil and balsamic vinegar to the frying pan and heat briefly until bubbling. Drizzle the warm dressing over the salad. For a special treat you could top the salad with a soft poached egg.

Suggestion for a green salad:

Combine the following: Mixed salad leaves, a few thin slices of green pepper, a 3 inch piece of cucumber cut into batons, half an avocado, peeled and sliced and a kiwi fruit, peeled and cut into chunks.

Serves 2
Preparation time: 10 minutes
Cooking time: 5 minutes

Chapter Eleven

A Sting in the Tale

In the aftermath of the mountain fire, our garden view had changed. A great swath of brown charred earth now loomed high in the distance, punctuated by an occasional skeletal pine tree.

Some of the surrounding countryside was beginning to take on a similar appearance, as it succumbed to the summer drought.

August arrived. The lush green bushes and vibrant wild flowers we'd enjoyed in spring were gradually transformed into withered tinder, needing only a spark to set them alight.

The thousands of almond trees which had painted the valley pink and white in March, turned autumn brown as the velvet green pods dried and split revealing the hard shell of the year's almond crop. Soon they would be ready for harvesting.

Roadside verges, only recently awash with colour, were now a uniform brittle beige, tilting inwards and narrowing the already restricted road space.

We read that it was an offence to be caught throwing a lighted cigarette from a car window: an offence the local police took very seriously. We looked out for such a thing but never saw it.

All this brown was in sharp contrast to the vast orange groves that had retained their bright green foliage throughout the summer, and now sparkled, aided by networks of irrigation pipes threaded between the trees.

The oranges themselves were swelling in the late summer heat as if absorbing the sunshine and storing it for winter. Despite a lack of irrigation, the olive trees remained in silver-green leaf, looking exactly as they had in January. The only difference, on closer inspection, was the season's crop of olives; already plump and swollen, they were still as hard as nuts.

The vines looked comfortable in their rigid ranks. Ancient roots still tapped into enough moisture to support wilting leaves that gave shade to the slowly ripening fruit. Already, roadside salesmen were setting up stalls with ancient weights and balances, boxes of sweet muscatel grapes and swarms of angry wasps. They were doing a roaring trade.

Shops and markets were awash with melons, heavy and hollow sounding, a clue to their ripeness.

Watermelons, *sandias*, were piled high in crates, for sale at every vantage point. Most were the size of footballs or bigger, with skin like camouflage jackets surrounding the luscious scarlet flesh. Nothing could be more thirst-quenching on a dust-dry day than a mouthful of ice cold dribbling watermelon, I thought, especially as they seem to have almost eliminated those annoying black seeds. I wondered, then, at the economics of producing these giant edible-drinks. Their very size and weight made them difficult to pack and transport, and yet here they were on sale for as little as thirty cents a kilo.

Even the watermelons were expensive compared to another of my favourite fruits – figs. I gathered these for free from trees we passed on our walks. No one seemed to be harvesting the overripe fruit, so it did no harm, I calculated, if I helped myself to handfuls each morning.

Nothing could be more exotic, even erotic, than a plump, ripe juicy fig, I thought. Perhaps it was the association with Adam and Eve.

The fig leaf is the ideal shape to cover a man's modesty and, growing in pairs, the fig itself resembles the embodiment of manhood with its wrinkled outer skin protecting the delicate flesh inside. (I told Viv all this but she didn't seem much interested – however, any man who has suffered a typical sporting injury will appreciate the simile, as the ripe skin of the fig is a rich purple turning black. So there. And: 'Don't rub 'em, count 'em,' as my old sports master would say.)

The new lemon tree in the garden of Casa Emelia was barely hanging on to life. Only a single one of the thirty or so embryonic lemons that had appeared in April, survived.

I still lived in hope, however, that it would ripen in time for the visit of Martin and Alison at the end of the month, so I could fulfil my promise of a gin and tonic, ice and *my own slice*.

The new lawn was in an even more sorry state. Still worried about the cost of water, I'd abandoned it to nature, hoping it would withstand the August scorching. Now it was a threadbare carpet, almost the same colour as the rock-hard earth from which it was trying to emerge, its tender roots shrivelling in the parched red soil... But someone up there took pity on it, and on us.

On Thursday, 1st August, it rained. A fierce electrical storm hovered over Parcent and lingered for several hours.

Within minutes the lawn was underwater; the baked surface initially provided an impervious layer. But not for long, as the water was sucked down by the sponge-like soil.

Salvation for the lawn also came in the form of a water bill, at last. Actually, it was not a bill but a statement from our bank to say that the water company had taken the money by direct debit.

The first deduction was for a two-month period, and amounted to just twenty-one Euros.

The trouble was, this first payment was for the period of July and August 2001 – two months before we owned the house. Jon, the 'Previous Owner' had taken revenge yet again, I told Viv. *'And look at this bill.'*

'Cheap, isn't it,' she said. 'Looks like we're in luck.'

'I'll believe that when I see it,' I said.

But the first bank statement was followed in quick succession by two more, both for similar amounts.

'At this price,' I said brightly, 'We can afford to give the lawn a helping hand.'

As things turned out, the weather remained *un poco loco* for the first ten days of August and we were spared the promised roasting; but it was not to last. I did water the lawn and the sight of it kept me going, but it is difficult to describe the intensity of the heat we endured for most of the rest of August.

Enough to say that one afternoon Viv was looking for some citronella candles to ward off the insects that were gradually eating us alive in the evenings.

She eventually found them in a wooden cabinet in the *naya*. The candles had melted.

In the village, excitement mounted. Preparations got under way for fiesta week in the middle of August.

Multicoloured bunting appeared in many of the narrow streets. Some of the houses were decorated with palm fronds that were placed at the side of doors and bent over to form an arch; many were decorated with flowers.

Whole streets had been painted – not the houses, but the road surface itself. One street had been decorated with giant cartoons of The Simpsons.

Each of the main streets leading into the village was festooned with fairy lights; strung between the houses these lights were arranged to wish visitors *Bones Festes* in Valenciano.

In the village square, la Placa del Poble, bunting stretched from the central drinking fountain to all the surrounding buildings, and a substantial stage appeared in one corner.

And then, disaster.

Four days before the start of festivities, a fire in the kitchen of Bar Moll! The main source of food and drink for the whole fiesta programme!

A refrigerator motor had burnt out in the night and, though the fire was quite small, there was considerable smoke damage. Everyone rallied to help in the clean-up operation, including me, so that food and drink service could be resumed in time.

I then popped into the *ayuntamiento* to see if I could have a programme of the week's events and was given a full colour brochure for the *Festes Patronais San Lorenzo* – complete with a photograph and message from King Juan Carlos and Queen Sofia and the Mayor of Parcent. But there was one catch. Juan, the main man in the town hall, explained that *I would have to pay*. Not for the programme, but as residents of Parcent: we had to pay a charge for the fiesta itself – 22 Euros each, 20 for *pensionistas*.

It was a toss-up between wanting to complain about being charged, and wanting to pay – since I was now being regarded officially as one of the locals, not a visitor.

A couple of days later we had an actual visitor: an English lady who, like us, was a resident. She had been commissioned to collect the 'fiesta tax' from all the outlying residents of Parcent, and she was having a torrid time.

Many of the residents she had called on were refusing to pay – and not just foreigners, she said.

I asked what would actually happen if foreigners didn't pay.

Pointing to the record book she'd been given by the *ayuntamiento*, she suggested that non-payment would not be in the interests of good relations with the town hall.

'Have you driven here, or did you come on foot?' I asked.

'I walked. Why do you ask?'

'It's just that I can't help thinking...'

'Don't start on *that* again,' Viv interrupted.

'But why should we pay for a week-long knees up, when our road is in a state of...'

'How much is it?' Viv said. 'Get her a cold drink, Mark.'

I did so. That went down well, then Viv rummaged in her handbag, paid up, and ushered the lady to the gate with me in tow.

'Mind you don't trip!' I called, as she wandered out of sight.

Viv belted me with her handbag.

'What? I just don't see why we should have to pay from our housekeeping budget when *public funds* are being squandered on *a fiesta, of all things we have absolutely no interest in...*'

'You owe me twenty-two euros,' said Viv.

'*Me?*'

'Cough up. You heard. In the interests of good relations.'

'No fair,' I said firmly (but who could resist?).

After that, we were both looking forward to the fiesta.

I pictured the whole village coming together as a community to participate in traditional pursuits – parades, music, dancing and games and a glance at the programme seemed to prove me right. Something was planned for every day and night for seven days. 'I marvel at the capacity,' I wrote to friends, 'of this small community to embark on such an ambitious programme of events.'

But all was not quite as it seemed.

Fiesta week kicked off on Friday evening, with a pilota match in the 'court' outside Bar Guay. This was followed by the parade of the Banda de Musica de Parcent.

We'd been listening to the practice sessions for most of the summer and the band were in good form to open the fiesta with the bull fighting tunes, many of which we knew by heart, by now.

Then the village band was followed at 23.00 hours by further musical entertainment from Orquesta La Petrulla, whose gentle tones wafted softly through the still night air to our terrace, where we sat and listened, by now convinced that it was a wonderful thing to have a fiesta on our doorstep.

All was quiet by midnight. Day one over. So far, so good.

Saturday was devoted almost exclusively to San Lorenzo, patron saint of the village and the village church. Just in case anyone had forgotten this prestigious day, a booming fireworks rocket was launched at 08.00 hours and the Banda de Musica struck up once more. A solemn mass in honour of San Lorenzo was scheduled for lunchtime, and a candlelight procession in the evening.

I stayed in village for most of the evening – and as I left, I noticed a van emerge from one of the side streets. Two men unloaded electrical equipment from it, before lifting several large amplifiers out and up onto a makeshift stage. I would find out later, I thought, what that was all about.

The day's proceedings were brought to a close with the *Gran Castillo de Fuegos Artificiales* (fireworks display) on the outskirts of the village, not far from our house.

My slow walk home was illuminated by these fireworks. They started at midnight and lasted for almost half-an-hour, and they put London to shame, I realised…and I couldn't help wondering, as I wandered up the rough track, how much they had cost, and whether the money might have been better spent on…

At that moment, I stubbed my toe on a rock.

I hobbled into the house, tired and hot, minutes later, to find Jessie housed in the shower and not willing to move, as usual.

Sunday was *almost* a repeat performance. Another wake-up boom at 08.00 hours, and the band was on parade once more.

Another pilota tournament was followed by another lunchtime Mass, this time in honour of Santisimo Christo de la Fe.

Another candlelight parade was scheduled for 21.00 hours.

Seen one, you've seen them all, I thought.

I stayed at home, and secured the doors to both bathrooms in case there were more fireworks. ('Not everyone appreciates dog hairs in the plug hole,' I shouted after Jessie, as she headed off to complain to Viv.)

The official fiesta programme listed the final event on Sunday as: '*24.00h Baile amenizado por la orquesta PLATINO.*' This sounded innocuous enough to me. I knew that *baile* was dancing and *amenizado* was entertainment. *Orquesta* seemed obvious and I pictured the gentlemen and ladies of Parcent tripping light-footed foxtrots, perhaps enlivened by a pasa doble, or even a daring tango or two.

'Platino' turned out to be a heavy metal rock band and now I discovered the reason for all the equipment I had seen unloaded the previous night.

Although our house is about one kilometre from the village we could hear every note as if it was coming from next door...It was a warm, humid night and shutting the windows would have made sleep impossible, so we lay awake.

The concert boomed on until 05.00 hours on Monday morning with a finale of Queen's 'We Are The Champions.'

Then someone let off another sub-atomic missile to confirm it was all over.

This didn't obviate the need for the usual wake-up call three hours later: the Banda de Musica de Parcent struck up once more.

'I suppose they've all gone to another village to get some sleep,' I grumbled to Jessie. Viv slept on.

Monday, Tuesday and Wednesday followed the same pattern. A Mass and procession in honour of la Divina Aurora, more pilota, early and late pyrotechnics and the band striking up at regular intervals repeating their now familiar repertoire.

A children's chocolate party sounded like fun, though we couldn't get in, and there was a dinner for the *pensionistas* (to which we were not invited, either) in the La Placa del Poble with catering provided by Bar Moll.

Wednesday evening saw the whole village come together once more; this was for the 'Popular Dinner of the People.'

Bar Moll catered, once again at full stretch, and tables and chairs filled the square. The whole population was involved in a mass eat-in. Those people who chose not to dine from Bar Moll, ate in the streets.

As I wandered around to see this event for myself, I had to pick my way through family gatherings and tables spread with all manner of food. Barbecues crackled with the sound of sizzling spicy sausages, kebabs and a variety of meats.

Huge trays of *coca* – a kind of thick pizza bread – were being carried out of houses, topped with tomatoes, peas, or anchovies. Warm *tortillas*, brimming with onions, potatoes, peppers and *chorizo* were placed on tables. Jugs of wine flowed as easily as the rapid-fire conversation in Valenciano.

This was what I had always imagined a 'real' fiesta to be like. The air was thick with the aroma of food and the sound of fellowship. It was wonderful to see and hear. Good old Spain. It would never change. I went home and told Viv, and she told me to close the bathroom window.

Even Parcent had moved with the times, I had to admit, when I saw there was more late night entertainment to come.

Monday was Orquesta Club Virginia (Disco Dance) and Tuesday was Los Astros (New Millennium Punk).

An unnamed band that was not listed in the official programme entertained us on Wednesday...

I can only describe this last group as a Status Quo tribute band. (I say this because they played that Quo song that goes: dee diddly dee dum dum, dee diddly dee dum dum, dee diddly dee, dee diddly dee, dee diddly dee dum dum. That seemed to be the only tune they knew, which is what made me think they were a Status Quo tribute band.)

For three nights we suffered varying volumes of modern Spanish rock music from midnight to 05.00 hours.

And to think we were, '*paying for the privilege*,' I groaned. 'I wonder how the old people in the village cope with sleep deprivation for such a prolonged period?'

That was certainly something to think about, Viv agreed.

Next day, I mentioned this to my friend Pepito. He shrugged his shoulders. 'It's for young people,' he said resignedly, 'I go to sleep. My only problem was a little too much wine at the dinner.'

I nodded. 'Me, too,' I said. 'It's only the old people I worry about. Not myself. Me and Viv, we both sleep like logs.' But when, I wondered, was the damn thing going to wind down? – *and they were getting noisier, I could tell* (Viv didn't agree with this, BUT WHAT DID SHE KNOW? SHE SLEPT THROUGH IT).

The final two days of fiesta were reserved exclusively for *Toros en la Placa del Poble*.

Like most people, I had read and heard of bull running at fiestas, and the local newspapers were full of stories of injuries, usually to young men or drunken tourists and usually to the groin or abdomen. Deaths were not uncommon.

Parcent's official programme contained a footnote at this point. '*El Ayuntamiento no se responsabilizan de los accidentes producidos por los toros.*'

I had reservations about bull fighting and all the rituals that surrounded it. I'd seen a bull fight in Palma Majorca many years earlier and had watched snippets on Spanish television. I'd read Hemingway's enthusiastic accounts, but always felt it was a one-sided fight and that the bull was set up to be on the wrong side.

But Spain was my adopted country, and I had vowed not to express an opinion on the subject – at least not to anyone Spanish.

I refused to visit Parcent's contribution to bull fighting culture, but midnight on Friday was my last opportunity to see for myself, so I decided I might as well walk into the village.

I'd not expected the spectacle of the famous bull running in Pamplona – but I was unprepared for what I witnessed.

Determined to keep calm and detached, I'd take up a position in a back corner, I decided.

My usual route to the la Placa del Poble was blocked at several places by heavy wooden barriers and I was forced to make a detour before emerging into the square.

The makeshift stage had been removed and tall wooden barriers lined most of the perimeter. They were each made of five thick planks bolted horizontally at intervals to an angled metal frame leaning outwards.

Looking like heavy-duty ladders, they seemed to fulfil a dual purpose as: a means of rapid escape from the bulls, should they charge, and a form of grandstand seating.

The doors and windows of houses were boarded up (though I doubted most of the flimsy timber could withstand an onslaught by an angry bull – and why would a bull target doors and windows, in any case?).

Even the telephone kiosk had the protection of some hastily-attached plywood for the benefit of anyone who felt the desperate need to phone home in the middle of proceedings.

Of course Bar Moll was fully operational, protected by a metal cage with bars set just far enough apart to allow a man to squeeze through, but presumably close enough together to give protection from the bull's horns.

Permanent wrought iron railings, no doubt purpose-designed with the evening's events in mind, already protected the central drinking fountain and its four surrounding trees.

A crowd of about two hundred had gathered.

The young men, and a few young women, were mostly seated on the tops of the wooden barriers.

Behind the barriers were older men and women; they had brought chairs onto the streets and sat in rows, five or six deep, to watch in relative safety through the gaps between the planks.

Underneath some of the more substantial barriers, small boys sat on the tarmac to get closer to the action.

Most of the more sensible men were corralled behind the bars at Bar Moll, with ready access to refreshments. I joined them.

The square was dimly lit. There was no music. Only the sound of conversation and a buzz of anticipation filled the balmy air.

I peered out through the bars. I had expected to see a herd of prime bulls career into the square, but I was told by someone standing alongside that there would be just four bulls released, one at a time, over the next two hours.

Without any kind of fanfare the first bull arrived on the scene, released from a truck that was parked in one of the side streets.

A muted ripple of applause sounded as the young black bull stood, startled, like an unrehearsed actor suddenly thrust onto a stage and into the spotlight...

Though small in stature, the animal was packed with muscle and its coat glistened in the phosphorescent lights. There was no doubting that its horns were capable of inflicting a fatal injury.

For a while there was inactivity as the bull took a few tentative steps into the temporary arena. It declined to show any interest in the shouts from the crowd.

The small boys under the barriers who poked out their hands to wave their red cloths provoked its first thrust. It charged half-heartedly but pulled up short, perhaps alarmed by squeals and screams as the red rags were rapidly withdrawn and the boys cowered away from the planks.

Then the action started.

I had noticed two young men in matching yellow T-shirts lurking by the drinking fountain. I later discovered that these were 'professional' bull men (I will not call them fighters) who were employed by the company that supplied the bulls.

As well as herding the bulls from the truck, their job was to make sure the animals performed for the crowd. They emerged from the railings and, through a series of rag-waving darts, eventually provoked the young bull into action.

As the animal charged, they deftly scrambled up to the top of the ladder-like barriers out of reach of the horns.

Some of the young men from the village began to join in, dangling a leg in front of the bull as they clung to the barriers. A few fearless, or foolish, adolescents ventured onto the street eager to demonstrate their courage by standing in the bull's eye-line – before retreating to safety.

Only one young man encapsulated the real bull fighting spirit by standing firm in the face of a charge and stepping aside at the last moment with a flourish of his makeshift cloak. This same young man roused a cheer from the crowd when he leapt in the air, his legs apart, as the bull ran beneath him.

In contrast to this bravado, the best that most young people could do was to prod the beast with a two-metre long pole, laughing as they stood on the barriers out of harm's way.

After thirty minutes the young bull looked more bored than tired, refusing to be further goaded by the provocation of the few people who ventured from safety. It was time for fresh stock.

The second bull was a full-grown, doe-eyed specimen with a mottled brown-and-white coat. This elderly beast was never going to grace the bullrings of Granada or Madrid, or anywhere else for that matter.

One horn protruded, proud and erect, as fine a horn as you could wish to see. The other was gnarled and bent downwards, almost like a ram's horn.

It looked more sad than comical. I guessed that this flaw, in an otherwise proud and courageous animal, meant it was destined to spend its time on the circus circuit of small village fiestas.

It rampaged as required, responding to the goading and prodding, before returning to the truck. Another performance over. Tomorrow: another town, another show.

The performance of the third bull was unremarkable; more of the same. I sensed the crowd was getting restless and so was I. By now I had taken up a position seated on the top rung of one of the barriers at the side of Bar Moll and the angled corner of the plank was making an impression in the cheeks of my backside.

Time for the climax.

At one-thirty in the morning the cattle wagon reversed slowly into the square. The tailgate dropped and side railings put in place.

A group of men thronged the back of the truck. It was difficult to see what was happening. Then the truck withdrew leaving just the group of about fifteen men grappling to subdue the bull and prevent any movement.

Suddenly, a match was struck and the men darted off in all directions, leaping to the top of the nearest barriers.

With the lights dimmed further, I could just make out two flaming torches on the far side of the square, wafting and waving in all directions. It was the bull.

The magnificent, jet-black animal was flailing about, wrenching its neck from side to side in wide-eyed panic as it tried to shake off the flaming adornments to its most effective weapons. It scraped its front hooves on the tarmac, demonstrating its anger.

After a few minutes the bull seemed to grow accustomed to the flames, or perhaps it was distracted by the actions of the bull men, who succeeded in provoking it into a series of charges. A few bold spectators joined in, but no one was taking any chances with this powerful beast. They kept their distance, doing just enough to cause the bull to turn towards them and start a charge before scurrying back to the top of the ramps.

The bull was at a significant disadvantage on the tarmac surface of the square.

I had seen other squares covered in dirt or sand for these events, but this was not done in Parcent. The bull slipped and slithered at the end of each charge, crashing with unintended force into the planks just below dangling feet.

Unable to hold its footing when its body changed direction, the bull stumbled and fell, legs splayed like a baby Bambi, with its chin on the ground.

One victim of a misdirected charge was the wheelie bin tucked away behind the telephone kiosk. Impaled on the flaming horns, the bin was dragged out into the arena and pushed all round the drinking fountain. It was as if, unable to extract its revenge on its tormentors, the bull was taking it out on the bin.

This raised by far the biggest cheer of the evening, more enthusiastic than any of the ovations given for the derring-do of the young runners.

I felt sick.

The bull lasted as long as the flames, and I saw it finally herded back to the transporter.

I left for home, more sad than angry at the scenes I'd witnessed. I would not be going to Toros en la Placa del Poble again.

What is it about the English that makes us want to export our way of life wherever we go?

There was a bar in Jalon called 'Bully's.' It sold English beer, full English breakfasts and curry, and had a pool table and Sky Television for the football.

Now, a new addition to Jalon's array of dining opportunities had been installed: the 'Mad Hatters Tea Shop.'

This was aggressively marketed by a plethora of blackboards and direction arrows planted at various points in the town. With cottage furniture, ladder-back chairs, lace tablecloths and china teacups and saucers, it was a little piece of England. You could be in the Lake District or the Cotswolds, eating cream tea with the American and Japanese tourists; but I wasn't really surprised when the business folded after just a few months, nor was I surprised when a fish and chip shop opened its doors in a prime location on Jalon's main thoroughfare.

This just wasn't the right setting for English tea, somehow.

Shortly afterwards, Parcent fell victim to redoubtable British entrepreneurial spirit. A new retail outlet called 'Open All Hours!' opened in a side street – immediately opposite one of the most renowned and traditional paella restaurants in this part of Spain.

In complete contrast to the understated appearance of most of the shops in the village, 'Open All Hours!' announced its presence with a large, brash perspex sign stating the availability of gifts, groceries, sweets, greeting cards and pet food.

In an effort to attract the native population, the sign was in Spanish as well as English.

'The idea,' someone explained to me, 'was that the shop would sell all those things we English can't live without and it would open when the village shops were closed. The service would also be much quicker.'

I entered this latest incursion into traditional village life to find everything any self-respecting Englishman would need – HP Sauce, Heinz tomato ketchup, Campbell's soups, sliced bread,

Marmite, Mars Bars, crumpets and frozen pork pies. What a sad lot we English are, I moaned to myself, buying a few crumpets.

It struck me that small retail outlets like this were struggling to survive in English villages, yet here it was, an old fashioned corner shop, seemingly thriving in the middle of rural Spain. I wanted to embrace everything Spanish and so, of course, I disapproved of this 'foreign' emporium.

I hid the crumpets inside my jacket until I got home, and vowed never to shop there again, but wondered if I would eventually succumb. Would I be tempted to remove my custom from the *panadería* in favour of *thin-sliced Mother's Pride* or forego my time-consuming trips to Udaco in favour of new-fangled convenience shopping?

Above all, I couldn't help wondering what the villagers would think about this latest attempt to export British culture. After all, Britain and Spain were old rivals when it came to colonising the rest of the world. More importantly, I realised I hadn't looked around the shop to be sure no one had seen me buy the crumpets.

As August drew to a close, the power of the sun diminished sufficiently for me to venture out, and onto the sun bed once again.

I needed to do this because most holidaymakers were now looking distinctly more tanned than me, and I had to catch up.

My favourite pastime after a morning spent labouring or arched over the computer, was to float on a lilo on the pool recharging my batteries in the solar rays and drifting in the breeze (for a photo I took of myself doing this, see the cover of this book). The only effort required was a gentle push off the side with my little finger or big toe to send me gliding serenely from one end to the other, constantly adjusting my orientation to the sun.

Was this a metaphor for my new life style, I wondered, one day? Drifting aimlessly, killing time, waiting for one day to expire before starting another and another until my own life expired at some point, hopefully in the distant future? Not at all, I assured myself. I felt invigorated, energised and fitter and healthier than for as long as I could remember. I had learnt to relax. I kicked myself off again, with a different toe.

We had adopted a series of routines that were necessary simply to get through everyday life...But my routine was far more interesting and challenging than the daily grind of the M25 and ten or twelve hours a day in the municipal mad house. There was food to buy and cook, a new language to learn, a garden to manage and maintain, a *casita* to build, new friends and acquaintances to discover and, above all, a book to write. Better still, we had barely begun to explore our surroundings or visit the vast hinterland of real Spain just a few minutes from our home...

So I didn't feel the least bit guilty snoozing on the sunbed that afternoon, then drying out after a final energetic swim, irritated by an occasional fly buzzing in my ear. I sat down to relax and felt something tickle the inside of my leg. I knew it wasn't Viv teasing with such energy, but rather than expend the energy myself, of sitting up to swat whatever it was, I simply rolled my leg over without even opening my eyes. That was when I felt the sting. I shot up, blinking in the brightness of the sunlight, but the aggressor had escaped.

I don't know whether it was one of the many long-legged wasps we had spotted in the garden, or one of the variety of almost tarantula-proportioned spiders I had previously fished out of the pool, but it hurt.

There was no sign of a sting in the wound, but over the next twelve hours my ankle swelled like a water-filled balloon, followed by my foot. My calf muscle set like concrete so that any attempt at walking felt as if I was tearing the skin.

For three days I hobbled around like a penguin with one leg twice the size of the other. An ice pack was my only relief. Perhaps my new life was not so perfect, after all.

'In the village, excitement was beginning to mount...
fiesta week.'

Aubergine Rarebit

A visit to Parcent market one week ended with an impromptu lunch with friends in one of the village bars (we only went in for coffee). I had bought some aubergines, which are excellent at this time of year, and over lunch we discussed ways of cooking them. We came up with this idea between us and I returned home to give it a try. If I say so myself, the result was absolutely delicious – perfect for a light lunch.

- *1-2 large aubergines*
- *75g cheddar-type cheese, grated*
- *1 medium tomatoes, diced*
- *1 small onion, finely chopped*
- *A dash of Worcester sauce*
- *1 tbls cream or crème fraîche*
- *Salt and black pepper*
- *Olive oil*

1. Pre-heat the oven to 200°C.
2. Remove the stalk from the aubergines and cut, from top to bottom, into slices about 1cm thick. Sprinkle both sides with salt and freshly ground pepper. Heat a little olive oil in a non-stick frying pan until it begins to smoke, then fry the aubergine slices over medium heat until both sides have begun to brown. You may need to do this in batches and add a little more oil as you go along.

3. Meanwhile, combine the cheese, tomatoes, onion, Worcester sauce and cream in a bowl and mix together. Place the fried aubergine slices on a non-stick baking tray and spread the cheese mixture onto each slice. (All this can be done in advance if you wish).

4. When ready to cook, place in the baking tray in the oven and bake for 10-15 minutes until the cheese has melted and begun to turn brown. Use a fish slice or spatula to slide the aubergines onto serving plates and eat whilst hot.

Serves 2
Preparation time: 15 minutes
Cooking time: 10 minutes plus 10 -15 minutes in the oven

Roast Chicken Salad

It's far too hot to be cooking in August, but we've still got to eat. So here's a simple idea for a special salad. I cheated a bit with a shop-bought blue cheese dressing, but you can use almost anything.

A blob of mayonnaise would be good or even – dare I say it – a generous helping of Heinz salad cream. Add a few green grapes if you like, or perhaps some fresh or jarred asparagus and a few green olives. Serve with crusty bread and alioli.

- *2 roast chicken breasts, cold*
- *Mixed salad leaves*
- *A green apple, quartered, cored and cut into wedges,*
- *A small avocado, peeled and cut into wedges*
- *½ a green pepper, thinly sliced*
- *A 2 inch piece of cucumber, peeled and cut into batons*
- *A handful of shelled walnuts*
- *Your favourite dressing*

Slice the chicken breasts and place around the edge of a serving plate. Pile a handful of salad leaves in the middle, then add the cucumber, green pepper, apple and avocado. Drizzle with your favourite dressing and sprinkle with walnuts.

Serves 2
Preparation time: 10 minutes

Chapter Twelve

Harvest Time

Everyone had told us July and August were the hottest months on the Costa Blanca, and their case had been proven long ago. We were counting the weeks to the arrival of September so we could say farewell to lethargic afternoons and hot, sleepless nights, but...

'Don't expect summer to end on 31st August,' I'd said to Viv on many occasions as September loomed. Now I repeated it, toward the end of the month. 'This will be a gradual process.'

'Stop saying that,' she replied. 'It's just to make me feel worse.' She went on unpacking her cardigans. 'Besides, I want to start wearing something different, and you're always wrong.'

'No, I am just stating a hard, cold fact. It's no use expecting a heavenly autumn day to arrive on the first day of September. It won't happen. So you might as well put that stuff away. I *am* right, for once.'

I was wrong. On the first day of September the heavens opened for a spectacular light show and several hours of glorious torrential rain. The wonderful smell of damp dust filled the air and I could almost hear the plants breathe a collective sigh of relief as the chlorophyll coursed through their veins, awakening them from their long-shrivelling sleep. At least, that's how I described the event to Viv, who said, 'ugh.' But we felt like celebrating. We'd survived our first Spanish summer ('without too much discomfort and with only a few moments of heat-induced disharmony,' I wrote to friends, prompting another 'ugh' from Viv when she sneaked up for a read while I composed. (She does that.)) But all this cheerful satisfaction did not last long.

We read in the Costa Blanca News that this had been the coolest summer since 1983. Temperatures had peaked at a mere thirty-eight degrees, well below the normal forty-five to be expected in this part of the world.

We had it all to do again, probably worse, next year.

'Oh, well,' Viv said, doing up the buttons on her new angora cardigan. 'At least we have autumn.'

But September's first day of rain was followed by a spell of cooler, cloudier weather and I soon found myself missing the monotonous predictability of hot summer days. Not for the first time, I was struck by a simple truth: the world looks a better place when the sun is shining.

Almost imperceptibly the path of the sun's arch crept daily ever closer to the top of the mountains. Autumn was here, and we needed to speak to Miguel-Ángel about some logs.

I drove into Jalon one day in early September.

I'd become used to negotiating the potholes, and the ponds that appeared every time it rained. It had been that way since I first visited the town more than a year ago, and I'd assumed that the road would remain in a state of partial completion for the foreseeable future. That morning, to my utter amazement, the road had been completely resurfaced in shiny black tarmac.

The footpaths still left a lot to be desired, but, 'Catering for pedestrians,' I said to Viv when I dashed back to report on this development, 'is always a bit of an afterthought in Spain.'

'Just be thankful we've got a road,' she said. 'And anyway, what do you care about footpaths? You never walk anywhere.'

The potholes had served the purpose of reducing driving speeds on the long straight stretch of road between the *bodegas* and the riverbed. Now that they'd disappeared, someone decided they needed man-made traffic-calming measures.

Traffic humps had been installed at 200 metre intervals.

Unfortunately, at the time of my drive into Jalon, these humps had not been painted, and it was near impossible to distinguish them from the new road surface; that was certainly the reason I hit the first one at about sixty kilometres an hour.

Luckily, Spanish traffic engineers, unlike their English counterparts, are not hell bent on smashing suspension systems. I suffered a bump on my head, but the shock absorbers survived. I soon decided, driving back, that fifty kilometres an hour was about the optimum speed to approach these platforms – 'After all,' I explained as I drove Viv into town the next day, 'it wouldn't do to slow down Spanish drivers too much – mind your head.'

A couple of weeks later a traffic jam on the way to Jalon brought on a hint of previous frustrations.

There were eight cars in front of me waiting to cross the one-way bridge over the dried-up riverbed. Nothing moved. I was delayed long enough to reminisce about the endless hours I had spent glaring at the scenery on the Kent/Surrey border as I crawled round the southern section of the M25.

My blood pressure had risen only slightly, I told myself, before the traffic slowly dissolved and the problem became clear.

On the other side of the bridge an array of agricultural transport vehicles had converged on the local wine co-operative. I soon saw that *in typical Spanish style*, they were *refusing* to form an orderly queue. Two farmers, their vehicles locked in combat, were squaring up to each other as they blocked the access to the winery. Behind them waited a chugging, rattling, smoking collection of thirty or more machines, from two-wheeled *mula mecánica* to miniature John Deere tractors and majestic Massey Fergusons. Each towed a trailer with bulging tyres and sagging springs, laden with the season's grape harvest oozing at the seams.

Like Bank Holiday day-trippers, it seemed they'd all been trying to get an early start, in the hope of avoiding the queue.

Some of them would have a long wait, I thought – with a mixture of frustration and satisfaction.

Each load had to be weighed and tested for sugar content, in order to fix a value on the crop. There'd no doubt be a few arguments along the way, I imagined with further satisfaction. Good. Let them fight it out. I could wait.

Tapping the steering wheel and rolling my eyes, however, it struck me that the price would determine the prosperity of many of the growers for the year to come, and I began, more soberly to calculate just what that meant...and I thought of old Pepito.

For the next few weeks the roads in the valley were clogged with tractors and trailers heading for the refinery's stainless steel silos.

I wondered, then, how long it would be before the young wine was being pumped into the wooden barrels in the aesthetically authentic *bodega* to be sold to the visiting coach loads from Benidorm; I began to warn Viv to expect tourists any day, and suggest ways for us to avoid running into any.

It was about this time that we bumped into Pepito and his wife gathering the grapes in their small vineyard just outside Parcent. Several deep rubber buckets overflowing with grapes were already standing on the edge of the stone terrace that formed the boundary between the vineyard and the adjacent olive grove.

'*¿Las uvas están bien este año?*' I called out. I should have known better. Like farmers the world over, Pepito launched into a tirade about the year's weather.

'*Demasiada lluvia, no suficiente lluvia, no suficiente sol. ¡Las uvas sólo valen para hacer vinagre!*'

Judging from the shrivelled bunch of tiny, greenish-purple grapes he tossed dismissively into a bucket, he was right to be so dismayed. Stripped of their fruit, the vines looked tired and forlorn, as if the intensive effort of dragging up moisture from deep within the rocky soil had left them exhausted. They were ready for their winter sleep and were already shedding their leaves.

The grapes were not the only crops being harvested.

It was time to gather the almonds, from trees that had long since lost their leaves and now looked distinctly autumnal.

The velvety-green husks of the almonds were crisp brown and split, leaving just the hard nuts clinging to the lifeless trees.

All across the valley men could be seen with long bamboo poles, tapping at the trees coercing the nuts to fall into nets placed below, ready to for collection. Traditionally, it is the women who pick the almonds from the ground; it is said to be bad luck for a man to gather his own nuts!

For some growers, tradition had given way to mechanisation.

I'd seen several tractors trundling along the country roads with complicated contraptions attached to the front, and one day I saw how this mechanisation worked. The attachment looked like a giant pelican's beak with expansive canvas gullets flopping beneath metal frames. In action, the tractor approached an almond tree and gobbled it up in its beak before shaking it to the roots with a vibrating arm that loosened the nuts and caught them in the billowing canvas shrouds. The men with the long poles had disappeared and, since *el tractor* is a masculine noun, I assumed the good luck associated with women collecting nuts had disappeared as well (and what a waste that was).

Around the rest of the valley, the other crops slumbered on in the gentle sunshine, still some way from maturity.

Bright green bulging olives with a dusty white coating clung to branches bowing under their weight. It would be November before they were ready for harvest; December or January before they turned black.

The unripe fruits on the orange trees were still hiding in the vast groves, camouflaged amongst vibrant green leaves. Just occasionally, we glimpsed the faintest hint of yellow as the ripening process began. Two, three or even four months more of soaking up the sun and they would be ready for harvest.

My lonely lemon still clung to the tree in our garden, determined to prove Vicente wrong, I thought; but the lemon is a peculiar tree. It flowers and fruits at least three times a year and at any time it's possible to see blossom, young green fruit, and mature lemons on the same tree. Our young sapling was having a second show of blossom, and I hoped for a lower mortality rate this time.

And the lawn? Well, the best that can be said is that it survived the summer scorching as well as we did, proving that no amount of artificial irrigation can match a good thunderstorm.

With the encouragement of the September rain and periods of cloudy weather – the lawn began to revive. Clumpy and patchy, it resembled a municipal football pitch at the end of a hard season, but the overall effect was almost green, I decided one day. I was quietly satisfied at having defied the forces of nature, and even pleased to bring the mower out of hibernation.

In early September Martin and Alison arrived for their second visit and announced they'd like to sample some authentic tapas.

'Right,' I said.

But simple as it may sound, it was not that easy...

In fact, it was easier to find roast beef, fish and chips or cream teas than to find good tapas in the Jalon Valley.

Many places had dishes in glass cabinets on the bar, but I could never tell if the cabinets were chilling the food or keeping it warm and I had my doubts about the sell-by dates. Some were an Environmental Heath Officer's worst nightmare, I often though, as habit kicked in and I mentally composed a report.

When ordered, the food on display was often taken out to be micro-waved in the back. Trial and error had led me to discover, finally, that the best tapas was rarely displayed in pre-cooked form, but listed on a chalk board at the back of the bar. This ensures it's freshly prepared, but you have to know what to order.

I spotted a promising little place in the tiny square just off the main street in the village of Lliber about ten minutes from home, and we decided to give it a try.

The weather was fine so we sat on the terrace in the dappled shade of a false pepper tree, taking the last unoccupied table.

The whole terrace sloped from one side to the other, and it was easy to see why this table was vacant. Even with several layers of folded cardboard wedged under one of the legs, it raked at an angle. The half-empty wine bottle stayed on the floor, under the pepper tree. But never mind, it was the food we were there for.

Martin and I entered to order the tapas, to find that only two of the listed items were within our limited comprehension.

I copped out. *'Ocho raciones de tapas variadas,'* I said quickly – leaving our fate in the hands of the cook.

The wonderful thing about eating tapas with friends is that there is always something one likes, and so it proved. Every dish was polished clean, the juices mopped up with hunks of fresh bread and washed down with *vino de la casa*. This wasn't fast food. The dishes came two at a time over twenty minutes or so, delivered personally by the cook, who enquired how we like them.

Dish after dish, the verdict was the same. *Delicioso!*

Although it's no longer harvested commercially, another crop is found in the valley – carob beans. Hundreds of these ancient trees dotted the fields, often tucked away in corners. At this time of year they were full of long black pods – like runner beans, only thicker, and brittle – dangling like earrings from the branches.

Most of the carob trees near our house were neglected and overgrown, but there were a few exceptions.

We often passed a small, fenced plot that appeared to be an allotment. Two ancient and very odd carob trees stood either side of the gated entrance. They were odd because they were carefully pruned, almost like pieces of topiary. The tops of the trees were crenellated, making them look for all the world like the turreted towers of a castle. A network of boards, accessed by a ladder, had been constructed between the boughs rather like a crude tree house. I often wondered why anyone would go to such trouble.

Then we made the acquaintance of the young man who tended the allotment. Wiry, wire-haired, in storybook-colourful layers of flapping coats, and at first shy to the point of furtiveness, slowly he began to give us a warm, welcoming smile.

We chatted occasionally, then, passing the time of day and commenting on the weather.

But late one Sunday afternoon, we encountered our friend closing the gates. He was in a talkative mood. Before we knew it, we were ushered through the gates for a guided tour of the plot.

With obvious pride he showed us his crops, stuffing a carrier bag as he went round.

Red and green peppers, cherry tomatoes, aubergines and a handful of basil leaves were generously handed over, along with *pimientos de padron* – small finger-like pale green chillies, which he warned us, were *'muy piquante.'*

I asked him his name.

'Antonio,' he replied.

At the far end of the plot I had spotted more castellated trees – a pine, two fruitless olives, and a prickly oak bearing tiny acorns.

Perhaps I should have known better, given my limited grasp of the language, but after we'd all introduced ourselves and become so friendly I couldn't resist asking about these strange creations. A slight shiftiness changed his demeanour, but his enthusiasm was undiminished. He tugged my elbow and led me towards a rickety wooden hut in the far corner. Viv and Jessie were left to wander.

Approaching the hut, I saw a musty old settee, some tins and cans, an assortment of sticks and rods, and a pile of crude wicker cages. There was a slatted wooden blind at the back of the hut. For a moment, I thought I heard something moving behind it.

At this stage my lack of comprehension was becoming clear. He babbled rapidly, then resorted to sign language. He flapped his arms, and clasped his forearm with his hand.

At last the picture was becoming clear. He was saying something about birds.

Ahhhh…I had it!

Putting two and two together, and imagining the effort required to manicure the trees into their idiosyncratic appearance, I presumed him to be a bird fancier. Pigeons, perhaps. Or parakeets.

Then he returned from the shed with one of the rods. It was about one metre long and had a shallow groove carved along its entire length. The groove was packed with plasticine.

Next he produced a bundle of thin sticks like spills, coated in a sticky substance which he inserted into the plasticine at an acute angle, almost parallel to the rod, so that they overlapped slightly. Again he motioned the clasping of his hand, this time around the rod, before easing it away from the sticky coating.

Only now did the penny drop.

He was motioning the trapping of a bird. He could not have noticed the look of horror on my face as he continued enthusiastically, tugging me towards one of the sculptured trees. The whole ritual was explained. The rods with the sticky sticks were lodged between the castellations at the tops of the trees. Birds would land on the ready-made perches and become ensnared on the adhesive before flopping over, exhausted, to be caught in nets placed around the base of the branches.

'*¿Qué tipo de pájaros?*' I said. I was still thinking pigeons and telling myself that, after all, they are remarkably good to eat.

Antonio tapped the side of his nose and led me back to the hut. He pointed to the slatted blind at the rear. I picked past the debris and peeked between the slats. Startled and frightened, a blackbird and a song thrush fluttered helplessly in a small wire cage.

'*¿Para comer?* (to eat?)' I asked incredulously.

'*Si, para comer. Están muy bien, una delicadeza!*'

Now Antonio sensed my reservations about his activities. He went on to explain that the practice of catching songbirds in this way had been outlawed some years ago. He was one of only a handful of people allowed to continue the ancient ritual. His father and grandfather had carefully sculpted the trees for the best part of a century in the days when food, especially meat, was hard to find in the mountains. He had a licence to trap the birds in the traditional way, but only for three weeks each year. Despite the time and effort required to maintain the trees in their fortress-like form, he felt it was his duty to continue the work of his forefathers. To him it was a labour of love, a piece of agrarian history, which would be lost forever if the trees fell into neglect.

I still found it difficult to share his passion, especially when I met him a few weeks later with a shotgun on his shoulder and two thrushes hanging from his cartridge belt.

The next day, still breathlessly indignant, I recounted this story, with flapping hand motions and a tear in my eye for the little birds, to Klaus and Marita next door.

'Bah,' said Klaus, counting on his fingers from what I could understand of his German. 'It would take at least four and twenty blackbirds birds to make a decent pie.'

'That may be true, but it is not, if may I say so, exactly the *point*,' I snapped, folding my arms and standing my ground.

'Come along, dear,' Viv said. 'It's time for you to get dinner going,' She added, 'He's making Dumkopf Stew.'

(Which was not funny, and they were wrong to laugh.)

'…missing the monotonous predictability of hot summer days.'

Chicken with Cashew Nuts
and
Quick Mango Chutney

I'm a real fan of cooking with nuts, and cashews are my favourites. I suppose you could call this dish a curry of sorts, but all the ingredients are commonly used in Mediterranean cooking. The mango chutney is quick and easy to make, but you can save time by using a ready-made chutney if you prefer.

- *4 chicken legs, skinned and boned and cut into chunks (use chicken breasts if you prefer)*
- *1 large onion, thinly sliced*
- *2 medium green peppers, de-seeded and sliced*
- *100g cashew nuts*
- *½ a red chilli, de-seeded and thinly sliced*
- *A thumb-sized piece of fresh ginger, peeled and chopped (or 1tsp ginger powder)*
- *1 tsp cumin seeds*
- *2 cloves of garlic, peeled and chopped*
- *1tsp hot pimenton or paprika*
- *4 cloves*
- *250g (2 small tubs) plain yoghurt*
- *50ml water*
- *Oil for frying*

Quick Mango Chutney

- *½ a fresh mango, peeled and cut into small cubes*
- *½ an onion finely chopped*
- *2 tsps sugar*
- *3 tbls balsamic vinegar*
- *1tsp ginger powder*

1. First make the chutney. Gently fry the chopped onion in a little oil with the sugar. When the onion is soft, add the ginger powder, mango and vinegar and boil rapidly for 4-5 minutes until the mixture turns sticky. Spoon into a bowl and refrigerate.

2. Place the cashew nuts, chilli, ginger, cumin, garlic, paprika and cloves in a blender and blend with the water until you have a smooth paste (add a little more water if necessary).

3. Heat the oil in a large frying pan and fry the chicken, onions and green pepper for 10 minutes until they are just cooked. Stir in the cashew nut paste and heat for a further 2-3 minutes.

4. Stir in the yoghurt and bring to a boil then simmer over a low heat for 3-4 minutes. Serve immediately with boiled rice and garnish with a few slivers of green pepper and chilli.

Serves 4
Preparation time: 15 minutes
Cooking time: 25 minutes

Caramelised Pineapple
with cardamom

Cardamom? Yes, cardamom. It's normally used in curries and other Indian cuisine (I KNOW), but its slightly scented flavour will really have your friends guessing.

- *4-6 slices of fresh pineapple, peeled, cored and cut into chunks*
- *125g soft brown sugar*
- *The seeds from 10-12 cardamom pods, crushed in a mortar and pestle*
- *A slug of brandy or other liqueur (optional)*
- *Thick cream, ice cream or marscapone to serve*

1. Mix all the ingredients together except the cream and warm over medium heat in a non-stick pan until the sugar melts and begins to go sticky (about 5-10 minutes).
2. Spoon into serving dishes and top with a blob of thick cream, ice cream or marscapone. Drizzle with a little of the syrup and serve immediately.

Serves 4-6
Preparation time: 10 minutes
Cooking time: 10 minutes

If you can't find cardamom, try adding a generous helping of freshly ground black pepper. The result will be totally different, but just as interesting.

Chapter Thirteen

A Return to Work

Could it really be 12th October already?...Was it really a full year since I bade farewell to the daily grind of the M25 and the frustrations of municipal administration?

Why did the past twelve months suddenly feel like just a dream?

Back then, I had so often indulged in wishful thinking – to counteract the boredom of a lifestyle entered into through inertia and a presumption that nothing could be changed.

But this was real, all right.

I awoke on my fifty-first birthday to see the sun streaming through the bedroom window. With Viv still fast asleep, and Jessie reluctant to stir, I ventured out of the house in the still silence of early morning, alone with my thoughts.

The backdrop of Carrascal was as uplifting as the first day I had seen it on my one and only inspection trip.

The silhouette never changed, yet the view seemed to vary each day, altered by the subtleties of light and shade striking the folds in the slopes at different hours and with the passing of the seasons.

I sat for a while beneath the Acropolis, marvelling at the jasmine which now engulfed the four columns, camouflaging the concrete sewer pipes coated with Miguel's expert rendering. They seemed straight enough to me, and visitors would find it hard to appreciate the reason for the structure's Athenian nickname, I was sure.

The flowers on the summer jasmine were just beginning to fade, along with the perfume they had released on balmy summer evenings.

The early autumn rain had rejuvenated the winter jasmine, and tiny buds were just beginning to form.

We'd spent some part of almost every day eating, drinking, talking beneath the fan shaped pergola.

I realised then that I'd derived more satisfaction from knowing this pergola was the product of my own imagination and labour than I'd ever got from any work I'd done in my office-bound career.

The lawn looked in pretty good shape too, recently mown and glistening with dew.

It was easy to forget the sloppy chocolate mousse of last winter and the birds that had gobbled up much of the seed.

It still had some way to go before it would win prizes, but the anachronistic patch of green was a source of great pride to me, even though I knew most of my neighbours thought I was completely barmy to have attempted the undertaking in the first place.

The planned dining room was still unfinished and remained home to a number of untouched packing cases, while the mahogany dining suite was covered in a thick layer of dust, some of it the residue of Cheli's handiwork more than five months earlier.

I'd begun to question whether we really needed a formal dining room, though. We ate outdoors for most of the year, or in the *naya*, or at the small table in the alcove of the lounge (or, like everyone else, although we didn't tell them so, off our laps in front of the television).

But Viv was adamant. The dining room *must* be ready for Christmas, no excuses, and I'd promised to make it my next priority, so knew I couldn't get out of the job.

The previous owner's makeshift light in the small toilet still dangled from the electric cable sheathed in insulating tape, too – and I had yet to fulfil my promise to install elegant new taps in the bathroom.

The small casita I'd started to construct in the corner of the garden was also unfinished after more than four months. Just one outside wall remained to be rendered and painted, but then there was the small matter of laying some two hundred roof tiles.

It was testimony to the way I had learnt to pace myself; labouring when I was in the mood, refusing to cut corners, walking away from problems when they arose, usually – but not always, as Viv sometimes went to the trouble of pointing out – to find that there was an easy solution the next day. Gone was the stress and frustration of constantly chasing deadlines and the fear of failure.

My only targets were the ones I set for myself, and only I would be the judge of whether my work was up to standard. (Well, almost. But luckily, Viv had a good sense of humour and seemed to enjoy the failures as much as the successes.)

Better still was the fact that I no longer had to take instructions from others, or judge other people's performance, or rely on anyone else to achieve my goals. *This was true job satisfaction*, I thought.

I walked around to the front of the house, to the spot earmarked for the second fossy – which was still on the cards, as we had heard nothing more from the *ayuntamiento* about the installation of main drains. Perhaps I'd install the fossy myself. After all, it was only a glorified hole in the ground.

The road outside the house was as bumpy as ever, bearing the scars of May's torrential rain, but I'd been sounding out some of the neighbours about buying a couple of lorry loads of gravel and organising a working party to shovel, barrow and spread twenty cubic metres of crushed rock. It needed doing.

Now, somehow I sensed I might live to regret being the architect of this particular idea when the inevitable squabbles broke out. Also, there would be deliveries to arrange, work schedules to plan, accounts to produce, records to maintain, money to collect, disputes to arbitrate.

It all sounded a bit too much like work, but there was such enthusiasm for the idea that I seemed to have landed myself with a job. All right, I'd do it.

However, I decided to follow the example of my new compatriots and leave it for *mañana.*

I remembered then that while writing this book, I gave the early chapters to Rosa, our neighbour, to help her practice English. One evening she read the passage where I described working ten or twelve hours a day in the closeted cloisters of Civic Offices.

'So many hours?' she remarked. 'You must have earned a lot of money.'

'Oh, I didn't get paid for the extra hours I put in. My contract was for thirty-six hours and I did the rest for nothing,' I explained.

'But why?' she asked.

I was about to embark on an explanation when the innocence of the question struck me. It would have been pointless trying to justify my motives; even I would find them less than convincing.

'Oh...we had long rest periods,' I said, and perhaps she imagined me snoozing in the office after a liquid lunch, since she nodded approval and went on reading.

Then I recalled a conversation I had with a colleague just before leaving work.

'Mark, I admire what you are doing and I wish you well, but I couldn't do it myself. I just have to work. I need the stimulation,' he said.

I had often thought about this comment, and occasionally wondered if I was lazy or selfish to leave the world of paid employment in the public service.

Over the past year, though, I had gradually been able to rationalise my situation. To me, work had always been a means to an end; a way of paying for a lifestyle that I enjoyed.

My modest roots had given me a degree of drive and ambition.

Blessed with a good education – well, with an education forced on me by my parents against my will – and a modicum of talent, I'd achieved a measure of success.

But I'd become materialistic. I wanted, even needed, the trappings of success as visible proof of my position and status.

My brief, almost inconsequential, illness in January 2001 had nudged Viv and I into an impromptu re-evaluation of our lives.

Fortunately, a few timely moves in the property market over the previous thirty years had given us choices not available to everyone.

So here I was in Spain; supposedly retired, and wondering how I would fill my time.

I needn't have worried.

As things turned out, I'd had more than enough to occupy my time, including work of a different kind. I had the means to live, albeit much more limited than before, but now I had different needs and new ambitions.

Shopping for food had become an almost daily task. The abandonment of ready-made meals (and my rules for 'real cooking') meant that planning and preparing sustenance was a constant daily challenge.

My forays with building projects (of which more were planned) gave me more than enough physical exercise, as did our labour intensive garden.

Walking with Viv and Jessie, observing the countryside and the changing seasons, was a source of enormous pleasure and relaxation.

Learning a new language and holding conversations with villagers was as much fun and as daunting as ever.

Then there was a book to write.

I'd never dreamt of embarking on such an ambitious undertaking – a few light-hearted e-mails to friends back home was all I ever planned. My two-fingered typing skills should have been enough to suppress any thoughts of becoming an author.

But somehow the idea took hold and I was driven to write, despite constant nagging doubts about my creative ability and whether I'd have the commitment to see it through.

Perhaps my colleague was right. I did need to work, after all. But this was work of a different kind.

As things turned out, I found 'gainful employment' almost by accident one day.

My birthday celebration involved a meal at La Tasca with a group of new friends, including Leny and Wil. (Wil and I had come to enjoy each other's company over a couple of beers in the Cooperativa in Parcent on Wednesday evenings. It was not the Hare and Hounds, but we found conversation easy and had a shared sense of humour. Wil called it his weekly English lesson and I told Viv I was picking up a few Dutch phrases.)

As we reached the end of my birthday meal, Pepe, the chef at La Tasca, asked if we knew a reliable gardener.

The small, raised front terrace of the restaurant was overgrown, with bougainvillea, jasmine and ivy wrapped around the wrought iron railings so as to almost obliterate the restaurant sign.

Pepe had tried several times to organise the work, but his compatriots had always let him down. It was pleasing to know that ex-pats were not the only victims of *mañana* culture. I grinned.

Wil and I looked at each other with a common understanding and went outside with Pepe to examine the scale of the task.

'*We'll do it for you,*' we said (in unison!).

'Yes, but when?'

'*Mañana,*' we both replied.

Pepe, perhaps mindful of the number of empty bottles on our table, looked less than convinced.

The next morning, unable to resist proving him wrong, Wil and I turned up for work at eleven o'clock; equipped like professionals with ladders, saws, secateurs, even a dustpan and brush.

An hour-and-a-half later, the terrace of La Tasca looked very prim with sculptured growth enhancing, rather than engulfing, the boundary rails. We called Pepe out.

Wil and I had never discussed payment for our work, but Pepe asked how much we wanted. We both said we'd settle for a couple of beers.

'I will pour the beers, but you must tell me how much I have to pay,' said Pepe.

We had no idea how much to ask, and when Pepe served the drinks, Wil suggested fifteen Euros. Pepe disappeared again and I wondered if we had overcharged.

'Here's ten Euros each,' said Pepe when he returned, 'and you must come with your wives for a free meal.'

I looked at my ten Euro note, my first pay packet in more than a year. I felt strangely proud to have profited from my own labour.

'Perhaps we should go into business,' I said to Wil.

'I don't think so,' he replied. 'You don't need the money, and remember – in Spain, the sunshine is free.'

He was right: the last thing I wanted was to embark on a new career...although that ten Euros felt very, very good.

As if to celebrate the anniversary of our first year in Spain, Jalon put on a spectacular party, and during it I remembered from my first few nights in Casa Emelia that this was fiesta time in the town at the centre of the valley. I reminded Viv that we should expect to hear more late night fireworks, and on the way home we noticed pieces of bunting were beginning to appear in some of the narrow streets.

But this was no ordinary celebration.

We paid a visit to the town to find out about it, early one Saturday evening.

The outskirts looked somehow different, with many more parked cars than usual, and the road into the town centre was blocked by a temporary barrier. We fringed the built-up area, then, and eventually found a parking space within walking distance of the main street.

The first thing we noticed there was a total absence of cars – not just being driven; there wasn't a parked car to be seen. The whole town had been cleared of traffic and sealed off.

Roads that were normally clogged with cars, vans and tractors abandoned indiscriminately wherever there was space, were now empty. Only a handful of pedestrians could be seen strolling quietly without the need to dodge between cars.

There was more to come. The main street, some five hundred metres in length, and all the side streets leading to the church square, had been painted in coloured emulsion. Roads were in blue, green or yellow, kerbs in contrasting shades; flower patterns or abstract symbols were painted every few metres. Blue-and-white bunting stretched between the buildings, and small trees in pots or columns wreathed in roses had been placed at intervals along both sides of the roads. Richly embroidered tapestries hung from many of the balconies and windows.

We sat for a while over coffees outside Bar Rull on the blue-painted road surface, and counted the decorations. On this street alone there were at least two hundred potted palms evenly spaced on the pavements, each topped with a torch waiting to be lit. More than three hundred pieces of bunting hung overhead, fluttering softly in the breeze.

The whole street looked like a carpeted boulevard and the bunting gave the appearance of a glazed arcade.

There were at least twenty streets decorated in exactly the same style, and each had a different theme.

What made the scene more amazing was the knowledge that the transformation had taken place over just a couple of days. We could only marvel at the effort and energy, not to mention the cost that must have been involved. Here was a town with something to celebrate, and I was sure it wasn't our first anniversary.

We asked some German people who joined us at our table if they knew what it was all about. They explained that many years ago, a valuable jewel-encrusted statue of the Virgin Mary had been removed from the town and hidden in the surrounding hillside, out of reach of marauding tribes. But it had been lost for centuries. Fifty years ago it had been found again, buried in the countryside, and reinstated in the Church. Its rediscovery was seen as a miracle of sorts and was celebrated every year in October.

The whole town was out to celebrate with a week-long programme of events, and that night we were treated to the spectacle of the Virgin Mary being paraded around the streets, followed by the town band and most of the local population out in their Sunday best.

As we lingered to enjoy the spectacle, the procession began to disperse and we felt a little like outsiders as whole families promenaded past our table, stopping to greet friends and neighbours.

But an odd thing happened.

Suddenly we spotted Teresa from the *panadería*, and could hardly recognise her without her beige and white apron and white hat. She wore a flattering, tailored black dress with matching patent leather high-heeled shoes, offset with a dainty gold handbag. Like many of the women, she was carrying a bunch of flowers –

red roses. Her hair was glossily styled and there was just a touch of makeup. She looked very elegant. Then we spotted Antonio the butcher – who we were used to seeing in a blood-stained apron behind the chops and sausages. Hair sleeked back, he wore black trousers and waistcoat over a crisp white shirt adorned with a red cummerbund.

'Viv, *look!*' I said. 'Teresa's *beautiful and elegant!*'

'Look at Antooonio,' she murmured back, taking a photograph. 'Bags I buy the next Christmas turkey.'

As an agnostic, if not an atheist, the religious significance of the festival escaped me. At the beginning of the third Millennium it would be easy to ridicule such an elaborate and expensive celebration of the rediscovery of a man-made artefact, I thought. But then I had no faith, and therefore no right, to question the faith of others. The people of Jalon clearly felt that their town had been blessed and enriched by this momentous event. Many other towns and villages in Catholic Spain had something similar to celebrate – and perhaps this was the glue that bound them together as communities.

So, one year on, what did I think of my adopted country and its people?

A year was hardly long enough to even begin to understand the complexities of a culture, when it is viewed by an outsider with only a limited grasp of the language.

Yet I never really felt like a complete outsider. It may have been something to do with the fact that there were so many expats here before me. Some of these were the real pathfinders, who came to the Jalon valley when it was off the beaten track, still a traditional agricultural community living in villages where foreigners were a rarity.

By the time I chose to make the break, a whole new infrastructure had followed in the wake of the first foreign settlers. English speaking doctors, dentists, lawyers and vets were easy to find. An army of English, Dutch, and German tradesmen had moved into the area finding plentiful work amongst the burgeoning ex-pat population. They were not necessarily cheaper or better than their Spanish counterparts, but as ever, people often felt more comfortable dealing with their own countrymen, not least because of a shared language.

New shops and restaurants had emerged to meet demand, many catering for national tastes with homespun products. A part of me felt a certain sadness about the colonisation of the valley, yet I was all too willing to take advantage of the services on offer and the advice of people who had been here much longer than me. A lack of confidence in my ability to communicate in Spanish had led me to the easy option of dealing with English speakers.

But I began to resent every new gouge in the countryside, carved out for the next urbanisation and the next influx of people just like me. I had serious concerns about the sustainability of development on this scale, but I never heard even a hint of anxiety from local people. Everywhere we went the Spanish people were warm and friendly, always willing to help and generously trying to understand me even though I was assassinating their language.

In the valley itself, and especially in the villages, life seemed to continue largely unchanged by the tide of immigrants. Yet the landscape had changed dramatically, as new developments encroached upon the wooded slopes and new houses sprang up amidst the vineyards and olive groves. Their visual impact had changed the whole atmosphere in the valley. It was no longer just a collection of small villages dotted amongst the vast swath of agricultural holdings nestling in the bed of the valley. There were the beginnings of urban sprawl.

I couldn't help thinking that there would be an outcry if this were happening in the Lake District or the Cotswolds. There would be consternation amongst the conservationists and outrage amongst the locals. But which was better – to live in an artificially preserved environment where it is easier to buy a souvenir than a loaf of bread, or to live in a place that accepts and adapts to change? The fact is, this is Spain, not England, and Spanish attitudes are not the same as English.

It seemed to me that Spanish people took life for what it was and adapted to the weather and the seasons. A few might hanker after the old ways and the preservation of an unspoilt landscape, but most seemed willing to accept progress and the new wealth it brought, at least in the short term. They saw their environment as an asset to be exploited, not just to be preserved for its own sake.

Beautiful as it was, the Jalon Valley was rather scruffy.

Wheeled refuse bins were on every prominent corner; often overflowing with rubbish or accompanied by abandoned mattresses, refrigerators or cookers – at least until the next collection. Crashed or abandoned cars could occasionally be seen amongst the olive and orange groves. Small piles of builders' rubble were abandoned by the roadside, and there seemed to be a heap of left-over sand, gravel, bricks and blocks outside every other house. I mused that there must be enough building materials lying around to construct a small urbanisation. Everywhere on the edge of villages and in the countryside were half-finished buildings, shells of concrete and breeze-block, seemingly abandoned for decades.

But this was an Englishman talking with a very English perspective. To Spanish eyes, I imagined these things went barely noticed. And there was the rub. It was because the Spanish people had such a relaxed approach to life, that immigrants such as me were accepted with such ease. The two went hand-in-hand.

Gradually I'd come to realise life was more important than order and tidiness; practicality more important than preservation.

If the bins were hidden away, if the unfinished buildings were completed, if holes in the roads were repaired, life would not change significantly. The sun would shine, the seasons would come and go, the oranges would ripen, the olives would fall and people would live and die. This was Spain after all, and I had learnt to love it and its people.

What could I say of Parcent?

A glance at the map would suggest it is well off the beaten track, remote from the pressure for development. In fact the sprawl of new urbanisations had reached beyond this sleepy little pueblo, though you wouldn't have to travel far to reach the last of the substantial ex-pat colonies. A part of me wished I were truly in 'the real Spain,' remote from fish and chips and steak and kidney pie. But that may have been a step too far for my first foray into life in a new country. Perhaps in a few years time I'd fulfil a wistful ambition to live in a remote location surrounded by my own oranges or olives...although, perhaps that was the real pipe dream.

For all the changes, Parcent still retained the essence of village life. Most local people had spent their whole lives in the village, as had their forefathers. Many still made a living off the surrounding land that had been in their families for generations.

Many of the village houses had belonged to the same families for decades, and three or more generations of the same families still lived together.

I never saw a wheelchair ramp and, to my knowledge, there was no old people's home; but elderly people were respected, valued and revered.

The local school thrived, despite falling pupil numbers that would have brought pressure for closure in England. Children were cherished and nurtured.

There was a real sense of community, and a range of services and facilities that would surpass those available in many a small English town.

People used and supported the weekly market, and the local shops, bars and co-operatives.

No one here drove miles to the supermarket, then complained about the demise of local shops or the closure of the village post office.

No one deserted the local bars in favour of mock Tudor fibreglass, steak and chips and the Charlie Chalk menu for the kids.

Even the Big Macs, available just half an hour away, had failed to make an impact.

Despite the admirable routine of taking wine or beer with breakfast, with lunch and even after work, I never saw anyone drunk. Nor did I encounter any of the yobbishness or rowdyism that seemed to plague even the most peaceful English villages.

There was much to be admired about this way of life.

Village people seemed to accept responsibility for their behaviour, instead of complaining to the authorities.

So was this truly Paraíso entre Montañas – Paradise between the Mountains?

Perhaps not...but it came close.

As we approached the exact date that marked the first anniversary of our arrival in Casa Emelia, the oranges and mandarins in the garden were beginning to ripen, just as they had the year before and would next year.

The olives were turning black and the leaves on the jacaranda tree were fading to gold.

The fresias were emerging from the rain-softened soil to compensate for the fuchsias, which had been a dismal failure. The lower fronds of the palms needed cutting away and the fruits of the prickly pear cactus lay in a mushy heap on the ground.

The pool was a chilly eighteen degrees, even colder than last year, and I had long since abandoned thoughts of taking a dip, even in the still-warm sunshine.

The last batch of blossom had failed to provide company for my one lonely lemon, which was stubbornly refusing to show any signs of ripening.

'To hell with it,' I thought.

The Gordon's gin trickled slowly over the ice cubes, making them crackle as they split.

The Schweppes tonic hissed as the top was prised away. It mingled with the gin, forming swirls like oil mixing with water until the bubbles had risen to the top leaving only tiny beads of liquid dancing on the surface.

Despite initial resistance to my sharpest kitchen knife, the skin of the still-green lemon eventually ruptured and the zest sprayed out in a momentary mist.

The rest of the hard yellow flesh yielded more easily and the bitter juice was released from the dissected segments.

Only a hard white pip defied the blade, until it, too, succumbed under a little added pressure.

The slice was complete and made a satisfying 'plink' as it was immersed in the effervescent fluid.

Carefully, I carried the glass to the Acropolis and placed it on the hardwood table, bathed in dappled sunlight. I examined it for a while wanting to savour the moment, before raising it to my lips...

Perhaps this was Paradise, after all.

Grilled Artichokes

I've struggled for years to find the best way of cooking artichokes, then I asked the lady on the fruit and vegetable stall at the market and she told me the secret – she cooks them in the microwave. So I gave it a try and the result was perfect. I decided to add a few extra flavours, and finish them off under the grill. You could serve these artichokes as a starter or as a vegetable with a main meal.

- *2-3 small artichokes*
- *The juice of a lemon*
- *25g cheddar-type cheese, grated*
- *1 tomato, sliced and roughly chopped*
- *1 tbls thick cream or crème fraîche*
- *Black pepper*

1. Prepare the artichokes (see tip) and dip them in the lemon juice. Place them on a flat dish then microwave on full power for 4-5 minutes or until soft when pierced with the point of a knife. Set aside to cool.

2. Meanwhile mix together the grated cheese, chopped tomato and cream and season with plenty of freshly ground black pepper.

3. Pre-heat the grill to maximum.

4. Cut each artichoke from top to bottom to form 4 slices. Lay all the slices on a shallow heatproof dish, then place a spoonful of the cheese mixture on top of each slice. Place under the grill for 4-5 minutes until the cheese begins to bubble and turn brown. Serve immediately.

Serves 2 as a starter
Preparation time: 15 minutes
Cooking time: 10 minutes

Tip:

Artichokes are notoriously hard to prepare, but they are not as difficult as they seem, especially if you buy small ones. There are two secrets. First, accept that there is going to be a lot of waste. Second, have a saucerful of lemon juice close at hand.

Pull off the outer leaves from the bottom of the artichoke until you reach pale green soft leaves. Trim off the top half of the artichoke and discard. Cut the stalk about 1cm below the bottom of the artichoke and trim to form a neat base.

Dip the cut edges of the trimmed artichoke in the lemon juice immediately and roll it around to coat all the cut surfaces, otherwise it will turn black within seconds. Microwave within ten minutes.

Roast Peppers
with cherry tomatoes and goat's cheese

This simple dish is easy to prepare and packed with flavours that somehow seem to epitomise Mediterranean food. I used a mixture of red, yellow and orange peppers, but you can use any colour you like. If you don't have soft goat's cheese, almost any melting cheese will do. Serve as a substantial starter or as a light meal perhaps with a few grilled artichokes and plenty of warm garlic bread.

- *3 medium peppers, cut in half through the stalk and seeds removed*
- *18 cherry tomatoes, halved*
- *Salt and freshly ground black peppers*
- *A handful of fresh basil leaves, roughly torn (or a tsp of dried basil)*
- *200g soft goat's cheese, cut into small cubes*
- *Olive oil*

1. Pre-heat the oven to 200°C.
2. Place the tomato pieces inside each of the halved peppers, sprinkle the basil over the top then season with salt and pepper.
3. Dot the cheese cubes on top of the filled peppers then place on a shallow, ovenproof dish. Drizzle with a generous amount of olive oil then roast in the oven for 35-40 minutes until the tomatoes have softened and the peppers have blackened at the edges. Serve immediately.

Serves 2
Preparation time: 5 minutes
Cooking time: 40 minutes

Thoughts About Food

In ten months I trimmed down from just over 15 stones to 12½. It wasn't difficult to begin with as I used to graze my way through boring days in the office and come home to something that took ten minutes in the microwave, usually with oven chips. But, more importantly, I've maintained my weight for more than two years. Viv has lost weight too, not that she really wanted to, but then I'm in charge of cooking. Now, I don't even think about what I eat, but I stick to a few simple rules.

NEVER go on a diet – you may lose weight, but if this is because you starve yourself or go without your favourite foods, you'll probably put it all back on as soon as you end your diet. Besides, you'll be boring and miserable while you are dieting and you'll lose all your friends. Then, you'll be even more boring and miserable as the pounds reappear but your friends don't.

INSTEAD, adjust your diet to something you can live with, if not forever then at least in the long term. It doesn't have to be rabbit food for the rest of your life, but hey, a good salad makes a nice change.

THE MEDITERRANEAN DIET. You don't have to live by the Med to enjoy it. Plenty of fresh fish, fruit and vegetables, lots of garlic and olive oil, but much less butter, cream and cheese.

INPUT – vs – OUTPUT. It's a simple fact that you never lose weight if you take in more fuel than you burn. And some bodies are more fuel efficient than others. You're lucky if you're a gas guzzler, but you need to take care if you have a lean burn engine, unless you put your foot to the floor occasionally and burn that extra fuel. Yes, that means exercise.

THE SECRET – and Viv will hate me for saying this – is portion control. I keep telling her that three roast potatoes taste as good as ten. And if you only cook three each there won't even be an argument. Eat whatever you want, but in modest quantities. That's modest – not tiny. We're not talking nouveau cuisine.

WHAT'S A MODEST QUANTITY? Most of us over-eat, so here's what to do.

- Put out your normal ration of food for any meal then take something away. It doesn't matter what: half a slice of toast, a scrape of butter, a potato or two, a scoop of ice cream, a few strands of spaghetti, a slice of ham, chunk of cheese – anything. Get used to seeing, and eating, smaller meals.
- Avoid most pre-prepared meals – pizzas, lasagne, steak and kidney pies – that sort of stuff. Apart from the fact that many are unhealthy, with too much salt, the portions are often too big or - worse still - too small (with the result that we buy a family sized portion and share it between two people).
- Go on, have a cake or a Mars bar if you want, they're so much nicer than those chewy muesli bars. But think about this: a cake or a sweet is nice, but you don't need to eat it all at once. Cut that strawberry tart in half and save the rest for tomorrow. Half a Mars bar tastes just as good as a whole one.
- Eat chocolate – it's good for you. But try to stick with plain dark chocolate with a high cocoa content. And don't eat a whole bar at once. I always have a few bars of chocolate in the house – usually in the fridge. When I fancy a bit, I go to the fridge, break off a just a couple of pieces of chocolate, replace the rest of the bar in the fridge, then sit down and munch – slowly. It doesn't take an iron will to say "enough is enough" and besides, I'm far too lazy to get out of the chair and go back to the fridge.
- Shop right – eat right. Twenty minutes of willpower in the supermarket is worth hours back home. Avoid buying all the things you know you don't really want to eat. If they're not in

the house you won't be tempted. "It's just in case we have visitors," I hear Viv say as the peppermint creams hit the trolley. Rubbish, you know you'll be tempted, and who really needs After Eight Mints anyway?

- Buy smaller portions. Chicken (you don't really want the fat old cage bird), minced beef (usually cleverly packed in portions that are not enough for three, but too much for two), steak (go for the best cut, not the biggest), lumps of cheese, duck breasts, guinea fowl, pâté de foie gras, fresh truffles, caviar – resist buying the biggest portion. The smaller ration will almost always be enough, and you'll save money.

ENJOY FISH. Don't walk past the fish counter. Buy some fish. If you don't like all those eyes staring at you, ask the fishmonger to cut the heads off. Or buy some fillets. And don't stick to salmon – that's cheating. Try sea bass, dorada, smoked haddock, sardines, cod, monk fish, tuna, anything even squid – yuck!. You know you'll enjoy it and, if you haven't got one already, buy a decent fish cookery book. Start with something by Rick Stein.

WHAT OIL? Cook with olive oil. Never mind polyunsaturated wotsits – olive oil is healthy and it tastes so much better, anyway.

WASTE DISPOSAL. Your body is a dustbin – or a very efficient composter to be more accurate. If you don't want, don't need or don't like what's on your plate at the end of a meal, don't feel guilty about leaving it. Throw it in the real dustbin instead of using your body as a trashcan.

BE FRUITY. Always (and this goes back to healthy shopping) have fruit in the house. If you're peckish between meals, don't make a cheese sandwich. Take an apple, peach, or a slice of melon. You'll have to eat the fruit anyway, or it'll go mouldy. Dried fruits are excellent, as well. Try apricots, figs or raisins.

NUTS, TOO: Nuts make a great snack – try walnuts, pecans, almonds or cashews. Don't eat them from the packet. Pour a small portion into a dish and put the packet back in the cupboard. Then sit down and nibble, doing your best impression of a squirrel.

BREAD. Try to avoid white, especially the pre-packed, thin-sliced variety. Choose wholegrain, seed bread or wholemeal. My one 'can't live without' luxury (apart from Marmite) is Hovis granary bread, frozen and shipped from the UK.

BREAKFAST. A good breakfast sets you up for the day. OK, so we still have bacon and eggs occasionally, and why not? But our regular breakfast consists of fresh fruit or fruit juice, a couple of dried figs or prunes (yes they do work!) and a slice of granary toast with honey or marmalade. Tea for Viv and a cup of strong black coffee for me.

IN RESTAURANTS – avoid value for money syndrome. I know that roast beef and Yorkshire pudding sounds better value than grilled sea bass with a green salad – BUT you can eat roast beef anytime and it will probably taste better if you cook it yourself. Try the fish, or the chicken, or the pasta and follow it with the fresh fruit brulee instead of the sticky toffee pudding. It's quality, not quantity that counts for value.

EATING OUT. Most menus list three courses, but if you're stuffed by the time it comes to pudding, say 'no' or ask for a piece of fruit. If the trashcan's full, don't sit on the lid!

AND FINALLY. Variety is the spice...
Enjoy your food and try something different every week. You'll find that eating interesting food is far more enjoyable than eating for the sake of it.

Eat for taste – not for fuel.

I've put up more of my recipe collection
(and photographs, including some of Jessie, and little Cheli)
on my website: http://vimark.50megs.com

Lightning Source UK Ltd.
Milton Keynes UK
UKOW041139080512

192159UK00001BA/214/A